Sustainability Stories

Brigitte Bernard-Rau
Editor

Sustainability Stories

The Power of Narratives to Understand Global Challenges

Editor
Brigitte Bernard-Rau
University of Hamburg
Hamburg, Germany

ISBN 978-3-031-52299-4   ISBN 978-3-031-52300-7   (eBook)
https://doi.org/10.1007/978-3-031-52300-7

© The Editor(s) (if applicable) and The Author(s), under exclusive license to Springer Nature Switzerland AG 2024

This work is subject to copyright. All rights are solely and exclusively licensed by the Publisher, whether the whole or part of the material is concerned, specifically the rights of translation, reprinting, reuse of illustrations, recitation, broadcasting, reproduction on microfilms or in any other physical way, and transmission or information storage and retrieval, electronic adaptation, computer software, or by similar or dissimilar methodology now known or hereafter developed.

The use of general descriptive names, registered names, trademarks, service marks, etc. in this publication does not imply, even in the absence of a specific statement, that such names are exempt from the relevant protective laws and regulations and therefore free for general use.

The publisher, the authors, and the editors are safe to assume that the advice and information in this book are believed to be true and accurate at the date of publication. Neither the publisher nor the authors or the editors give a warranty, expressed or implied, with respect to the material contained herein or for any errors or omissions that may have been made. The publisher remains neutral with regard to jurisdictional claims in published maps and institutional affiliations.

This Springer imprint is published by the registered company Springer Nature Switzerland AG
The registered company address is: Gewerbestrasse 11, 6330 Cham, Switzerland

If disposing of this product, please recycle the paper.

*To the unsung heroes of sustainability,
the change agents working tirelessly in the shadows,
determined to make the world a better place*

Preface

2030 is widely recognized as a pivotal milestone within the frameworks of both the United Nations (UN) Sustainable Development Goals (SDGs) and the 2015 Paris Agreement on climate change. These initiatives outline a comprehensive and interconnected agenda, establishing specific targets and deadlines across economic, social, and environmental domains to address global challenges. Addressing various sustainability issues such as poverty eradication, quality education, clean water and sanitation, climate action, gender diversity, and more, these frameworks underscore the need and urgency to find solutions.

In a notable trend, initiatives aimed at promoting sustainable and responsible action are steadily gaining momentum, demonstrating some level of success. The pressing grand challenge of climate change stands prominently at the forefront of global concerns, sparking extensive studies and analyses. Innovative forms of climate activism, including the emerging realm of digital climate activism, have emerged as dynamic tools that showcase how the relationship between business and society can be strengthened (Belotti et al., 2022; Fisher & Nasrin, 2020).

However, five years away from 2030, it becomes evident that progress is not being made at the speed or scale required. The urgency of addressing global challenges has never been more apparent as noted by UN Secretary-General Antonio Guterres: "We need to wake up—and get to work" (Guterres, 2023). The unprecedented COVID-19 pandemic, ongoing violent geopolitical conflicts, and natural disasters, from floods to earthquakes, further underscore the fragility of our interconnected world, testing our resilience as a global community.

In this era of polycrisis, characterized by extreme uncertainty, the need to solve societal grand challenges has become a top priority for both national and international entities (World Economic Forum, 2023). For instance, Gen Z and Millennials, concerned about their uncertain futures, are drawing attention to issues beyond climate change, including racial justice, mental health, work–life balance, the cost of living crisis, and inequality in general (Deloitte, 2023).

Increasingly, public organizations are turning to private organizations to drive meaningful change and to address a unique combination of challenges. One powerful avenue for transformative change involves tapping into the potential of financial markets. The landmark Paris Agreement dedicated to combatting the climate crisis establishes a foundation for redirecting investments toward sustainable, low-carbon initiatives. Similarly, the strategic European Green Deal recognizes the crucial role of the private sector in financing the transition toward a sustainable economy.

In recent years, the field of sustainable finance has therefore witnessed innovative strategies and collaborative efforts among various stakeholders, including financial institutions, governments, NGOs and corporations, among others. The attempt to reconcile the utilitarian approach of the financial markets with the need to solve major societal challenges has emerged as a key way forward. Responsible and sustainable investors promote explicit social and environmental agendas and serve as advocates for social and environmental needs. More specifically, impact investors have adopted an investment style that considers not only financial returns but also the social and environmental consequences of the allocation of their funds. Many policy makers see this investment approach as a source of hope and vision for the future (e.g., Logue & Grimes, 2022).

This is, however, a journey where each of us has a role to play. So, my question is this: How can we, as individuals, contribute efficiently to solving long-standing societal problems and effecting real change? And my proposition: Should not we consider new epistemological and ontological approaches, new codes of ethics, new altruistic ways of living, new imagined futures, and new narratives, to bring about real change (Beckert, 2016; Gabriel et al., 2022; Pelluchon, 2021)?

I embed my proposition in the idea of a purposeful, sustainable world in which human beings and their social and ecological concerns prevail. In their seminal book, On Justification, Boltanski and Thévenot (2006 [1991]) refer to several "common worlds" that are in constant competition and experience situation of disputes. Among them, the "market" world is typically opposed to the "civic" world. The former emphasizes competition, efficiency, and profit-making, contrasting with the latter, which focuses on equality, cooperation, and public interest. Boltanski and Thévenot claim that their "Economies of Worth" framework can, through "higher order principles" such as "common good" and "justice" resolve these tensions. This approach necessarily introduces ethical values into the relationship between financial and social commitments in terms of values and beliefs. It not only changes the current narrative around the opposition between two paradigms—profit maximization vs. social impact contribution—it goes beyond it by supporting the perspective of a post-materialistic world in a "new enlightenment" paradigm (Pelluchon, 2023).

The relationship with oneself and with others remains an essential notion for a just perception of the world, the world in all its complexity, but ethical, poetic, and real (Glissant, 1990, 1997, 1999; Ricoeur, 1992). There is, therefore, not only hope but an urgent need to reflect, discuss, and propose, together with a reformulation of the SDGs, a profound reorientation of traditional material assumptions based on targets, metrics and performance indicators, by introducing normative and ethical assumptions and integrating future-oriented visions for the common good. This should not be a mere ideal, but the result of concrete, direct, tangible actions aimed at establishing the foundations for a future full of hope in which all human beings can flourish (Pelluchon, 2023).

The contributors to this edited volume answer this call for action by pursuing individual and collaborative efforts that lay the groundwork for an optimistic future for humanity. They navigate the complex web of issues threatening our world and proactively engage to drive meaningful social change. In their narratives, the authors show how governments, businesses, investors, and individuals must work together to create an ecosystem that rewards responsible practices, encourages innovation, and accelerates the transition to a more sustainable future. The clock is ticking, but it is through collective and individual commitment that we can bring about lasting positive social change.

References

Belotti, F., Donato, S., Bussoletti, A., and Comunello, F., (2022). Youth activism for climate on and beyond social media: Insights from FridaysForFuture-Rome. *The International Journal of Press/Politics, 27*(3) 718–737.

Boltanski, L., & Thévenot, L. (2006[1991]). *On justification: Economies of worth*. Princeton University Press.

Busch, T., Bruce-Clark, P., Derwall, J., Eccles, R., Hebb, T., Hoepner, A., Klein, C., Krueger, P., Paetzold, F., Scholtens, B., & Weber, O. (2021). Impact investments: a call for (re)orientation. *SN Business & Economics, 1*(2), 1–13.

Deloitte. (2023). Deloitte Global 2023 Gen Z and Millennial Survey.

Gabriel, M., Horn, C., Katsman, A., Krull, W., Lippold, A. L., Pelluchon, C., & Venzke, I. (2022). *Towards a new enlightment.* The New Institute.

George, G., Howard-Grenville, J., Joshi, A., & Tihanyi, L. (2016). Understanding and Tackling Societal Grand Challenges Through Management Research. *Academy of Management Journal, 59*(6), 1880–1895.

Glissant, É. (1990). *Poétique de la Relation.* Gallimard.

Glissant, É. (1997). *Traité du Tout-Monde.* Poétique IV. Gallimard.

Glissant, É. (1999). *Philosophie de la Relation.* Poésie en étendue. Gallimard.

Gutteres, Antonio (2023). United Nations Secretary-General's briefing to the General Assembly on Priorities for 2023. 06 February 2023.

Fisher, D., & Nasrin, S. (2020). Climate activism and its effects. WIREs Clim Change. 2020. https://doi.org/10.1002/wcc.683.

Kölbel, J. F., Heeb, F., Paetzold, F., & Busch, T. (2020). Can sustainable investing save the world? Reviewing the mechanisms of investor impact. *Organization & Environment, 33*(4), 554–574.

Logue, D., & Grimes, M. (2022). Living up to the hype: How new ventures manage the resource and liability of future-oriented visions within the nascent market of impact investing. *Academy of Management Journal, 65*(3), 1055–1082.

Pelluchon, C. (2023). *L'espérance ou la traversée de l'impossible.* Bibliothèque Rivages, Editions Payot & Rivages.

Pelluchon, C. (2021). *Les Lumières à l'âge du vivant* (first edn.). Seuil. ISBN: 978–2,021,425,017.

Ricœur, P. (1992). *Oneself as another* (first edn.). University of Chicago Press. ISBN: 97802267.

World Economic Forum. (2023). *The global risks report 2023* (18th edn.). Insight Report.

Hamburg, Germany   Brigitte Bernard-Rau

Credits

I extend my sincere thanks to the following individuals and organization for granting me permission to reproduce previously published content in this edited volume:

Corine Pelluchon: "Ecology as New Enlightenment," copyright at Global Solutions Initiative Foundation. Used by permission of Amy Pradell, Director of Communications at Global Solutions Initiative Foundation.

Acknowledgments

The completion of "Sustainability Stories" is a testament to the wonderful support and dedication of countless individuals who have contributed their time, knowledge, and inspiration. This collection of narratives on sustainability-related topics has been a labor of love, dedication, and relentless determination and I would like to express my heartfelt gratitude to everyone who made this project possible.

First and foremost, I extend my sincere appreciation to my fellow authors whose distinctive and authentic voices have shown how sustainability manifests itself in our daily lives. Through their narratives, they have shed light on how they are confronting and navigating the multifaceted implications of the social and environmental challenges of our era, enriching the understanding of readers.

A special appreciation also goes to those who introduced me to some of these authors: Sandrine Benattar, Franky de Cooman, Jean Martin Herbecq, Anna Kaschke, Beatrice King, Nicole Lappe, Pascal Léger, Karmele Fernández de Larrea, Christine Taylor, Flora Balet-Schnerring, and Janice Vogel. Your trust and enthusiasm helped me bring this collected work to fruition.

I would also like to express my gratitude to Beatrice King and Janine Kaiser, the two graphic and layout designers, as well as to all the copy editors, whose meticulous work ensured the quality and visual appeal of this collective work. Thank you for your invaluable support.

At Springer, I wish to thank Prashanth Mahagaonkar and Ruth Milewski for making this book project possible. There is nothing like having a dedicated team at a professional publishing house.

To my husband Christian, your unwavering support and encouragement have sustained me through the challenges and triumphs of this endeavor. Your belief in the importance of sharing these narratives with a wide audience and in my ability to contribute to the field of sustainability has been a constant source of motivation and inspiration throughout this project.

I must here also express my deep gratitude to my mother, Marie, who instilled in me the values of empathy, responsibility, and stewardship from a young age. Your legacy of caring for the vulnerable ones in our world has been an invisible but driving force behind this collection.

Lastly, to all the pioneers and role models in the field of sustainability who paved the way for the work we continue to do. Your dedication and vision have provided a foundation upon which we can build a more sustainable future. Thank you.

About the Book

The idea of collecting narratives for this book originated from a spontaneous desire to connect with sustainability-minded individuals and encourage them to share their knowledge with a broader audience. Terms such as sustainability, sustainable development, Corporate Social Responsibility (CSR), and ESG (environment, social and governance) have become prevalent in public discourse, politics, media, marketing, and advertising. However, few grasp the wide and complex issues these terms encompass. While numerous books and articles exist on sustainability and CSR, to the best of my knowledge, none uses a narrative approach to reach a broader public.

Amid the global spread of COVID-19 in 2020, I took the opportunity to contact friends and colleagues, inviting them to join me in writing a collective book on sustainability, sustainable development, business ethics, CSR, ESG issues, and sustainable finance, sharing short sustainability stories. Many welcomed the idea and contributed with their stories to help build a more informed sustainable world.

In this collective book, artists, entrepreneurs, lawyers, professors, sustainability experts, and change advocates from all over the world share their observations, suggestions, and solutions for a sustainable future. These unheard voices, very active in their fields, will inspire readers of all backgrounds, young or old, educated or not, from the North or the South hemisphere, to care for our planet and society at large. Driven by optimism and determination to bring about change in society, they will edify readers on a series of sustainability issues, acting as communicators of vision, connectors, or responsible leaders.

I believe that sharing the sustainability stories of this book with a broader audience can help better understand and tackle the complex grand challenges of our times. By leveraging the power of storytelling, these stories contribute to a more compassionate, environmentally aware, and collectively responsible world. They can empower managers seeking to make a difference in their organizations and also influence us, individually, to adopt a prosocial behavior. It is my sincere hope that these stories will resonate deeply within the hearts and minds of every reader and challenge us all to contribute to an enjoyable, equitable, and sustainable world. In fact, I truly believe that every individual, regardless of background, can contribute to make the world a better place. Reflection and sharing are exceptionally powerful ways to connect us and inspire change through personal experiences. These narratives demonstrate that with passion, determination, and a genuine desire to create a more harmonious world, together, we can drive positive change and transform the world.

The book categorizes the sustainability stories into four main parts: (1) Calling for Change—in Theory and In Practice, (2) Exploring Environmental and Social Challenges, (3) Addressing Governance and Financial Matters, and (4) Art as a Driver for Transformation.

In an age where good news is scarce, these stories remind us that it is the heart and the mind that can make the most profound impact on people and the planet.

Contents

Part I Calling for Change: In Theory and in Practice

1 Ecology as New Enlightenment ... 3
  Corine Pelluchon

2 Challenging the "Gloom and Doom" Narrative Begins
  in the Classroom ... 11
  Graeme Mitchell

3 Slipping Sustainability into Higher Education. Take One! ... 19
  Elisa Baraibar-Diez and Maria D. Odriozola

4 Approaching Wicked Issues in Practice, in Theory,
  and in the Wild ... 27
  Katinka Quintelier

5 How to Become a Sustainability Ambassador and
  Changemaker in Five Steps? ... 37
  Susanne Preiss

6 Lessons Learned from CSR Managers in the Retail Industry
  in France ... 49
  Sandrine Benattar

7 Not All Businesses Are CSR Friendly. Good News: This Can
  Be Fixed! ... 57
  Marine Le Picard

8	**Regenerative by Design: Building Regenerative Business Models** *Leon Seefeld*	63
9	**Prometea: A Participative Way Toward Social Transformation** *Iciar Montejo Romero*	71
10	**Hanging on to a Dream** *Franky De Cooman*	81
11	**Sustainability Professionals as Ambassadors for Change: Redefining Communication** *Stella Blohmke*	95
12	**The Ten Essentials of Responsible Business Conduct** *Brigitte Bernard-Rau*	101
13	**Synergies for Hope: Partnering for Sustainable Development in Kenya** *Janine Kaiser and Peter Wanderi*	109
14	**The Power of Fellowships** *Claire Coletti*	121

Part II Exploring Environmental and Social Challenges

15	**Earth Restore: A Story of Resilience Among Adversities** *Nayan Mitra*	131
16	**What Is a Climate Neutral Company and How Do You Become One?** *Bernhard Schwager and Gabriele Renner*	141
17	**Mass Reforestation: Combining Tech and Nature to Fight Climate Change** *Fernanda Tsujiguchi and Diego M. Coraiola*	149
18	**As Simple as a Lady's Slipper** *Bonnie Lewtas*	159
19	**The Tourism Paradox: Can Tourists Improve an Area They Visit?** *Khalid El Housni*	165

20	**Plugging Zimbabwe's Brain Drain** *Fungai Mettler*	177
21	**Gender Equality Is Essential for Establishing a Climate Just World** *Annika Degen*	181
22	**Our People Make Our Firm** *Raquel Flórez Escobar*	189
23	**Women at the Margins: Organizations, Social Structures, and Gender Norms in Rural India** *Hemalatha Venkataraman*	195
24	**Empowering Communities Through Social Entrepreneurship: The Label Créole Project** *Marie-Lou Nazaire*	207
25	**"Entgrenzung": De-Bordering & Breaking Down Barriers** *Sigrid Berenberg*	213
26	**An Idealistic Approach to Temp Work** *Ingrid Verduyn*	223

Part III   Addressing Governance and Financial Matters

27	**What Is Compliance: An Open Conversation** *Christian Rau*	233
28	**Navigating Artificial Intelligence Governance Challenges in Organizations** *Blanca Escribano Cañas*	239
29	**International Climate Negotiations: "Blabla" or Key Forum to Solve the Climate Crisis?** *Axel Michaelowa*	249
30	**More Than A Seat: Building Sustainable Ecosystems for Youth in Government** *Ashley Priore*	257
31	**After ESG: Is Impact Investment the New Frontier for Responsible Investing?** *Grégoire Cousté*	263

32	Why and How We Should Start Measuring Real Impact *Jan Moellmann*	269

Part IV Art as a Driver for Transformation

33	From KALABATOLA to TO BE: A Transformative Journey in the Twenty-First Century *Joël Nankin*	279
34	Planetary Perspectives: Making Sense of the Sustainability Transformation through Art *Samuel Huber*	287
35	Chernobyl: The Path to Healing Human and Ecological Scars *Laurent Michelot*	297
36	The Colour Fools: Communicating Sustainability Through Music *Igor Shishlov*	307
37	An Ecological Path: From Science to Music and Painting *Emilia Jücker*	313
38	Art of Change 21: Uniting Art and Ecology for a More Sustainable Future! *Alice Audouin*	321
39	Who Am I? A Plural Identity, Hybrid, Ambiguous, Interconnected *Brigitte Bernard-Rau*	331

I Have a Dream   335

About the Editor and Contributors

About the Editor

Brigitte Bernard-Rau is a sustainability expert, lecturer and researcher at the Chair of Management and Sustainability at the University of Hamburg in Germany. She teaches sustainable finance with a focus on impact investing, environmental, social, and governance (ESG) issues, and corporate social responsibility (CSR) to Bachelor and Master students. A French native, born and raised in the French West Indies (Martinique and Guadeloupe), Brigitte has extensive international experience in business corporations, transnational public administrations, and not-for-profit organizations. Thriving in multicultural environments, she enjoys establishing connections with positive and inspiring individuals.

Firmly believing in the synergy between knowledge and action, Brigitte dedicates herself to initiatives promoting sustainability awareness and driving significant social change. Her motto, "Better Be Responsible," fuels her aspirations for a more harmonious, equitable, and respectful world. With an ultimate vision of progress built on shared understanding and cooperative efforts for the common good, Brigitte aims to inform the public about global societal challenges sharing observations, studies, suggestions, and innovative solutions from sustainability-minded actors of society and change advocates.

Brigitte's interest in the field of sustainability was sparked during her tenure at the nonfinancial rating agency oekom research AG (now ISS-ESG) in Munich, Germany, where she worked as an ESG analyst. This experience deepened her understanding of the importance of thorough assessments and precise evaluations of companies and countries from social and environmental standpoints for a sustainable future. Brigitte conducted extensive research on the role of social rating agencies, culminating in the successful defense of her Ph.D. thesis in management sciences at Radboud University in Nijmegen, the Netherlands. The title of her thesis is "Better Be Responsible—The Impact of Social Ratings on Bringing about Change in Organizations."

Brigitte has a diverse academic background, including graduate studies in English, Spanish, and International Business Development from Novancia Business School in Paris, France, and an LL.M. in European and Comparative Law from the University Carlos III in Madrid, Spain. She worked as an international business development executive in Paris and Madrid and served as a public procurement officer at the European Commission in Brussels, Belgium, overseeing contracts and financing at the External Aid General Directorate for Latin America. Brigitte is fluent in English, French, German, and Spanish.

Contributors

Alice Audouin Art of Change 21, Paris, France

Elisa Baraibar-Diez Department of Business Administration, University of Cantabria, Santander, Cantabria, Spain

Sandrine Benattar Paris, France

Sigrid Berenberg Schotstek, Hamburg, Germany

Brigitte Bernard-Rau Hamburg University, Hamburg, Germany

Stella Blohmke KYBELE, Hamburg, Germany

Blanca Escribano Cañas Carlos III Madrid University, Madrid, Spain

Claire Coletti Ecodesign, Neuilly-Plaisance, France

Diego M. Coraiola Peter B. Gustavson School of Business, University of Victoria, Victoria, BC, Canada

IAE Business School, Universidad Austral, Pilar, Argentina

Grégoire Cousté Forum pour l'Investissement Responsable (FIR)— Sustainable Investment Forum (French SIF), Paris, France

Franky De Cooman MENSJ, Lovenjoel, Belgium

Annika Degen Podcast "Gender & Climate", Hamburg, Germany

Khalid El Housni Cadi Ayyad University, Marrakech, Morocco

Raquel Flórez Escobar Freshfields Bruckhaus Deringer, Madrid, Spain

Frédéric Faure Unilever, Rueil-Malmaison, France

Samuel Huber Zurich University of the Arts (ZHdK), Zurich, Switzerland

Emilia Jücker Hamburg, Germany

Janine Kaiser University of Hamburg, Hamburg, Germany

Marine Le Picard My Little Green Star, Paris, France

Bonnie Letwas TurtlCo, Amsterdam, The Netherlands

Fungai Mettler SwiZim Trust, Kilchberg, Switzerland

Axel Michaelowa University of Zurich, Zurich, Switzerland

Laurent Michelot Brussels, Belgium

Graeme Mitchell Institute for Global Solutions, Victoria, BC, Canada

Nayan Mitra Sustainable Advancements (OPC) Private Limited, Salt Lake City, Kolkata, India

Jan Moellmann Leonardo, Frankfurt am Main, Germany

Joël Nankin Paris, France

Marie-Lou Nazaire Label Créole, La Hulpe, Belgium

María D. Odriozola Department of Business Administration, University of Cantabria, Santander, Cantabria, Spain

Corine Pelluchon Global Solutions Initiative Foundation, Berlin, Germany

Susanne Preiss Hamburg, Germany

Gut Haidehof, Wedel, Schleswig-Holstein, Germany

Ashley Priore Queenside Ventures & Queens Gambit, Pittsburgh, PA, USA

Katinka Quintelier Vrije Universiteit Amsterdam, Amsterdam, The Netherlands

Christian Rau GRC EMEA, Hamburg, Germany

Gabriele Renner Pervormance International, Ulm, Germany

Iciar Montejo Romero Prometea, Vitoria-Gasteiz, Spain

Bernhard Schwager Pervormance International GmbH, Ulm, Germany

Leon Seefeld reframe.ventures, Tettnang, Germany

Igor Shishlov Perspectives Climate Group, Freiburg im Breisgau, Germany

The Colour Fools, Barcelona, Spain

HEC Paris, France

Fernanda Tsujiguchi London South Bank University (LSBU) Business School, London, UK

Hemalatha Venkataraman An Independent Researcher, Coimbatore, Tamil Nadu, India

Ingrid Verduyn WaW Jobs, Meise, Belgium

Peter Wanderi Mount Kenya University (MKU), Thika, Kenya

Part I

Calling for Change: In Theory and in Practice

1

Ecology as New Enlightenment

Corine Pelluchon

The Reversal of Reason into Irrationality and the Scheme of Domination

The COVID-19 pandemic and the threat of collapse due to climate change and the erosion of biodiversity point to the aberrations of a development model that is based on the unlimited exploitation of natural resources and other living beings. More than ever, it appears necessary to reorient the economy in order to put it at the service of people and the preservation of the common world.

To understand why ecological transition is a chance for re-initiating a civilizational process, we must explain the reversal of progress into regression, of rationalism into irrationality. A double amputation of reason explains its degradation. First, during late modernity, that is, after the eighteenth century, rationalism became instrumental and gave rise to the era of quantification. Whereas reason in Kant or Rousseau was viewed as the most appropriate way to develop a common project, it gradually became an instrument at the service of individual desires. By being cut off from truth, reason was reduced to

---

This story was previously featured in the Global Solutions Journal. (GSJ, The World Policy Forum, 7, p. 218–223). We extend our sincere gratitude to the Global Solutions Journal for granting us permission to republish it in "Sustainability Stories."

C. Pelluchon (✉)
Global Solutions Initiative Foundation, Berlin, Germany

calculation. It lost its moral dimension as well as its capacity to distinguish the just and the unjust and could support the most barbaric and disproportionate enterprises. The second amputation of reason is more ancient since it is a consequence of the radical separation between civilization and nature that is specific to the Western world. It underpins the will to master inherited from the Enlightenment, and we realize today that it could lead to the ruin of our civilization.

The global crisis to which we are confronted is a crisis of reason. The latter is trapped in the net of domination, which is exercised over others and nature, but is also rooted in the rejection of our vulnerability and in the repression of our carnal condition. This largely explains our obsession for control and our contempt for other living beings.

This process of self-destruction of reason and civilization is not a fatality. However, to interrupt it, we need to identify its mechanisms and characterize what we call the Scheme of Domination. A Scheme is the organizing principle of a society. It is made up of all the conscious and unconscious representations that guide our economic, social, and political choices and also determines our values and desires as well as our behavior (Pelluchon, 2021: 98–100). The Scheme of Domination transforms everything (agriculture, husbandry, politics) into war. It elicits an attitude of predation toward nature and other living creatures and turns techniques into ends that are disconnected from any civilizational purposes. When we are aware of the Scheme of Domination, we understand the connections between apparently distinct phenomena, such as totalitarianism and capitalism, the destruction of nature and the exploitation of other human beings, animal abuse, and our inability to coexist with people who are different from us. This awareness prevents us from limiting ourselves to the mere denunciation of a single economic or political system and helps us to decolonize our imaginary.

It therefore becomes clear that positioning ecology at the center of public policies not only implies combatting global warming and the erosion of biodiversity. The required changes in our modes of production and lifestyles depend on a radical questioning of our representations and our relationship with other living beings. So, what makes ecology an emancipation project and the translation, in terms of public policy, of a new Enlightenment? What enables the latter to lay the foundations of a common project which, while being radically ecological and avoiding the pitfalls of the hegemonic universalism of the past, also strengthens the fundamental principles of the Enlightenment, namely autonomy, democracy, and the idea that there is one humanity and one planet?

Eco-phenomenology as the Foundation for a New Social Contract

Ecology cannot be reduced to its environmental dimension, which is mostly associated with the fight against global warming. It entails a social dimension linked to the organization of work and the fair allocation of resources and has a subjective meaning (Guattari, 2000). More precisely, ecology is the wisdom or the rationality of our habitation of the Earth and our cohabitation with others, human and non-human. Thus, it is part of our existence.

An inquiry into human existence that takes our carnal and earthly condition seriously highlights our dependence on nature and other human and non-human beings. As a consequence, ecology is a major component of ethics and politics. We can no longer ground the political association upon an atomistic and abstract subject, considered only in light of freedom conceived as the ability to make choices and to change them. The phenomenological description of eating, dwelling, living in a place, and being co-residents with other humans and animals leads to an eco-phenomenology which shows that the subject is always relational and dependent on natural and cultural things that nourish his or her life, giving it meaning and flavor. This philosophy of corporeality provides the foundation for a new political theory. The goals of the State are not only security between people and the reduction of unfair inequalities. The protection of the finite biosphere, the alleviation of animal suffering, the concern for future generations, and the consideration of all the dimensions that enable us to flourish frame a new social contract (Pelluchon, 2019a: 254–262).

Ethics defines my ability to make room for others, be they human or non-human, present and future. Additionally, justice supposes that my right to use whatever is good for my own preservation is not only limited by my fellow citizens. The impact of our lifestyles and activities on future generations and other cultures, the respect of the ethological norms and the subjectivity of animals, and the attention to the irreversible nature of certain technologies are to be taken into account by laws and public policies. Thus, the declaration of human rights which is based on the individual moral agent is no longer sufficient to guarantee equity, justice, and peace in the present ecological, technological, and demographical context. Moreover, globalization and our ecological footprint have changed the structure of our responsibility because we may unintentionally inflict damage on unborn beings and on people we never encounter. This is why the 2015 Universal Declaration of Humankind Rights proposed at the Paris Climate Summit in 2015 complements the former philosophy of human rights by proclaiming the right of humanity and of all living species to exist and live in a healthy environment and describes our duties to preserve the common goods. (http://droitshumanite.fr/).

These criteria of justice can provide guidance both at the individual and collective level. They are not values but structures of existence that proceed from the phenomenological description of the human being considered in his geographical, social, and technological environment and in his interactions with other forms of life. Phenomenology then offers an alternative to relativism, but also to the abstract and hegemonic universalism of the past Enlightenment, which has been accused by postmodernism of hiding behind so-called general principles to impose a model of civilization. Thinking about our carnal and earthly condition restores the ideal unity of humanity while recognizing the diversity of cultures. Everyone can admit the validity of these principles, which stress the centrality of ecology. However, even if they are universalizable, their application must be contextualized and put to a debate. Public policies cannot be the product of arrogant reasoning that seeks to impose fixed conceptions of good and evil, just and unjust, in a vertical and homogeneous manner. The universalism constructed here is in context and lateral: it is not the result of an overarching reason but is nourished by multiple perspectives on the world (Pelluchon, 2021: 72; Merleau-Ponty, 1964).

However, acknowledging that the duties of the State entail an extension of the common good to other generations, other cultures, and other species is still insufficient. We are only halfway there. In fact, everyone knows what is wrong and numerous reports and discourses explain how to concretely execute the ecological transition. Yet, few people are changing their lifestyles and most governments still opt for an extractivist and productivist model or support intensive livestock farming. In addition, the ecological transition appears as a burden from which everyone tries to escape. The current challenge is therefore to bridge the gap between theory and practice, awareness and action, and to make the ecological transition a stimulating project. Does the current pandemic, by highlighting the counterproductive nature of our development model in environmental, health, economic, and social terms, provide an opportunity for a profound reshaping of our representations and a change of scheme that could lead to an ecological realignment?

The Emancipatory Strength of Ecology and the Scheme of Consideration

In order to respect planetary limits and other living beings, we must overcome the separation between nature and civilization and the narrow anthropocentrism in which we have been brought up. Today, ecology is at the center of the reflexive attitude that defines Enlightenment, which is the ability to relate critically to the present in order to define its challenges and to meet them. We need to know what has to be preserved and what has to be abandoned. In other words, we must initiate a civilizational *époché*.[1] Admitting the aberrations of our model of development, which testifies to the irrationality of our dwelling on Earth, obliges us to examine our practices in agriculture, trade, urbanism, and health care one by one. It also implies freeing ourselves from the prejudices and ways of beings that support our predatory attitude toward nature and encourage our addiction to consumption. By combatting the ideas and attitudes responsible for the radical separation between nature and culture and for the denial of the community of vulnerability that unites us with others, human and non-human, we can gradually dismantle the Scheme of Domination and make room for other forms of life and culture.

Ecology is an emancipatory force, because it is impossible to respect nature and other living beings while continuing to conceive oneself as an empire within an empire. Ecology which involves the respect of planetary boundaries in our ways of producing and consuming presupposes the acceptance of our own limits. The latter are primarily related to our carnal and earthly condition, our vulnerability and finitude, but they also refer to our fallibility and to the fact that our knowledge is always limited. Ecology therefore implies humility, without which we cannot cooperate with others or institute the common good. To operate the ecological transition, we ought to carefully formulate what risks not to run and have a cautious response to the unexpected events emerging from the interactions of humans with their environment and technologies. Ecology is the political translation of the Scheme of Consideration, for which individual creativity and the preservation of the common world are the two main criteria of justice (Pelluchon, 2021:141–148). These criteria impose to invest in specific areas of research and to refuse technologies and products that can degrade the conditions of life of other beings or cause our own extinction.

Consideration means recognizing the value of things and beings, in order to make good use of them or to treat them with respect. It is based on an experience of something that is incommensurable: the common world (Pelluchon, 2019b:106–115) The latter welcomes me at my birth and will survive my individual death. It is made up of generations and encompasses the living and the cultural and technological heritage. The awareness of

---

[1] E. Husserl defines *époché* as the first operation of phenomenology understood as a way to accomplish the Enlightenment, whose spiritual figure is Socrates. *Époché* means that we put into brackets the "natural attitude" which is characterized by a certain dogmatism, leading people to believe that their representations are reality and to naively adhere to them.

belonging to a world which is older and larger than ourselves gives depth to our existence and makes us feel the bond which unites us with other living beings. It transforms our desires to the point that we have pleasure in consuming less – and in a different way. The desire to transmit a habitable world becomes a concrete motivation of our actions. Living means "living from" natural and cultural things, "living with" others, be they human and non-human, and "living for," that is, having the common world as the horizon of one's thoughts and actions. To eat, work, produce, or create a company, having in mind the preservation of the common world, and respecting the dignity and creativity of people contributes to a development model based on the Scheme of consideration.

This scheme corresponds to an enlargement of the self at several levels, ranging from civic-mindedness to a commitment to the protection of other living beings. It actually answers the aspirations of many individuals who are convinced that the current development model is outdated and would like to find meaning and conviviality in all aspects of their lives. The growing interest manifested by numerous people for the environment and the fate of animals are the harbingers of the age of the living. Gradually substituting the Scheme of Domination for the Scheme of Consideration to guide our social, economic, and political choices would enable us to build a common project that responds to these aspirations instead of disappointing them and nurturing resentment and racism, hatred of reason, and rejection of democracy. Therefore, ecology is at the center of the new Enlightenment, which goes hand in hand with a form of humanism that is based on the recognition of our carnal and earthly condition upon which our responsibility toward others, human and non-human, is grounded.

References

Guattari, F. (2000). *The three ecologies*, trans. I. Pindar and P. Sutton. The Athlone Press.
Merleau-Ponty, M. (1964). *Signs. Studies in phenomenology and existential philosophy*, trans. R. C. McCleary. Northwestern University Press.
Pelluchon, C. (2019a). Nourishment. Philosophy of the political body, trans. J. E. Smith. Bloomsbury.
Pelluchon, Corine (2019b). *Ethik der Wertschätzung. Tugenden für eine ungewissene Welt*, trans. H. Jatho. WBG.
Pelluchon, C. (2021). *Les Lumières à l'âge du vivant*. Le Seuil. *Das Zeitalter des Lebendigen. Eine neue Philosophie der Aufklärung*, trad. U. Bishoff, WHB, 2021.

1 Ecology as New Enlightenment

Corine Pelluchon is a French philosopher and professor at Gustave Eiffel University. A specialist in political philosophy, her research interests include phenomenology, moral and political philosophy and applied ethics (bioethics, philosophy of the environment, and animal ethics). She developped a philosophy of corporeality which has two parts, one centered on vulnerability, the other on our habitation of the Earth which is always a cohabitation with other living beings. This philosophy of phenomenological inspiration underlines the relation dimension of the subject and articulates a philosophical anthropology with a political theory that leads to install ecology and the animal cause at the center of ethics and politics. In this work, which is part of the heritage of the Enlightenment while going beyond its anthropocentric and dualistic foundations, ecology and justice towards animals are not dissociable from the promotion of a new humanism. Pelluchon has published about fifteen books, including on Leo Strauss, Emmanuel Levinas, and Paul Ricoeur.

In 2020, Corine Pelluchon received the Günther Anders Prize for Critical Thinking in recognition of her significant body of work. Website: corine-pelluchon.fr

2

Challenging the "Gloom and Doom" Narrative Begins in the Classroom

Graeme Mitchell

> *Education can never be apolitical, "objective" or "value neutral":*
> *it is—and ever must be—a political endeavour.*
> *It either moulds the young to fit in with traditional beliefs,*
> *or it critiques those beliefs and helps to create new ones.*
> Mary E. Clark (1989. *Ariadne's Thread: The Search for New Modes of Thinking*)

"What's the Point? We're Screwed"

This was a statement made by one of my brightest 15-year-old students at the end of a classwide discussion on the impacts of climate change in the spring of 2008. While hearing apathetic comments from teenage boys is nothing new, this particular statement was different. No sooner had the words left his mouth, the bell sounded, and the 29 learners quietly dispersed. The tension in the air was palpable. His statement seemed to have touched a collective nerve, and it lingered with me for the rest of the day.

When the class reassembled the following morning, the students took their spots in a pre-arranged circle for our weekly Socratic-style seminar. I was determined to gain some clarity. I wrote the young man's statement in the middle of the whiteboard in bright, red marker and asked the students to spend a minute reflecting on his words. When I prompted them to share their

---

G. Mitchell (✉)
Institute for Global Solutions, Victoria, BC, Canada
e-mail: gmitchell@saanichschools.ca

thoughts, the floodgates opened, and unbeknownst to me at the time, the path of my teaching career was about to take an unexpected turn.

For nearly 45 min, the students spoke passionately and led the seminar in a remarkable fashion. Throughout, I uttered only a handful of words, and when the discussion finally wound down, the main takeaway was clear. While it became apparent that my students were concerned about the receding ice caps, projected water shortages, and mounds of plastics clogging our oceans, they were simply overwhelmed by the thought and scale of so many seemingly intractable problems. It turns out that they were not so much apathetic but afraid. Apathy suggests not caring, existing in a state of indifference. What my students shared was rooted in fear.

Fear is a tricky thing—for some, it can motivate and spark a fighting reaction, but for others, it can produce the exact opposite effect and generate paralysis, or, perhaps worse still, the urge to run and hide. Either way, the class discussion made one thing very clear: perception matters. How we perceive the world and the events unfolding around us contributes to our likelihood of leaning in, stalling out, or turning to flee.

As I write this in the spring of 2021, many contend that our world seems to be on the brink of collapse. The daily news cycle bombards us with stories about pandemics, divisive politics, poverty, terrorism, and environmental degradation. From Syria to sweatshops and melting ice caps to #MeToo—all you have to do is flip on your social media feed to see that we are living in a period of conflict and uncertainty.

Or Perhaps We Are Not

Despite the influx of negative news, there are numerous scholars, activists, and entrepreneurs who challenge the prevailing "doom and gloom" narrative, asserting that it does not provide an accurate reflection of the world we live in. Interestingly, our perceptions often diverge from reality, as we tend to exhibit a negative bias when assessing the world around us. Given that adverse events tend to stick in our memories more persistently, negative incidents frequently overshadow our perceptions. Many contend that this skewing effect is intensified by the fiercely competitive media landscape, which must capture our attention to remain lucrative. Sensational stories of earthquakes, kidnappings, and bombings dominate headlines, while mundane realities do not.

The emergence of social media platforms has arguably worsened the situation. These platforms often reinforce existing beliefs in sensationalized echo chambers, further entrenching preconceived negative perspectives. To illustrate the magnitude of this influence, I recently conducted a survey among my 44 Grade 10 IGS students, revealing an astounding collective total of 46,000 h spent on social media within the span of a year by my single class.

Tech tycoon and philanthropist Bill Gates, eminent statistician Hans Rosling, and celebrated authors Steven Pinker and Johan Norberg represent some notable figures disputing the pessimistic headlines. They assert that not only is the prevailing negativity baseless but also that data from the United Nations and World Bank offer solid proof that humanity is currently healthier, happier, cleaner, freer, and more peaceful than at any previous time. Their guidance is straightforward: trust the data. The cognitive psychologist Steven Pinker emphasizes that "there has been a remarkable improvement in every single measure of human well-being. And here's the surprising part: almost nobody is aware of it."

However, successive surveys consistently show that most people believe the world is getting worse. There is no denying the multitude of challenges affecting our planet. The frequency of conflict-related deaths, which has been progressively declining since World War II, is now increasing due to persistent conflicts in Syria and Ukraine. The impacts of climate change, human-made pollution, and overfishing on our oceans are of great concern. The list of endangered species continues to expand.

Despite our tendency to focus on the stream of discouraging events surrounding us, it is worth considering what the trajectory of our planet looks like when we assess well-being over time using a consistent benchmark. The data is unequivocally clear. Factors such as life expectancy, health, prosperity, safety, peace, knowledge, and happiness are all trending upward, not just in the West but across the planet.

There is no doubt that we have to educate students about the world's biggest challenges, especially at a time when we face a seeming convergence of unprecedented crises. However, I believe that it all depends on how we present the challenges. Terrible news catches people's attention, but a raft of research demonstrates that this approach is not especially good at changing minds or motivating people. In fact, many studies suggest that it may do the exact opposite and paralyze rather than empower. In regard to how feelings of fear impact learning, the research is unequivocal: youth cannot absorb information and think critically if they are anxious, frightened, or in trauma.

After discovering how feelings of fear were holding back my own learners, I decided to try and flip the narrative by designing a learning experience that would highlight scalable solutions, innovation, and human potential—one that would serve as a road map toward a more attractive and exciting future.

In short, I hoped to build a model around evidence-based optimism. My goal was to juxtapose the conventional doom and gloom forecasts against solutions already at work in the realms of technology, economics, psychology, health care, and conservation. I sought to shed light on pockets of hope that could provide the foundations for a sustainable and resilient future. In my mind, I envisioned a class that would push students to grasp that the following three "big ideas" could be true simultaneously:

1. By almost all metrics (health, environment, economy, etc.), humanity is doing better than most people think.
2. Collectively, humanity still faces a number of "wicked" challenges.
3. There is still much room for future improvement.

In short, the goal was to highlight many of the amazing ways humanity has vastly improved over the past few decades in the hopes that learners would be filled with optimism and conviction that further progress is possible and that they would feel empowered to become part of the solution. To be clear, my perception of hope aligned closely with that put forth by systems scholar Thomas Homer-Dixon. According to Dixon, for hope to be a powerful force, it must be rooted in honesty in terms of the challenges ahead and provide a clear path forward.

Looking back, it would seem as if I began my quest to overhaul my tiny niche of the educational landscape on Vancouver Island, British Columbia, at an ideal moment in time. External and internal forces appeared to align as groundswell of support from my colleagues, administration, and trustees converged with growing calls for educational reform at the provincial level. What follows is the story of how my journey, inspired by the fateful question of "What's the point?" unfolded and how the successes and pitfalls over the past 15 years have helped to galvanize a new educational framework that my colleagues and I call the Institute for Global Solutions.

If It Ain't Broke ... Blow It Up!

The volume of education has increased and continues to increase, as has pollution, exhaustion of resources, and the dangers of ecological catastrophe. If still more education is to save us, it would have to be education of a different kind: an education that takes us into the depth of things (Schumacher, 1997, p. 208).

In the fall of 2007, I began to design a locally developed course entitled Sustainability 11/12.

The course, which was developed at Stelly's Secondary School in Saanich, BC,[1] was created to increase awareness, commitment, and competence in students around sustainability principles and provide a platform to develop initiatives for meaningful change. The course was designed to be a hands-on, participatory experience that gave learners an understanding of sustainability topics. The impetus for this program was a realization that while we had certain courses (Social Studies, Geography, Earth Science, Biology, Chemistry, Civics, Law, etc.) that highlighted issues of sustainability in BC, the prescribed content was often incomplete, fragmented by subject area, and emphasized challenges over solutions. In short, I felt there was a niche for a cohesive solutions-based offering that focused on the practical skills and thinking required to address the ecological, economic, and social challenges of the twenty-first century. The course was given school board approval and launched in September 2008, with 87 students taking part in the initial offering. The curriculum was rooted in systems thinking, with the understanding that what happens in one part of a system affects every other part, and incorporated aspects of the science-based frameworks from the Natural Step and the Center for Ecoliteracy. Initially, students explored eight overlapping modules examining consumption, energy, population, poverty and health, governance, food and water, climate change, and sustainable design.

Sustainability 11/12 seemed to resonate with learners; by year 2, 140 Grade 11 and 12 students)[2] at Stelly's Secondary School in Saanich had taken part. As a result, I was invited to help design the BC Ministry of Education's Sustainability Framework in 2008 and promote professional development opportunities around sustainability education. While Sustainability 11/12 proved popular among students at Stelly's and was exciting to teach, I began to realize that as a stand-alone elective offering, it was not accomplishing two fundamental objectives. First, the course was still only accessing 25% of enrolled senior students. Second, the interdisciplinary scope of the content was limited—both in terms of instruction time and by my own area of expertise. After conducting a qualitative review of the program, I was convinced that to maximize its efficacy, the curriculum needed to be delivered not as an isolated course but as part of a comprehensive, cross-curricular model.

Twelve years later, this stand-alone course has transformed into an interdisciplinary program with more than 200 learners taking part annually and is

---

[1] Saanich is a municipality in Greater Victoria, on the southern tip of Vancouver Island, British Columbia (BC).
[2] Secondary schools in British Columbia encompass Grades 9 through 12, similar to American high schools. Students are usually 13–17 years old, respectively. After successfully completing Grade 12, students receive their Dogwood Diploma, a high school graduation diploma.

known as the Institute for Global Solutions (IGS) at Claremont Secondary School, also in the Saanich School District.

The design of IGS stemmed from a collective belief that achieving sustainability is a matter of transformation, requiring fundamental changes in perspectives and behavior, and was based on two overarching ideas. The first is that the places where our students study, play, and work are the centers of their experiences. These experiences, in turn, help to inform how the world works and where they fit within it. As such, we felt the need to design the program purposively to expose students to sustainability education inside the classroom and outside the local community. The second idea is that all curricula are loaded or embedded with values. In the face of critical environmental and social justice challenges, our IGS team felt that it was incumbent upon educators to take an active role in encouraging and imparting values that contribute to a more sustainable present and future.

Given the cross-curricular nature of sustainability education, our IGS team decided that in addition to bringing teachers from distinct subject areas together within the building, we needed to reach out to experts around the province of BC. After meeting with educational practitioners from both secondary and postsecondary institutions as well as the Ministry of Education, we settled on a framework that would allow us to run the offering within the confines of our school's daily four-block timetable. At the senior levels, we combined the prescribed learning outcomes from four distinct Grade 11 and 12 semester-long courses: Social Studies 11 and Political Studies in the fall and Environmental Science 12 in the spring. These senior-level offerings combined the 80-min classes before and after lunch (giving us nearly 3 h each day when the 40-min lunch break is included). At the Grade 9 and 10 levels, we combined Social Studies and Science into year-long linear offerings. To justify having two educators from different subject areas team-teach the curriculum in the same class simultaneously, our board required that we double the number of students in each offering. As a result, we typically run Grade 9 classes of 50 students and Grade 10–12 classes of 50–55.

We started from the core belief that our primary job was to create the conditions to bring people together and organize a point of contact that would allow the curriculum to come to life and take on relevance. The IGS Program would rely on three main pillar activities: action projects, speaker series, and field studies. A central component of IGS is student-driven action projects. The program is designed to support project-based learning experiences in the local community, such as habitat restoration and awareness campaigns. These projects take learning outside of the classroom where students' contributions make a difference to the community's well-being. We ask students to select a social/ecological challenge that interests them, conduct research on the topic, plan and implement a solution, and showcase their final outcome. Some of the more memorable projects include the installation of solar panels on the school, the construction of an outdoor classroom, fundraising for microcredit institutions, and annual education campaigns around climate change and watershed restoration for elementary students.

In addition to the focus on action projects, we offer a biweekly Speaker Series that exposes students to many of the region's most prominent leaders and innovators, from academics and politicians to entrepreneurs and activists. This interactive series format provides students with an amazing opportunity to engage with a number of inspirational individuals. Since its inception in 2013, we have put our learners in front of over 50 prominent speakers, including Prime Minister Justin Trudeau, environmentalist Dr. David Suzuki, journalist Gwynne Dyer, indigenous activist Wab Kinew, and systems scholar Dr. Thomas Homer-Dixon.

While we initially focused on connecting our learners with experts in our region, we began broadening our scope with our first "Rails to Relevance" trip in 2013. To engage our students with Canada's structure of government and democratic institutions, our teaching team came up with the idea of taking our Grade 11 cohort on a cross-Canada train trip. On our inaugural voyage, 40 students were given two central questions to explore: (1) What does it mean to be a citizen of Canada? (2) What is Canada's responsibility to the world? Along the way, students interviewed Canadians of all stripes and were tasked with creating documentaries to showcase their findings. Our Member of the Legislative Assembly, Lana Popham, and Member of Parliament, Elizabeth May, accompanied us along the way and taught classes on governance and civic engagement as we sped along in our moving classroom. By the time we reached Ottawa, word of our unique field trip had spread, and we were granted access to politicians and leaders from all the major parties. Since 2013, "Rails to Relevance" has become a mainstay of our Grade 11 offering and inspired a Grade 12 excursion that takes students to Haida Gwaii (Rails to Resilience).[3]

As we embark upon the tenth anniversary of the founding of the IGS program, we are proud of many of our accomplishments. We are still learning (and failing) every day, but students are voting with their feet, and what

---

[3] Haidi Gwaii, often referred to as the Canadian Galápagos, is an archipelago located off the northern coast of British Columbia, south of the Alaska panhandle. Known as The Queen Charlotte Islands until 2010, the islands regained their original name Haida Gwaii, the home of the Indigenous Haida First Nations. This rugged island group is blessed with a mystic beauty and rich Haida culture, which are protected by the remote location (Takei, 2021).

started as a small niche offering has grown to a program that includes approximately 200 learners every year. While we are still hearing anxious comments from teenagers about the state of our world on a regular basis, what we have found is that our space seems to provide an opportunity for our learners to voice their concerns while also giving them opportunities to dive into evidence-based optimism. By engaging our students with stories, ideas, and concepts about what is working in our world and articulating the potential that exists, we feel that we are on to something special. Our experiment has shown us that more than anything else, hope is what galvanizes our students and seems to be the most powerful tool for change and collective action.

References

Schumacher, E. F. (1997). *This I believe: And other essays*. Green Books.
Takei, M. (2021). *Haida Gwaii. Travel*. https://www.nationalgeographic.com/travel/article/haida-gwaii-british-columbia

Graeme Mitchell is an educator based in Saanich, British Columbia, Canada, who has dedicated his career to empowering youth and addressing the pressing ecological and social challenges of our time. In 2012, Graeme co-founded the Institute for Global Solutions (IGS) at Claremont Secondary School. This innovative program inspires youth to develop and implement solutions for a more resilient and equitable future. Over the past decade, the IGS program has experienced remarkable growth, expanding from an initial enrollment of 23 students to nearly 200. In addition to his work at IGS, Graeme is an Associate Professor at the University of Victoria and Royal Roads University.

3

Slipping Sustainability into Higher Education. Take One!

Elisa Baraibar-Diez ⓘ and Maria D. Odriozola ⓘ

Teaching Sustainability: A Script for Change

Imagine that you are the director of a film about sustainability. If education were a character, what role would it play? Surely it would have a leading role, don't you think? And what about the title "The Future Will Be Sustainable or It Won't Be" for that film?

Let me tell you something: the truth is that this film is already being shot, and it is on this premise of a "sustainable future" that we have to work in all areas of society. Most importantly, it is something we have to show to young people, teaching them responsible and sustainable behavior and consumption habits. Actually, if we stop for a minute to think about it, there is no other option because there is currently a lot of pressure (from international entities but also from the planet and society itself) to achieve long-term economic, social, and environmental objectives.

In this sense, educational institutions have a great responsibility, since the weight falls on them for training at all stages of life, from kindergarten to higher education, through a lifelong learning context.

As active university lecturers, it is comforting to witness the interest that more and more students have in sustainability issues, students who are accustomed to terms such as ESG (environmental, social, and governance

---

E. Baraibar-Diez (✉) • M. D. Odriozola
Department of Business Administration, University of Cantabria, Santander Cantabria, Spain
e-mail: elisa.baraibar@unican.es; odriozolamd@unican.es

© The Author(s), under exclusive license to Springer Nature Switzerland AG 2024
B. Bernard-Rau (ed.), *Sustainability Stories*, https://doi.org/10.1007/978-3-031-52300-7_3

factors for sustainable investing), SDGs (Sustainable Development Goals), GRI (Global Reporting Initiative), KPIs (key performance indicators), OKR (objective and key results), materiality, and environmental or social impact. Additionally, we applaud small habits that we observe in and outside the classroom in relation to more sustainable food choices (reusable bottles on the tables, less processed food), sustainable transportation (walking, bicycles, public transportation, carpooling initiatives), conscious shopping (reusable bags), and green campus initiatives such as environmental volunteering.

However, we are aware that it is not enough, and international studies reflect this, showing that the habits of students who finish their degrees are slightly less sustainable than those of freshmen or sophomores (Chuvieco et al., 2018). What are we doing wrong, then? How can we rewrite the script of our film? The students who enroll in our classes are obviously not the sponges that they used to be at the beginning of their studies, and we cannot ask them to unlearn what they have learned. The main problem is not so much conceptual as it is how to materialize those concepts, that is, the problem is in not knowing what to do to achieve sustainability. And what's more important, what to do so that students truly internalize the truth about the impact they have on everything around them. It is here that higher education institutions (HEIs) can contribute to solidifying and actualizing effective practices that, first, awaken awareness in students; second, increase their participation; and third, let them know the consequences of their behavior. Universities are the perfect place for this, so … lights, camera, action!

What can universities do for sustainability? The power they have as vectors for the transmission of sustainability ideas is immense (it could be said that this sustainability film is going to be released in every theater in the world), and the template can be adjusted for "plot twists" in the script. These "plot twists" include actions such as (1) be sustainable, (2) integrate sustainability into the curricula and training, (3) research, and (4) promote sustainability in the relationship with stakeholders.

Be Sustainable

Set an example by acting sustainably. If we want the entire university community to develop sustainable habits, we have to demand that the university itself is also sustainable (the directors of the film have to be models of flawless behavior, and they should always keep the complete storyline in mind). Therefore, sustainable principles must be adopted by university management.

In fact, having a committed university is directly related to a positive attitude in the university community (Dagiliūtė et al. 2018). Like liquid seeping into a crack, sustainable initiatives need to cover all aspects of student life and engage students on a day-to-day basis:

(a) Sustainability in the use of materials and resources (e.g., paper, utilities, telematics, research materials, waste, and recycling).
(b) Sustainability in consumption (e.g., sustainable and local supplies in canteens and cafeterias, healthy lifestyle habits, food planning, and responsible purchasing).
(c) Environmental sustainability (e.g., electric bikes, public transport, and beach and park cleaning initiatives).
(d) Social sustainability (e.g., responsible human resource practices, promotion of inclusive education, care for vulnerable groups, and respect for diversity).

For example, at the University of Cantabria, we have the Ecocampus Project, which is the formalization of the university's commitment to environmental management and sustainable development. Furthermore, the Equality, Conciliation, and Social Responsibility Area has a supporting role, whose objective is to promote transversal measures (visibility, seminars, conferences, case studies, fair trade promotion) and to ensure their compliance. The Energy Sustainability unit is part of the Vice-Rectorate for Campus, Services, and Sustainability, with the goal of developing an energy plan that prioritizes energy security, social equality, and environmental impact reduction.

Integrate Sustainability into the Curricula and Training

We are very fortunate within a university setting. What other institutions have the structure and capacity to disseminate knowledge at such a transversal level? And where can we find an audience as engaged as university students? In each and every one of the scientific disciplines found within the university, the integration and promotion of sustainability are not only possible but essential. It is true that universities are sometimes seen as rigid and unyielding institutions, and it is our responsibility as lecturers or educators to do our bit and contribute as much as we can. We have multiple tools at our disposal, such as activities, simulations, essays, discussions, storytelling, case studies, course topics, full courses, seminars, massive open online courses (MOOCs), specialization classes, and master's degrees. The possibilities are limitless, given that we have all the actors in our film willing to promote sustainability. Furthermore, by educating future doctors, engineers, economists, teachers, and more in sustainability, we ensure that they will develop and carry forward these principles into their professional and personal lives, using the skills that they have acquired.

This need has received recognition and support at the central government level in Spain. Royal Decree 822/2021, of 28 September, which establishes the organization of university education and the procedure for quality assurance, states that curricula (Bachelor's, Master's, Doctorate) must be based on democratic principles and values and the Sustainable Development Goals (SDGs).

Research

What about research? We can consider research the best part of our film, as it supports and enhances continued learning, promoting long-term thinking. Research is one of the pillars of a university, and as such, creating knowledge in any field (humanities, social sciences, medicine, engineering, etc.) will only favor innovation and technological improvement, promoting the development of solutions for the challenges that sustainability poses. Our university has five leading research institutes, two foundations, and more than 150 research groups that support research advances and the transfer of knowledge not only regionally and nationally but also internationally.

Promote Sustainability in the Relationship with Stakeholders

In a world where cinema has certainly become outdated in reaching a certain audience, what if we release our sustainability film not only in theaters but also on other platforms and streaming services to reach an even wider audience? Strengthening and working on commitment with internal and external stakeholders (such as government, policymakers, practitioners, and the community) is key to promoting alliances and guaranteeing innovative practices. Bringing the university's activities to the general public will only reinforce visibility and enhance the transformative power of a sustainable university. Thus, events such as Researchers' Night, Pint of Science, Campus for Children, and UC-Enterprises Forum help show what goes on "behind the scenes" of our sustainability film. A continuous dialog with stakeholders ensures that their perspectives and concerns are considered in HEIs' sustainability efforts.

The mere act of becoming the scriptwriters of this film has made us realize that our universities have a great responsibility that is probably not being realized (as at many other institutions) precisely because it is not understood. One of our main weaknesses has been our inability to impart concise and meaningful information that is worth reading. In a hyper-informative environment, we are so focused on reading our part of the script that we forget the whole story and do not interact with the other actors who may have a more important role than ours. Therefore, we should work on more effective means of communication that are especially dedicated to sustainability (stories are a perfect example) that put our values into action and quantify their impact.

Shooting the film of sustainability requires the collaboration of very diverse actors, and we must bear in mind that our university students are very demanding spectators.

But wait, a cliffhanger! Our students must be aware that they are the ones who will film the sequel to "The Future Will Be Sustainable or It Won't Be", and they will go from being spectators to being the leading roles in the picture. For this reason, in addition to engaging with students to encourage awareness, we need to put special emphasis on communication, storytelling, and the impact both generate, ultimately promoting a spirit of responsibility and cooperation.

References

Chuvieco, E., Burgui-Burgui, M., Da Silva, E. V., Hussein, K., & Alkaabi, K. (2018). Factors Affecting Environmental Sustainability Habits of University Students: Intercomparison Analysis in Three Countries (Spain, Brazil and UAE). *Journal of Cleaner Production, 198,* 1372–1380. https://doi.org/10.1016/j.jclepro.2018.07.121

Dagiliūtė, R., Liobikienė, G., & Minelgaitė, A. (2018). Sustainability at Universities: Students' Perceptions from Green and Non-Green Universities. *Journal of Cleaner Production, 181,* 473–482. https://doi.org/10.1016/j.jclepro.2018.01.2

Elisa Baraibar-Diez is a tenured lecturer in the Department of Business Administration at the University of Cantabria, earning her PhD in 2013. She lectures both in Spanish and in English in the fields of business administration, entrepreneurship, international business, and simulation in business administration. Her research interests focus on sustainability and CSR, corporate transparency, teaching innovation, social entrepreneurship, and social impact. She belongs to the research group Economic Management for the Sustainable Development of the Primary Sector, and her research has generated a number of papers in national and international journals, sharing her contributions at various national and international conferences. She has visited the Institut für Management at Humboldt Universität (Berlin), Sun Yat-sen University (Guangzhou, China), and La Trobe University (Melbourne, Australia). She has coordinated the official MBA program at the University of Cantabria for 3 years, and she is now vice dean of Planning, Digitization, and International Relations GADE at the Faculty of Economics and Business Administration.

María D. Odriozola is a tenured lecturer in the Department of Business Administration at the University of Cantabria, earning a PhD in 2015 (awarded in 2016 by the CSR Santander chair at the University of Málaga). She lectures in the area of human resource management, management skills, new management models, and entrepreneurship. She belongs to the research group Economic Management for the Sustainable Development of the Primary Sector. Her main lines of research are on aspects of corporate and labor social responsibility, labor practices, corporate reputation, teaching innovation and the dissemination of social information. Her research has been part of several papers, book chapters, and proceedings at national and international conferences, and she has visited the University of Bath (UK) and the University of Bretagne Occidentale (Brest, France). Now she is the academic coordinator of the master's degree in human resources: The Value of People, director of the University Expert Degree in Guidance, Entrepreneurship, Accompaniment and Innovation for Employment and Director of the UC Summer Courses in the municipalities of Suances and Los Corrales de Buelna (Cantabria, Spain).

4

Approaching Wicked Issues in Practice, in Theory, and in the Wild

Katinka Quintelier

Throughout history, philosophers and scientists have come up with life-saving solutions to socio-environmental problems. We can prevent polio and smallpox, we have antibiotics, and we rely on technology to clean water. However, equally often, possible solutions are not timely or broadly implemented. Physicians know how to cure and prevent tuberculosis, but it is still the deadliest infectious disease in the world (Foster, 2020). Climate and food scientists expect that a more plant-based food production system and diet would drastically reduce greenhouse gas emissions (Hayek et al., 2020), land use (Stehfest et al., 2009), and diseases (American Dietetic Association, and Dietitians of Canada, 2009), but every year, only approximately 1% of the population in the Netherlands decides to become vegetarian (de Waart, 2020). While epidemiologists and microbiologists have developed models and vaccines to stop a pandemic, the fight against COVID-19 has been hampered by vaccination skepticism. Why is implementing a possible solution to our problems so hard? How can we improve this situation?

This chapter argues how current socio-environmental problems require social solutions, where multiple stakeholders are involved in finding and implementing solutions. To illustrate this, I will fast-track you through a course on multistakeholder management. This course offers basic guidelines for approaching problems where the solution seems obvious, but the path

---

K. Quintelier (✉)
Vrije Universiteit Amsterdam, Amsterdam, The Netherlands
e-mail: k.j.p.quintelier@vu.nl

toward it is a challenge. Every year, students in business administration choose this 4-week course and work on a problem of their own choice. I will ask you, the reader, to imagine yourself as a student who participates in the course with a problem you care about. After laying out methods to approach your problem, these methods are generalized to theoretical principles. The chapter ends by exploring what previous students learned from the course and how that helped them or an organization they worked for. But, first, we need to understand the nature of the problem.

Wicked Problems and the Social Sciences

Natural scientists develop technical solutions to socio-environmental problems. However, implementing technical solutions requires social solutions, where people change their behavior. Let's illustrate the difficulty of this implementation process with an example from the medical sciences. A group of UK-based researchers interviewed 232 medical professionals to find out why medical interventions did or did not get implemented in practice (Ferlie et al., 2005). Surprisingly, the strength of the evidence did not matter: medical interventions with stronger evidence were not more likely to be implemented than medical interventions with weaker evidence. What did matter were social attitudes, such as the extent to which people from different professional groups agreed on the evidence, trusted other group members' intentions and competence, communicated expectations, and understood others' values. For instance, an intervention, where nurses would by default provide patients with information about anticoagulation drugs, is an evidence-based intervention. However, nurses did not take up this intervention. Reasons were that the evidence for it seemed contested, and doctors and nurses did not trust each other's competence or intentions. As a consequence, information about the intervention did not pass from doctors to nurses, and the intervention was not implemented. What this example illustrates is that even a simple behavioral change—nurses informing patients—is actually a very complex process consisting of many changing interactions between different people. The process of implementing a possible solution is socially complex, requiring cooperative interactions between people with different and conflicting interests. We can say that implementing a solution is often a wicked problem (Peters, 2017).

To approach wicked problems, we need the social sciences. Traditionally, strategic management, as a social science, investigates how to implement solutions to a problem. However, strategic management also tends to underestimate the social complexity of a situation. Stakeholder management, instead, is a specific approach to strategic management that explicitly acknowledges social complexity. It builds on the observation that different people have different stakes in a situation. In other words, there are different stakeholders. Stakeholders are individuals or groups with a vested interest in the situation who are affected or can affect the solution to a problem (Freeman, 1984). Getting these stakeholders to interact in a cooperative way is one of the central problems in stakeholder management. When stakeholder management is applied to wicked problems, scholars tend to speak of multistakeholder management (Rühli et al., 2017).

Multistakeholder Management in Practice

Multistakeholder management is a practical affair: you have to practice it in order to learn it. Therefore, when following this course, student teams choose an existing case to work on while learning the theory. The case ideally contributes to a socio-environmental problem that the students care about. Next, student teams choose an organization that addresses the problem. Organizations, compared to individuals, carry a stronger potential to have an impact. Most people, including students, can have noticeable effects on organizational processes, and organizational processes have a strong influence on people's behavior. A good example is an organization's food options. Most employees, at least in Western Europe, can start a campaign at work to influence which food options the organization offers. The potential impact of such a strategy is considerable. If a campaign gets one organization to commit to Meatless Mondays—offering its employees only vegetarian options for one day every week—most employees would eat one vegetarian meal once every week. Up to 5% of employees' meals (during their lifetime as an employee) would then become vegetarian. In comparison, at the moment, only 2% of the current population in the Netherlands considers themselves vegetarian. Having a meat-free Monday at work is therefore comparable in impact to at least doubling the number of vegetarian employees.

Another way for an individual to have an impact is to start one's own organization. For instance, one student was the co-founder of an NGO that attended to the needs of hospitalized children. Because of political instability, funding was uncertain. A team of students therefore considered how to transition the NGO to a social enterprise—this is an organization that engages in commercial activity to make a profit and then reinvests the profit in the organization's social mission (European Commission, 2016). The NGO has existed for more than 8 years now and has expanded its activities to online hospital visits and language courses. Hence, by choosing a problem and addressing it at the organizational level, one can make a clear difference.

Of course, people vary in what they care about, so you might choose an entirely different problem and organization than the ones illustrated. Once you have in mind which problem and which organization sparks your interest, we can conduct a stakeholder analysis to determine whose behavior should change. There are different approaches to this step, ranging from a more top-down approach to a more bottom-up approach. In a more top-down approach, who the stakeholders are is decided by a leader, in a theoretical manner, and the scope is usually exclusive—focusing mostly on the most powerful stakeholders. For instance, in US healthcare management, a top-down stakeholder analysis leads executives to see powerful health organizations as important stakeholders, while patients—who are not very powerful—are deemed less important (Brugha & Varvasovszky, 2000). In the case of anticoagulation drug information, the nurses were deemed the most powerful stakeholders because they had to implement the practice.

Is a top-down approach the right approach to your problem? In our examples, it seems to overlook stakeholders that are important, notably patients. In the case of health care management, it is difficult to see how health care can be called a success if patients do not comply with their treatment. Intuitively, when addressing social problems, beneficiaries such as patients appear as the most crucial stakeholders, even when they have no power. A top-down approach also overlooks stakeholders that turn out to be important during the implementation process. In the case of anticoagulation drug information, the situation was in hindsight more complex because the implementation also depended on doctors' behavior, which was unforeseen. Importantly, many apparently simple social situations are complex in hindsight. For these reasons, we better try out a more bottom-up and inclusive approach.

Bottom-up methods include determining who is involved in a more informal manner, and the scope is inclusive. We can ask the stakeholders whom they interact with, we can observe stakeholders' interactions, or we can actively participate as stakeholder ourselves. Bottom-up methods ensure that everyone who has an interest in the matter can be included, even if they do not seem to have much power to influence the process. During the course, students apply bottom-up techniques such as interviewing or observing stakeholders. However, students are also encouraged to choose a problem they are knowledgeable about. For instance, a case about capital investments in Eastern Africa was undertaken by a team comprising a student with a professional background in capital investments and another student with an Eastern African cultural background. These diverse backgrounds provided the students with valuable implicit knowledge about the situation and its stakeholders, offering an additional bottom-up method for stakeholder analysis. We can expect that applying bottom-up methods to the anticoagulation drug information case would have led to the recognition of nurses, doctors, and patients as significant stakeholders. A good idea might be to start with a top-down approach and then further deepen the analysis through a bottom-up approach.

Now that we have analyzed the stakeholders, the question is how stakeholders should change their interactions. This step also has different approaches, ranging from a more unidirectional to a more participative approach. In a unidirectional approach, a strategic team uses the results of the stakeholder analysis to develop a solution and a plan. Stakeholders are then instructed, trained, and incentivized to carry out that plan. When looking at past attempts, students often find that unidirectional approaches have been tried and failed. For instance, our university experimented with Meatless Mondays by instructing a reluctant caterer. Immediately though, some meat-eating students and employees complained about the unexpected and unexplained lack of meat. The caterer then used these complaints as a reason to stop the experiment. Following instructions is not a very motivating task.

Instead, we can try out a more participatory approach, which implicates all the stakeholders in finding a solution and in instructing, training, and incentivizing each other to carry out the agreed-upon solution. In the case of unsustainable food, this was simulated by having all teams in class interact with the team that wanted to increase the number of vegetarian food options. That way, students with a stake in eating meat (Leenaert, 2021)—the majority of them—engaged with the problem of unsustainable food and participated in finding solutions to that problem. While challenging, this also led to more creative solutions, such as eliminating ruminant meat only because it has a higher carbon footprint than other meat (Ripple et al., 2014).

How successful was the bottom-up, inclusive approach? This is a difficult question. A few years later, the number of vegetarian food options had increased, but we cannot know to what extent the student project contributed to this. However, we do know that this project made students engage with the sustainability of their food choices. For other projects, students conducted interviews and became aware of stakes that cannot be found in textbooks. In addition, alumni felt that in their current jobs, multistakeholder management helped the organization better understand the stakeholders and offered creative insights. While these outcomes are not yet implementations of a solution, they do seem valuable as such and can be useful in the long term when addressing a social or environmental problem.

Multistakeholder Management in Theory

Now that we have a bird's eye view of the practice, we can infer theoretical principles. In fact, you already know the essence. When engaging in multistakeholder management, you have to ask yourself three questions: why, who, and how. Why do you want to change people's interactions, or what is the socio-environmental problem? Who should be involved in solving it, or who are the stakeholders? And finally, how will you spur the stakeholders to change their interactions? These three questions can be asked iteratively. For instance, when stakeholders leave or join the interaction process, one should again analyze the stakeholders and check how stakeholders can participate. This is illustrated in the case of the NGO for hospitalized children. With donating political parties gaining and losing power, the organization had to reconsider who could donate money to the organization, and this question was coupled with how funders would interact with the organization. In complex situations, iteratively asking why, who, and how helps to guide you through the process.

In addition to these three questions, you already know that there are different approaches. We can put them on a continuum ranging from a more "organization-centric" to a more "issue-centric" approach (Roloff, 2008). An organization-centric approach aims to achieve the organization's goals and tends to be more top-down, exclusive, and unidirectional. We have seen how it fails, but it also has benefits. An organization-centric approach works well if the organization's performance is a major concern. It is also fast, and it works well in a hierarchical context when the issue is truly simple or complexity can be ignored. For instance, one study investigated how the Helsinki school district instructed schools to have a weekly vegetarian day (Lombardini & Lankoski, 2013). This worked, in the sense that schools complied with the instructions. If an organizational goal such as compliance with a principle is the only problem you want to solve, then you might opt for an organization-centric approach.

In contrast, an issue-centric approach aims to achieve a solution to an issue instead of an organization's goal and tends to be more bottom-up, inclusive, and participative. This is a slow and complex process, but again, it has its own benefits. If the problem is larger than one organization, it is better to cooperate with a more inclusive set of stakeholders. An issue-centric approach also provides more sustainable solutions, and it works well in complex situations where stakeholder interactions need to be taken into account. We can again look at the Helsinki school district. If, in that case, the school district wanted to increase the sustainability of children's food consumption, the sketched top-down approach was not optimal. That may come as a surprise because schools complied. However, the forced food restrictions led children to throw away their food and decreased participation in school lunches in the short term. In order to increase sustainable food consumption, schools and the district might have done better by participating with the community and its children.

So far, we can conclude that if you want to tackle a socio-environmental problem, you need to engage in issue-centric stakeholder management, which is a bottom-up, inclusive, participative approach. At least, this seems a better fit for the situation. However, does an issue-centric approach also lead to better results? This is hard to find out. On the one hand, the process of issue-centric multi-stakeholder management is dynamic and unpredictable and therefore does not lend itself easily to controlled experiments (WHO, 2013). On the other hand, qualitative research does show that issue-centric multi-stakeholder management, if done right, leads to intrinsic benefits to the involved parties, such as increased trust and respect, empowerment, the development of new institutions that increase democracy and accountability, and acceptance of proposed solutions (Coulby, 2009; Reed, 2008). In other words, while it is unclear if issue-centric multistakeholder management leads to the implementation of a proposed solution (no matter how flawed), it does lead to the formulation of more acceptable, sustainable, and feasible solutions (WHO, 2013). This is at least a good basis for the long-term resolution of a problem.

Multistakeholder Management in the Wild

This leads us to the final question: Did these methods and theories help students approach wicked problems in their professional lives? To find out, I got in touch with former students. I asked what they learned, and if what they learned helped them or their organization.

Students learned a few things that are intrinsically valuable. For instance, students remembered from the course that stakeholders are "not just people who earn money." Instead, stakeholders have a wide variety of interests. This was also recalled as the snaildarter controversy, where people's interest in a tiny but endangered fish (the snaildarter) delayed the building of a dam for 6 years but saved the fish from extinction (Freeman, 1984). Each stakeholder has a variety of interests beyond earning money, and this can help in solving a variety of problems. A related point is that different stakeholders have diverse interests. While this diversity can lead to conflict, it can also lead to more creative formulations of the same problem or possible solutions. In sum, the course seemed to foster the recognition of stakeholders as complex and diverse human beings (Freeman et al., 2010).

How does multistakeholder management help an organization? More than one student is now more focused on what organizations do for society. Another student felt empowered to explain to a colleague why Fridays For Future is a relevant stakeholder for a bank. Hence, this course also made some students acknowledge and defend the societal role of organizations. In addition, students remarked that organizations should engage in multistakeholder management more often. Other students conducted stakeholder analyses themselves and found that taking time to analyze the stakeholders in a structured way is very helpful, can make stakeholders happy, and helps them convince colleagues.

Mirroring practice and theory, students' responses mentioned intrinsic benefits of learning about multistakeholder management but no specific successes in solving social and environmental problems. The opposite would have been a surprise. Students are just starting their careers, and changing organizational processes takes many years. However, the existence of intrinsic benefits is very promising. The creation of more trusting, respectful, and empowering interactions lays a foundation for agreeing on possible solutions. We can say that multistakeholder management is a decent approach to wicked problems, in practice, in theory, and in the wild.

References

American Dietetic Association, & Dietitians of Canada. (2009). Position of the American Dietetic Association: Vegetarian diets. *Journal of the American Dietetic Association, 109*(7), 1266–1282. https://doi.org/10.1016/j.jada.2009.05.027

Brugha, R., & Varvasovszky, Z. (2000). Stakeholder analysis: A review. *Health Policy and Planning, 15*(3), 239–246. https://doi.org/10.1093/heapol/15.3.239

Coulby, H. (2009). *A guide to multistakeholder work: Lessons from the water dialogues*. Accessed http://www.mspguide.org/resource/guide-multistakeholder-work-lessons-water-dialogues, from 30 December 2017.

De Waart, S. (2020). *Factsheet Consumptiecijfers en aantallen vegetariërs*. https://www.vegetariers.nl/bewust/veelgestelde-vragen/factsheet-consumptiecijfers-en-aantallen-vegetariers-

European Commission. (2016). *Social enterprises* [Text]. Internal Market, Industry, Entrepreneurship and SMEs - European Commission. https://ec.europa.eu/growth/sectors/social-economy/enterprises_en

Ferlie, E., Fitzgerald, L., Wood, M., & Hawkins, C. (2005). The nonspread of innovations: The mediating role of professionals. *Academy of Management Journal, 48*(1), 117–134.

Foster, L. (2020). 5 of the world's deadliest infectious diseases. *World Economic Forum*. https://www.weforum.org/agenda/2020/04/covid-19-infectious-diseases-tuberculosis-measles-malaria/

Freeman, R. E. (1984). *Strategic management: A stakeholder approach*. Cambridge University Press.

Freeman, R. E., Harrison, J. S., Wicks, A. C., Parmar, B. L., & De Colle, S. (2010). *Stakeholder theory: The state of the art*. Cambridge University Press.

Hayek, M. N., Harwatt, H., Ripple, W. J., & Mueller, N. D. (2020). The carbon opportunity cost of animal-sourced food production on land. *Nature Sustainability, 1–4*. https://doi.org/10.1038/s41893-020-00603-4

Leenaert, T. (2021). Steakholders. In K. Dhont & G. Hodson (Red.), *Why we love and exploit animals: Bridging insights from academia and advocacy*.

Lombardini, C., & Lankoski, L. (2013). Forced choice restriction in promoting sustainable food consumption: Intended and unintended effects of the mandatory vegetarian day in Helsinki Schools. *Journal of Consumer Policy, 36*(2), 159–178. https://doi.org/10.1007/s10603-013-9221-5

Peters, B. G. (2017). What is so wicked about wicked problems? A conceptual analysis and a research program. *Policy and Society, 36*(3), 385–396. https://doi.org/10.1080/14494035.2017.1361633

Reed, M. S. (2008). Stakeholder participation for environmental management: A literature review. *Biological Conservation, 141*(10), 2417–2431. https://doi.org/10.1016/j.biocon.2008.07.014

Ripple, W. J., Smith, P., Haberl, H., Montzka, S. A., McAlpine, C., & Boucher, D. H. (2014). Ruminants, climate change and climate policy. *Nature Climate Change, 4*(1), 2–5.

Roloff, J. (2008). Learning from multi-stakeholder networks: Issue-focussed stakeholder management. *Journal of Business Ethics, 82*(1), 233–250. https://doi.org/10.1007/s10551-007-9573-3

Rühli, E., Sachs, S., Schmitt, R., & Schneider, T. (2017). Innovation in multistakeholder settings: The case of a wicked issue in health care. *Journal of Business Ethics, 143*(2), 289–305. https://doi.org/10.1007/s10551-015-2589-1

Stehfest, E., Bouwman, L., van Vuuren, D. P., den Elzen, M. G. J., Eickhout, B., & Kabat, P. (2009). Climate benefits of changing diet. *Climatic Change, 95*(1), 83–102. https://doi.org/10.1007/s10584-008-9534-6

WHO. (2013). *Implementation research in health: A practical guide*. World Health Organization. http://www.who.int/alliance-hpsr/resources/implementationresearchguide/en/

Katinka Quintelier is a researcher and associate professor in Strategy and Ethics at the Vrije Universiteit Amsterdam. In her research, she aims to develop scientific insights that foster sustainability in an inclusive way. Her area of expertise is at the intersection of stakeholder theory and the circular economy, with a special focus on how stakeholders (including organizations) can create value for (1) people and (2) the environment, while (3) being financially sustainable. She looks at the circular economy through the lens of stakeholder theory, which was the topic of her PhD in strategy (2020), and through the lens of moral psychology, which was the topic of her PhD in philosophy (2011). Currently, she is involved in research projects about the circular economy in the construction industry. Previous research shows her broad interest in all things human and natural and resulted in high-impact scientific, professional, and popular publications and in three awarded or nominated contributions to conferences.

5

How to Become a Sustainability Ambassador and Changemaker in Five Steps?

Susanne Preiss

Amid the widespread conversation about the climate crisis and the growing awareness of its pressing nature, books such as the one you hold take on vital significance for both individuals and organizations. They serve as invaluable resources, aiding us in the crucial task of pinpointing practical solutions. However, the question remains: how and where do we start addressing the biggest change of all time? How do we turn cognitive awareness into action? Moreover, how can we instill the urge for sustainable transformation into the minds, and then the veins, of some of the main actors—the CEOs and entrepreneurs?

I would like to share our experience in conducting our Future Thinking workshops, designed to precisely achieve these objectives. I will provide a detailed account of the process to immerse you in the experience, prompting you to integrate and customize these methods for your own workshops. Please feel free to E-mail me, ask any questions, and request further details. Ultimately, we are all colleagues, united in our common pursuit of a shared climate goal: ensuring that our planet stays below a 2 °C global temperature increase. We collaborate, not compete, on this critical mission.

S. Preiss (✉)
Strandweg 98a, Hamburg, Germany

Gut Haidehof, Wedel, Schleswig-Holstein, Germany
e-mail: preiss@susanne-preiss.de

Who Attended the Workshop and What Were Their Business and Organizational Expectations?

Workshop participants included directors of large- and medium-sized companies, senior managers, hotel owners, professionals from the advertising world, and entrepreneurs. All participants confirmed that the topic of sustainability has become more present and urgent in their businesses. However, they could not judge whether this was part of a conscious and practiced corporate culture.

During the workshop preparations, we sent participants a few questions about their expectations for the workshop. Here are some of their answers:

- *We are a pure service company. Our customers are placing increasing importance on sustainability. In this workshop, I would like to learn the minimum requirements for our organization to be classified as a sustainable organization.*
- *In our area of IT, it is not easy to find qualified people. Young and highly skilled applicants ask more frequently about a sense of purpose and sustainability. After this workshop, I would like to leave with concrete ideas or recommendations for implementing sustainable procedures and policies.*
- *We are facing extreme challenges with our logistics company. We want to gradually make the entire company—the management, our products, and services—sustainable. By attending this workshop, I hope to better understand what sustainability is and where we should start.*
- *We have gone public with our globally active company. Fund managers invest almost exclusively in companies that have a sustainability track record. Quite simply, I am interested in the quickest way to produce a sustainability report.*
- *We are a family-owned company in the media sector. We already have many sustainable initiatives, and the employees love to participate in them. However, these initiatives are not specifically part of a strategic approach. The CEOs think these issues are costly and of secondary importance. I am particularly interested in convincing my fellow shareholders that this topic is necessary for our company's survival and part of our social responsibility.*
- *Others want to address and raise sustainability issues at the leadership level and present themselves as sustainable transformation managers shaping their company's future. Another driving motivation is how sustainability could generate new ideas for products and markets.*

- *Some current board members wish to make this topic their own and be identified with it as a manager, leading the company into a sustainable future. One of the entrepreneurs would like to gain concrete experience in sustainable thinking and receive an orientation on the topic, while others would like to find out to what extent sustainability could also open up new business areas.*

With these expectations in mind, we recognized that the success of our Future Thinking Workshops successfully relied on creating an environment that would bring participants into direct contact with vital natural resources—soil, water, air, plants, and animals—engaging all their senses. Such an immersive setting was essential to facilitate a transformative shift in mindset among our participants.

Embodied Recognition as a Key to Making the Shift to a Sustainable Mindset

My husband and I bought a farm together with friends a few years ago (www.gut-haidehof.de). Experiencing sustainable processes with all five senses has proven very beneficial to our workshop idea, infusing the issue of sustainability with the emotional energy needed to initiate major change. Here, at our organic farm, we have a motivated team of experts from around the world. We show how regenerative agriculture works and why our soils are an essential part of the solution for CO_2 sequestration. We follow the rule of "no digging." We focus on soil regeneration, pasture management, growing healthy food, and cultivating a beautiful market garden. The buildings on the farm are all a bit run down, nothing fancy. Our animal husbandry is already almost CO_2-neutral, which is due to our pasture management. We are the German Hub (official holistic reference center) of the Savory Institute. Together with Leuphana University in Lüneburg and its Chair of Biodiversity, we are scientifically proving the extremely positive and rapid impact that applied regenerative agriculture has on biodiversity.

We begin our workshop with a pure body experience. We stand with our participants outside, stroke the animals, and examine the soil and its consistency very closely. We do this because this broad topic is about our beautiful world. We should live in harmony with it and do everything we can to preserve it. What better way to develop a feeling for this than by getting right up close to nature and perceiving it with all of our senses! (Figs. 5.1 and 5.2).

Fig. 5.1 City dwellers are (re)connecting with nature on the farm. (Photograph by: Anita Merzbacher. All rights reserved)

Fig. 5.2 Happy with chicken! Chicken love cuddles; workshop participants get a chance to interact with them in a more affectionate context, which they otherwise only know as a source of food (Photograph by: Anita Merzbacher. All rights reserved)

Our organic farm, Gut Haidehof, exudes sustainability. It provides the perfect environment for shifting your perspective and mind while being supported by our network of coaches and consultants who specialize in accompanying organizations in their transformation toward sustainability. We call ourselves UNO INO. The name arose from a common observation: Sustainability is on our minds and on everyone's lips. That is all well and good, but how does sustainability become anchored in our hearts, our neural pathways, and our hands? How does insight become a reflex? It is time to act. Today. Now. You Know. I Know. This is how UNO INO was born. You can do the same!

How to Conduct a Future Thinking Workshop

I will now provide a step-by-step breakdown of our workshop process, covering the different stages spanning one and a half days.

Step 1: Establishing a Framework and Learning to Speak the Same Language

In the first part of the workshop, we develop a common understanding of what sustainability is. We build a foundation for the group to start a discussion and talk about the same things. We provide input about the Triple Bottom Line (TBL) accounting theory, Sustainable Development Goals (SDGs), Inner Development Goals (IDGs), CO_2 measurements according to the Greenhouse Gas Protocol, reporting according to the Global Reporting Initiative's GRI Standards, and becoming a CO_2-neutral company. Understanding these theories, accounting systems, and standards is essential for those people who think, analyze, and make decisions based primarily on numbers and data. After introducing and discussing these standards and tools, I like to show the movie *Tomorrow—The world is full of solutions* to convey some of the great initiatives already operating successfully around the world and to highlight the bigger picture of sustainability. We watch the movie in the old barn, sitting on benches with our feet in the dirt. Afterward, we stand around the campfire. The topic is no longer whether we have to change something, but instead, what it could be. What specific changes should be made? Conversations focus on the new insights gained, the first new ideas, and the best cases presented in the movie.

By the end of the day, participants had acquired a foundational understanding of basic knowledge and had developed an emotional connection or investment in the subject.

> **Lessons from Step 1**
>
> We initially underestimated the strong desire for exchange and discussion. In particular, the film, ignited lively dialogs. As a result, we ran out of time during the first part of the workshop. Our lesson here: Allot more time for exchange and provide more space to explore these very personal attitudes about the topic.

Step 2: Embodied Recognition—Getting in Touch with Nature, Feeling the Earth, the Soil, and Stroking our Animals

When the sun rises, the mist is still hovering over the meadow. This is the setting for the second part of our workshop. It is 7:00 a.m.; rubber boots and work clothes have replaced business attire. We do not wait for latecomers because nature does not wait for us. We move the herd of cows from one piece of pasture to the next. We cuddle with our hens, who love that. We leave our comfort zones and learn how leadership works within the herd of cows and brood of hens. Additionally, we learn everything about CO_2 sequestration through proper pasture management and that even meat production can be CO_2 positive. The participants learn that we aim beyond just sustainability—our goal is to be regenerative. It is a different way of looking at business. It is not about maximizing profit and exploiting nature or people. It is about taking good care of what mother earth offers and keeping this wonderful system nourished so we may be able to coexist in harmony.

Participants learn about the hidden champions, the microorganisms. What do they need, and how do they want to be treated to be able to give our plants the best environment to grow big and strong and be full of life? We show how each bug and worm performs an important job, even if they are shy and rather unattractive from our perspective.

At this point, we reflect on how we can transfer this knowledge to our teams and incorporate it into the way we work.

> **Lessons from Step 2**
>
> This experience in nature is the key to opening the hearts of the participants. There is no longer the question of whether to do something or not but rather what concrete measures can be undertaken.

Step 3: Purpose—My Values, and What Are My Driving Forces?

After a simple but healthy oatmeal breakfast, we assemble in our seminar room (a former horse stable) and define our personal sustainability values according to the 17 SDGs. The SDG cards are highly effective for this kind of work because they are visually striking. We can tactilely experience them by holding them in our hands. They serve as inspiring illustrations of the SDG categories upon which it is rather easy to define personal and company sustainability values. Are the personal and company values the same, or do they differ? The important question here is: What matters most to my company and me, and why? By looking at the best practice cases of small, mid-size, and large companies, we expand our outlook and horizons and stimulate ourselves to develop our own ideas. For example, the participants learn the following: sustainability and profit are not necessarily contradictory; sustainability and digitalization go very well together; sustainability creates resilience; sustainable companies are more likely to win the battle for talent; sustainable business transformation is inevitable; and the cost of not becoming sustainable is much higher than the investment costs now (Figs. 5.3 and 5.4).

Fig. 5.3 Workshop participants embark on an exciting journey of self-discovery as they align their sustainability values with the SDGs (Photograph by: Susanne Preiss. All rights reserved)

Fig. 5.4 Workshop participants embark on an exciting journey of self-discovery as they align their sustainability values with the SDGs (Photograph by: Susanne Preiss. All rights reserved)

Nevertheless, the most important question to answer here is: Why do I want to get involved? What drives me to do this?

> **Lessons from Step 3**
>
> It is interesting to note that the large-format SDG cards we prepared are excellent for reflection work. They are even better than we had expected.

Step 4: Inventory and Stakeholder Analysis

Many companies are already acting sustainably without knowing or communicating it. A good first step is to acknowledge which activities are already in place and take stock of things that might count as aspects of sustainable management. Alternatively, with best practice examples in mind, participants gather initial ideas about what they would love to do first. Having the SDGs and IDGs as a guideline makes it easy to determine which idea or activity already matches the respective goals. Some companies already have a written strategy, while others do not. One objective of compiling these short inventory lists is to determine whether there is already a visible strategy behind the sustainability activities or that this still needs to be developed.

Next, we look at the most important stakeholders: consumers, suppliers, clients, government, community, and employees. Who are they? What do they expect? What would they need for them to decide in favor of my company, product, or community?

> **Lessons from Step 4**
>
> This segment of the workshop operates extremely well when using the prepared worksheets. This is also a great opportunity to build a bridge with an essential tool—the materiality matrix, which illustrates the different needs of various stakeholders.

Step 5: Designing a Sustainable Future. My Vision—My Story

After lunch, we need courage, unbridled imagination, and productive group work. Participants visualize their company in 7 months, 2 years, and 7 years from now. They describe these phases precisely, employing a mixture of optimism and realism. We raise the following questions: What should my company stand for? What stories should people tell if they talk about me? How will I change my product, my business, and my company's culture to meet the environmental, social, and economic requirements of sustainability?

We reflect on the question of how attractive that future would be on a scale from 1 to 10. How would I recognize that I am on the right path? What would be different?

Then a very important question needs to be answered by each participant:

Just imagine, everything you have envisioned becomes a reality: How would you feel about that? What would that mean for you? What difference would it make in your life? At this point, we need to "fish" for everything that comes to the participants' minds because this is the WHY. It is the purpose—the driving force for transformation. It is the core source of energy.

> **Lessons from Step 5**
>
> This step is very suitable for a team from the same organization. For our open workshop, this was too ambitious for some individuals. Nevertheless, some of the participants developed great ideas here.

Step 6: The Next Steps—Making It Happen!

In this last part of the workshop, we aim to transform the ideas and stories into a serious commitment.

The objective is to go beyond mere declarations of intent and instead forge a commitment toward implementation and the next steps. At this stage, we become quite pragmatic and motivate our participants to commit by making binding statements, including specific timelines, for implementing the respective parts of their plan. We notice that we often need additional people, skills, and resources to implement the goals that have been set. Therefore, the question is: who or what do I need to turn my ideas into reality? In this last part of the workshop, we also want to look at the possible obstacles and sources of resistance to bring one's ideas to fruition and try to find possible solutions right away. How can I succeed in convincing important players about the idea? What makes these people tick, and which arguments could most effectively convince them?

Follow-up

During individual coaching sessions approximately 6 weeks later, we collectively assess with each individual participant the progress made in implementing the measures required to achieve their expressed goals. Together, we determine the steps required to establish a long-term transformation process toward sustainable management within the company. This approach enables the company to assume responsibility and contribute to achieving the goal of holding global warming to +1.5 °C.

Summary Our post-workshop assessment reveals the following: Less is more. For the topics we aim to convey, an ideal timeframe would encompass two days, complemented by an evening session for viewing the film upon arrival. Nevertheless, the single-day format was a pivotal criterion for many participants to engage.

Susanne Preiss , a certified business coach, regenerative organization consultant and sustainability transformation manager, is passionate about guiding organizations in sustainable business transformations. She firmly believes that sustainability is a holistic endeavor, with the people driving change being the linchpin of success. Collaborating with her husband and other partners, she also operates a pioneering regenerative agriculture farm in Germany, showcasing how intelligent pasture management and animal husbandry can yield a CO_2-positive balance (www.gut-haidehof.de). Beyond her professional pursuits, Susanne also initiated a transformative school project near the Somali border in Kenya, offering underprivileged children quality education to deter radicalization (www.mwendobora.org). Born in 1967, Susanne resides in Hamburg, Germany. A mother of four, she has spent over 9 years living in Latin America and Southeast Asia. Photograph by: Andreas Lühmann. All rights reserved.

6

Lessons Learned from CSR Managers in the Retail Industry in France

Sandrine Benattar

I worked for "*Collectif Génération Responsable*" (Responsible Generation Collective, later referred to as Collectif) from 2018 to 2020. The Collectif is a nonprofit association that has been contributing to the development of concrete policies and actions in the business field for over 15 years, both in the societal and environmental aspects, through the implementation of continuous improvement processes. The members of this club are CSR managers from the retail sector who convene monthly with a shared commitment to enter a labeling process and to make progress in a systematic way. During these gatherings, they actively share best practices, engage in discussions with solution experts, facilitate workshops, find solutions, and foster valuable networking connections.

These CSR managers are personally committed to driving positive change within their organizations, despite being well aware of the challenges they face. Whether dealing with varying budgets, levels of support from their management, or positions, meaning power, within the organizational hierarchy, their determination remains unwavering.

They are happy to share their progress with their peers, as they think that sharing and even "mutualizing" their ideas collectively is useful.

The brands they work for touch all sorts of industrial sectors, which also have their own challenges, tempos, and legislative frameworks (e.g., food, cosmetics, decoration, and fashion).

S. Benattar (✉)
ESSEC, Paris, France

Testimonials

Among these remarkable individuals, a few have dedicated themselves to CSR endeavors for over a decade. They stand as pioneers and experts, having lent their expertise to renowned brands such as the store chain "Nature et Découvertes." The chain is inspired by the former Californian company, The Nature Company. In addition to selling products centered around a nature-themed concept, the brand develops a nature education program and establishes connections between naturalist associations and its customers. Take, for instance, Etienne, whose innovative approach turned CSR into an "event." He made a bold statement during European Mobility Week by summoning an excavator to eliminate two parking spaces exclusively reserved for management, symbolizing the transformative power of CSR.

In contrast, some of their peers, particularly those in the fast fashion sector, have embarked on a relatively recent journey to catalyze CSR within their organizations. These individuals came from diverse backgrounds, including communications departments and business units, lacking specialized CSR knowledge initially. However, their personal commitment to environmental change and transition sparked a remarkable transformation, including at a personal level. They successfully infiltrated the organizational hierarchy, becoming catalysts for change from within—and it is their inspiring stories that I will delve into further.

Consider the transformational journey of Gabrielle as an illustrative example. She initially held a strategic development role in Russia, but a growing personal awareness of environmental issues prompted her to ponder a career with Greenpeace. However, Gabrielle ultimately chose a different path, opting to catalyze change from within her organization. She proactively proposed an internal consulting initiative to her management, which organically evolved into a pivotal role as a Corporate Social Responsibility (CSR) manager, leading to the establishment of a dedicated team to drive sustainable practices and positive environmental impact.

Or take Simon, who in search of purpose transitioned from the role of a social media manager to a CSR conductor, quietly influencing and advising the management from within.

Significant changes have occurred since 2015, spurred by various factors, including the landmark COP 21 Conference and the subsequent Paris Agreement. Pivotal events in the field of CSR, such as those listed below, have catalyzed these changes:

- External triggers such as the scandals in the food industry or the textile industry (e.g., Rana Plaza)
- Consumer-driven pressure is compelling B-to-C companies to exert influence on B-to-B enterprises, creating a cascade of demand throughout the supply chain.
- Internal pressure stemming from employees or prospective candidates during interviews
- Pressure from shareholders, competitors, NGOs, the media, and other stakeholders
- Awareness of the leaders (in politics and in business)
- Regulation

Let's focus on some determinant factors.

Today, the legislative framework is indeed favorable for accelerating progress in the CSR field, both at the national and European levels. See, for example:

1. The French Loi Pacte, which helps companies move from subjugated CSR to strategic CSR
2. The French Anti-Waste Waste and for a Circular Economy Law, also called AGEC Law
3. The European CSRD (Corporate Sustainability Reporting Directive)
4. The EU Taxonomy, a European classification system that helps identify socially and environmentally sustainable economic activities.

In addition, internal pressures originating from employees at the company level are drive significant change. But how? Over the past few years, I conducted interviews with a select group of individuals to uncover their CSR journey inside their company and the challenges they faced in building CSR from the ground up. My goal was to collect valuable insights and seek advice they could share with their colleagues. Here are some lessons learned from their stories:

1. **In terms of mindset and posture**

    - Humility: Begin with modest steps and maintain patience and determination.
    - Service Orientation: Place oneself in service of the various professions.
    - Transparency: Embrace transparency as a guiding principle.

- Roles Evolution: Progress from the role of an auditor and internal consultant in the diagnostic phase to that of a facilitator and conductor as the journey unfolds.

2. **In terms of approach**
   In the initial phase:
   - Begin with a comprehensive internal assessment.
   - Conduct an audit of all existing initiatives, even those not previously synthesized or well documented.
   - Engage in discussions with business managers, support function leaders, and passionate volunteers who have personal involvement.
   - Compile a detailed record of past efforts, their requirements, and more.
   - Establishing a roadmap:
   - Develop a structured framework around identified issues.
   - Catalog the issues that are commonly acknowledged.
   - Integrate CSR considerations into their daily roles and responsibilities.
   - Formation (setting up ?) (of) Working Groups:
   - Define working groups comprising 10–15 volunteer managers from various backgrounds, expertise levels, professions, and brand affiliations.
   - Collaboratively agree upon and internally prioritize the identified issues.
   - Commitment to Key Initiatives:
   - Secure commitment to prominent core business projects.
   - Additionally, focus on a selection of smaller, visible actions.
   - Concretize the action plan with a formalized document.
   - Embark on a path of incremental accomplishments.
   - Align these accomplishments with key events in the company's internal communications calendar and noteworthy annual highlights, such as European Sustainable Development Week, Mobility Week, or even occasions such as Black Friday.

In the second phase:
Environmental Impact Focus:

- Shift the focus toward measuring and reducing the organization's carbon footprint.
- Conduct comprehensive life cycle product assessments to gauge their environmental impact.
- Undertake a materiality analysis after establishing a meaningful dialog with stakeholders.

External Validation:

- Strive for continuous improvement through a robust labeling process, which includes the involvement of an independent third-party organization for validation.

Effective External Communication:

- Begin external communication efforts, either through corporate communication channels or dedicated CSR platforms.
- Ensure that the communication is both engaging and authentic, avoiding the pitfalls of being either mundane or engaging in greenwashing.

Recognition and Internal Engagement:

- Participate in industry awards and accolades to foster internal team motivation and engagement, celebrating achievements collectively.

3. **And now, what contributes to success:**

- Stay Informed: Continuously gather information from relevant organizations and solution experts to stay updated on CSR trends and best practices.
- Benchmarking: Analyze CSR reports, websites, and newsletters of other organizations to benchmark and learn from their experiences.
- Networking: Actively engage with peers and professionals in the field by attending events and networking opportunities.
- Build Internal Relationships: Foster positive relationships with all internal stakeholders and strive to listen to and understand management's perspectives.
- Effective Communication: Tailor your communication to resonate with various stakeholders, speaking their language in terms of performance, market expectations, cost savings, talent acquisition, and retention, among other key areas.
- Discovering Surprises: Seek out pleasant surprises by uncovering existing CSR efforts and identifying opportunities for internal communication. Rely on influential ambassadors and individuals with organizational influence.
- Partnerships: Forge partnerships with relevant associations by participating in events such as Anti-Waste Day or collaborating with initiatives such as "Too Good to Go."

4. **Points to Keep in Mind:**

- Balanced Input: Avoid soliciting input from everyone without the capacity to fulfill all requests, preventing potential disappointments.
- Realistic Timeframes: Exercise prudent arbitration while considering realistic time perspectives. Acknowledge that we frequently overestimate what can accomplish in a single year while simultaneously underestimating our long-term potential over a decade.

In summary:
For an individual or an organization to make progress in the field of CSR, the following critical elements need to be set on the agenda:

- Management Conviction: Cultivate a deep-seated commitment from management to go beyond mere compliance with regulations. Encourage a transformative approach to reshape the business model.
- Transparency: Uphold a culture of openness and transparency in all actions and communications.
- Evidence-Based Discourse: Embrace a discourse founded on tangible evidence and results, demonstrating the efficacy of CSR initiatives.
- Strategic Prioritization: Prioritize issues that demand sustained effort and unwavering dedication, aligning them with the broader organizational strategy.
- External Validation: Seek external validation through labels, assessments, or awards, reinforcing the journey of continuous progress.

Sandrine Benattar is a corporate social responsibility (CSR) trainer and consultant, who works passionately with her clients. Since September 2020, she has been the coordinator of ESSEC (French Business School) Transition Alumni Club, collaborating closely with ESSEC Alumni to drive synergy within the global Alumni community.

In the period from 2018 to 2020, Sandrine Benattar took on the rewarding task of developing Club Génération Responsable, where she played an instrumental role in fostering a community of individuals committed to responsible practices and sustainability.

Sandrine serves as a Board Member for Social 3.0, where her focus is on facilitating effective networking and support for young social enterprises. In this role, she dedicates her energy to creating meaningful connections and empowering social entrepreneurs.

7

Not All Businesses Are CSR Friendly. Good News: This Can Be Fixed!

Marine Le Picard

In an ideal company, social impact would be the raison d'être of every business, the driving force behind innovation, and the main vector for employee engagement, to the point where the topic of corporate social responsibility (CSR) would fall into disuse. What if this is not the case in your company? Here are a few tips to make it happen.

In the meantime, it is clear that the maturity of companies regarding social and environmental issues remains extremely variable. When I began my conversion to sustainable development a few years ago, I was struck by the repetition of the idea that the commitment of top management was an indispensable prerequisite for the deployment of a CSR approach worthy of the name. While top management's dedication is undeniably a powerful driver, can you achieve your goals when you don't have this favorable situation? By operating a few simple levers and with a good dose of perseverance, I have experienced the feasibility of the following approach, and I am able to confirm that, yes, you can!

M. Le Picard (✉)
My Little Green Star, Paris, France
e-mail: marine@mylittlegreenstar.com

CSR Does Not Exist? Create It!

There are many ways to introduce this idea into an organization. It is, for example, possible to rely on the growing number of legal obligations everywhere around the world (extrafinancial reporting, duty of care, conflict minerals, etc.). It is entirely possible to take up these subjects without occupying a position with an official CSR stamp on it. Once this has been done, going back is almost impossible, and you can legitimately plead for a more structured approach.

Say What You Do and Do What You Say!

Communication is key to strengthening the place of CSR within a company. By taking care to avoid the pitfalls of social- or greenwashing, a company that communicates transparently about its actions and results in this area implicitly makes a commitment to maintain and even improve its CSR performance. It thus enters a virtuous circle encouraged by its stakeholders, who are the targets of its communication. In this way, CSR gradually becomes one of the company's strategic issues.

Internally, communication is also essential to establish an approach, give it credibility, raise awareness, and mobilize all employees. It is necessary to anchor social and environmental issues in the company's culture. The icing on the cake: these cross-cutting issues that affect both professional and personal life are formidable vectors of connection and relationship.

Pick Your Battles: The Importance of Impact

In addition to the social and environmental issues identified in a conventional way, e.g., through materiality analysis, it is wise for a company to place at the heart of its strategy those issues just where it thinks it has the capacity to significantly enact change. This reflects a sincere commitment and the desire to have a positive impact on the world.

In the context of the COVID-19 crisis, the rapid mobilization of a number of companies has been remarkable, whether in the cosmetics sector for the production of hydroalcoholic gel, in the fashion industry for the manufacture of masks, or in the sports industry for the conversion of equipment into respirators. Likewise, in the field of banking and financial services, efforts have focused, in particular, on the expansion of contactless payment technology for sanitary reasons, and small businesses' support to engage in distance-selling activities with their customers in order to maintain their activity. In this way, everyone was contributing to the common good in the best possible way. Regardless of exceptional situations such as the COVID-19 pandemic, the question of "impact" should be regularly revisited by a company to maintain a specific, relevant CSR approach that is in line with societal needs. For example, electronic payment solutions for businesses and consumers are formidable tools that facilitate access to banking services for populations located far from cities or excluded from traditional banking systems. In line with the UN Sustainable Development Goals (SDGs), specifically SDGs 8 and 10, when installed at merchants' premises, payment terminals become real bank counters for day-to-day transactions, thus contributing to the reduction of inequalities and economic growth (Figs. 7.1).

Digital payment solutions can also be used to collect donations and provide public-interest organizations with new sources of funding. It is easy to understand the specific value provided by a company that puts its technologies, its capacity for innovation, and its know-how to the service of the common good. By supporting NGOs (nongovernmental organizations) in financing their missions, it acts in line with the partnership logic of Agenda 2030 and SDG 16.

Now, I had to overcome some internal resistance to the large-scale deployment of this type of payment solutions due to the false assumption of an antagonistic relationship between impact logic and business logic. The solution finally laid in the creation of a position solely dedicated to the deployment of these payment solutions with a positive impact, which allowed me to build a bridge between the marketing and CSR functions and to erase the gaps between these two forms of logic, a gap that was essentially due to different time approaches. In the long term, the return on investment is confirmed: innovation, new customer sectors, loyalty, etc.

What is good for Society is also good for the Company!

Fig. 7.1 The 17 United Nations Sustainable Development Goals also known as the Global Goals (Source: UN Department of Global Communications)

Takeaways: A Message to Internal Actors

Awareness of the need to mobilize companies to address environmental and social issues is growing. It is also rightly welcomed by the new generation. Some companies have been thinking about this for a long time. For others, there is still time to sow the seeds for this necessary transformation, which will be exciting to see germinate, hatch, and develop.

Let's act from within for a sustainable transformation!

Marine Le Picard 's career started in 2000 at Société Générale in Cameroon, where she launched the first payment cards, ATMs (automated teller machines or cash machines), and POS networks (point-of-sale locations or payment terminals) in the country. After 15 years of experience playing various roles in the payment industry, she decided to add a new dimension to her career with a focus on sustainability. She pled for the creation of a global CSR function at Ingenico Group and led its related strategy from 2015 to 2020. Whether at an individual or at an organizational level, Marine strongly believes we all have a role to play in building the world we want.

Now, with My Little Green Star, Marine aims to help citizens move to a greener way of life, and companies propel this change among employees thanks to an app that makes the ecological transition easy and fun. LinkedIn: https://www.linkedin.com/in/marinelpmailnet/

8

Regenerative by Design: Building Regenerative Business Models

Leon Seefeld

To avoid the catastrophic, cascading risks of crises such as climate change, biodiversity loss, and soil degradation, as well as global pandemics, inequality, and mass migration, it is paramount to fundamentally change most of the systems that we rely on today. Anything from our food, housing, and transport systems to our health, education, financial, and legal systems will sooner rather than later have to undergo unprecedented transformation to avoid societal and ecological collapse. Foundational to this superscale transformation is not only policy and regulatory innovation but also the courage and contribution of each and every one of us, including the institutions and businesses that we work for and buy from. This chapter explores how we can help to build a holistically regenerative economy through business model innovation with small and medium-sized enterprises (SMEs).

In recent years, we have seen a substantial rise in genuine interest from businesses to shift their operations toward alignment with sustainable development objectives, including the UN Sustainable Development Goals (SDGs). However, to shift systems at the scale outlined above, businesses will have to go beyond incremental operational improvements and holistically rethink the core logic of their economic activity, their business model. Corporate Social Responsibility (CSR), Environmental Social Governance (ESG), and corporate citizenship activities are worthless if a business model is structurally designed to privatize gains and socialize costs, i.e., to generate

L. Seefeld (✉)
reframe.ventures, Tettnang, Germany
e-mail: leon.seefeld@reframe-rt.de

company profits from the systemic degradation of natural ecosystems and/or undermining of societal thriving.

Rethinking the logic of core business models requires a holistic view beyond sustainability. One emerging concept that proves promising for reverting the above-described logic of systematic degeneration is *regenerative business models*.[1,2] Regenerative business models, although almost impossible to fully achieve, allow businesses to earn company profits while also generating system-level value for the ecosystems they are nested in and the stakeholders that surround them (see Fig. 8.1). Much like how bees not only extract pollen to produce honey for their own personal benefit but play an integral part in the complex stocks and flows of natural ecosystems and the web of life, companies can create more value for the system than they extract.

While a holistically regenerative approach to business model design is difficult to achieve in the short term, businesses can begin to embrace certain elements that are common to regenerative business models. One of these includes the principle of circularity, i.e., the circular design of material and energy flows.

> **Example: From Waste to Value**
>
> *About one-third of the food produced on this planet is never eaten. It takes an area larger than China to produce all that wasted food. If it were a country, food waste would be the third-largest emitter of greenhouse gases after China and the USA. This is what makes tackling the issue of food waste such an important objective in the context of combating climate change, let alone global food security and inequality. So far, a lot of businesses have benefited from externalizing the costs of wasted food from their balance sheets to our common balance sheet.*
>
> *At reframe.ventures, one of our clients, a German family-owned bakery, aspired to tackle this issue within its sphere of influence. We worked with them and developed a beer made from leftover and unsold bread, which a nearby brewery produced. In so doing, we created a demand for something previously deemed worthless and built a circular business model around a global sustainability issue at the microscale. Today, with every bottle sold at this bakery, food waste is reduced and company profit is generated.*

The example of the beer made from leftover bread is one of the models that we are talking about when we propose the idea of *regenerative business*. The concept should not be confused with the steps many businesses have taken to, e.g., reduce water and electricity usage, avoid unnecessary printing, separate

---

[1] Konietzko, J., Das, A. and Bocken, N. (2023) 'Towards regenerative business models: A necessary shift?', *Sustainable Production and Consumption*, 38, pp. 372–388. doi:10.1016/j.spc.2023.04.014.

[2] Caldera, S. *et al.* (2022) 'Moving beyond business as usual toward regenerative business practice in small and medium-sized enterprises', *Frontiers in Sustainability*, 3. doi:10.3389/frsus.2022.799359.

8 Regenerative by Design: Building Regenerative Business Models

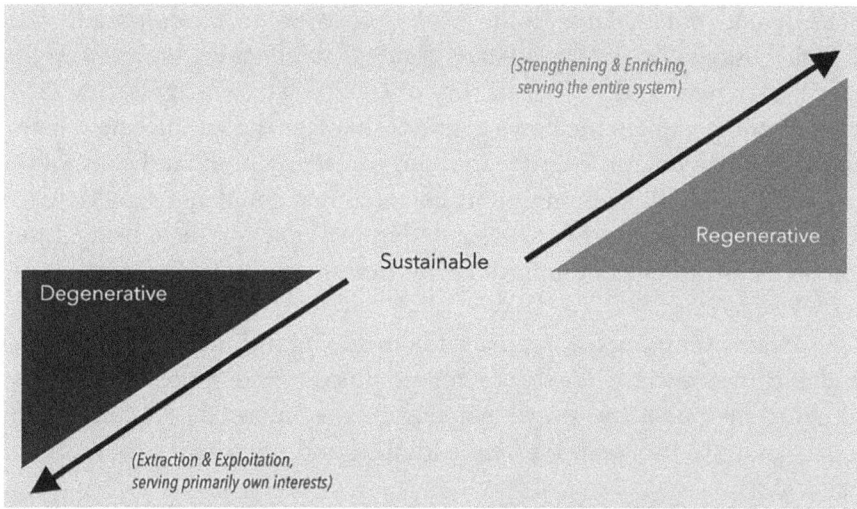

Fig. 8.1 From degeneration, beyond sustainability to regeneration (Image by: reframe.ventures. All rights reserved)

waste, implement corporate volunteer days, donate a percentage of profits to charity, and offer employee health checks. These steps are worthwhile, of course, but to catalyze systemic change, businesses need to rethink the logic on which they generate their profits. By adopting regenerative business models, companies can sell products and services that benefit both the business in economic terms and society/the environment at large.

To identify the different elements that can help construct a truly regenerative business model, company decision makers can, for example, look to start-ups for inspiration. According to the German Start-up Monitor 2022, more than 40% of new businesses consider themselves social start-ups, meaning that tackling a specific social or environmental problem is as important to them as turning a profit.[3] Their high success rate illustrates how valuable societal impact can be for business success. However, not only start-ups, but also multinationals such as Patagonia, Interface, Danone, PepsiCo, Walmart, Unilever, and Nestlé are starting to support regenerative business practices.

We believe that much more can be done, though. The German economy is known for its small to medium-sized enterprises (SMEs). SMEs account for approximately 45% of the total economic output and employ approximately 60% of the workforce in Germany.[4] Many of these businesses are family owned and rooted in models that were developed generations ago. Most of

---

[3] German Start-up Monitor 2022: https://startupverband.de/fileadmin/startupverband/mediaarchiv/research/dsm/DSM_2022.pdf
[4] Federal Agency for Civic Education of Germany (www.bpb.de).

them are not yet familiar with the concept of *regenerative business*, and many of their business leaders have never heard of regenerative business models. Even if they have heard about it, they often struggle to imagine how such a concept would work in their own context. They lack the specific know-how of a business model that is effective for both generating profit and contributing to societal good. There is enormous potential that could and should be harnessed to shift systems from being very dysfunctional for life to being in support of life—through the innovation of new, regenerative business models. But where to start?

At reframe.ventures, our approach to developing such regenerative business models is rooted in the Double Diamond process model used in the Design Thinking methodology, which emphasizes the importance of thoroughly understanding a problem first before ideating and prototyping solutions (see Fig. 8.2).

So, in a nutshell, how do we work?

The process always starts with an interest, vision, and commitment of key decision makers in the company for the business to be a force for good in the world. For the success of regenerative business model innovation, genuine, intrinsic, and strong leadership commitment is essential and, thus, a precondition for our work.

After having started the joint engagement, we begin with a carefully curated and structured process of identifying degenerative, social, or environmental problems that are relevant to the SMEs' core business, those that the leadership team is willing to help alleviate. It is vital that the business is committed to addressing the root cause of this problem, rather than just treating the symptoms. We have developed a set of comprehensive frameworks to guide our clients through this stage of orientation, focus setting, and selection (see 1a–1d in Fig. 8.2).

Only once the issue is clearly defined and thoroughly understood can a business begin to develop ideas of how the new business model can systematically contribute to holistic value creation and betterment. Often, these new business models will not immediately replace the core business. They are usually incubated on the side first, before they mature and eventually (could) phase out the degenerative business model. Creative workshops and interactive brainstorming tools help to shape rough pictures of what a solution to be incubated could look like (see 2a in Fig. 8.2). At this stage, we introduce a sophisticated proprietary database of real-life regenerative business model examples for inspiration. We developed our database by analyzing +600 best-practice examples of social and regenerative enterprises around the world, identifying their business model—how they generate profits—as well as their

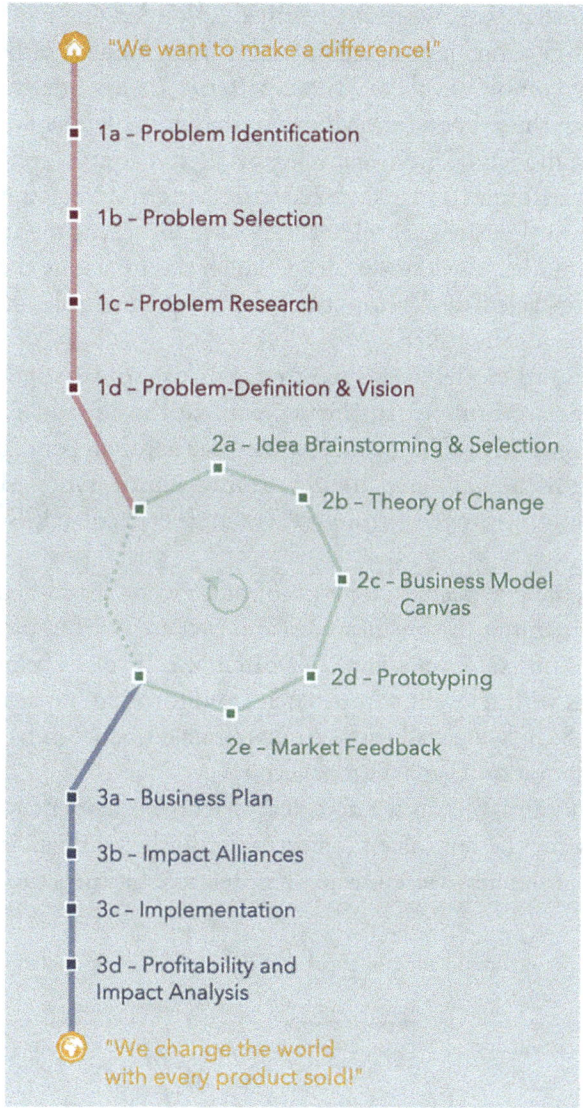

Fig. 8.2 A typical client journey to innovating Regenerative Business Models (Image by: reframe.ventures. All rights reserved.)

impact model—how they create a positive societal impact.[5] This allows us to abstract patterns that describe the different ways in which business and impact models form the foundations of new regenerative business models.

---

[5] Business Model Patterns by reframe.ventures: https://www.reframe-rt.de/grundtypen

Through our database, we have identified 24 underlying patterns that help to design and develop new regenerative business models, either within the patterns or by combining them. These patterns are essential for structuring and simplifying the process for SMEs and, therefore, democratizing access to such business models. Three examples of such patterns are illustrated in Fig. 8.3: basic patterns 01, 16, and 22. Basic pattern 22 illustrates the model that was used in the case example of the German bakery mentioned earlier: the upcycling model. The leftover bread, which was for a long time considered "waste," was upcycled to develop a beer that was then sold, hence creating economic value for the bakery.

Once a business model idea is selected, a Theory of Change and Business Model Canvas are built to further crystallize the idea in its conceptual stage (see 2b and 2c in Fig. 8.2). Designed on paper, regenerative business models can now be validated by developing a prototype, which is iteratively tested and improved through early market feedback (see 2d and 2e in Fig. 8.2).

As soon as there appears to be a proof of concept, a full-fledged business plan helps to manifest the business idea and prepare it for implementation or launch to the final target market. This often also involves bringing in additional partners with relevant competencies and forming impact alliances (see 3a–3c in Fig. 8.2). We usually act as a matchmaker between parties and help facilitate collaboration to maximize success.

The job is not finished until a holistic impact measurement system is developed to allow for the constant monitoring of both the financial and impact performance of the newly established regenerative business model (see 3d in

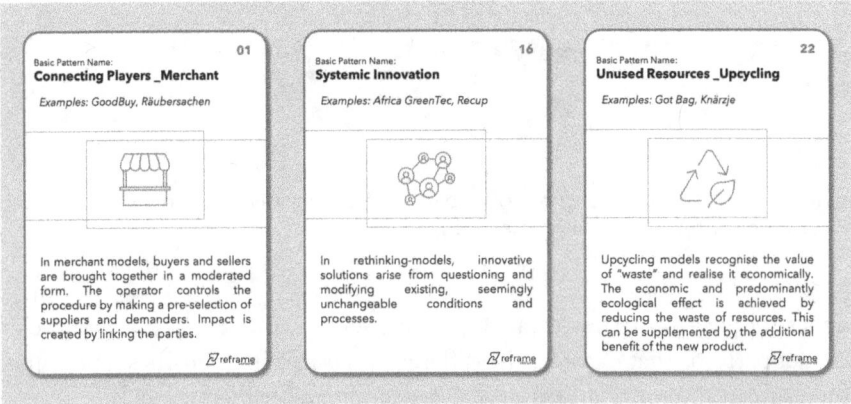

Fig. 8.3 Three of twenty-four basic business model patterns (Image by: reframe.ventures . All rights reserved.)

Fig. 8.2). This ensures that positive impact is scaled up over time and that potential negative impact is avoided by incremental adjustments to the new business model based on gathered data.

The ultimate goal is always to design new business models that allow positive system value with every unit sold and every unit of company profit made.

Understanding the elements of regenerative business models and how to apply them is still in its infancy. Many business schools still teach the same old degenerative paradigms of economics and business management. There is still a widespread belief that one either does business or charitable work, and never the two shall meet. However, where holistic sustainability and regeneration are adopted as fundamental paradigms, they can foster unseen economic success and make companies more resilient in times of crisis, as pioneering examples such as VAUDE and Werner & Mertz in the German SME market vividly show.

However, in the minds of many people, there is still a disconnect between the actions of individuals and those of businesses. People may realize that they need to change their own behavior or lifestyle but often fail to make the link between the current poly-crisis and the business world.

For businesses to become part of the solution, we need business leaders who understand their responsibility and acquire the skills and knowledge to address the enormous challenges mankind is facing. We need to educate young talent to make decisions based on clearly defined values that prioritize the greater social good over selfish wealth-maximization pursuits. Regenerative business models have a transformative role to play as they bridge the gap between impact and profit.

> Sustainability is not a problem to be solved, but a future to be created, together.—Peter Senge, MIT Sloan School of Management.

In the face of the complex and superscale crises that we find ourselves in today, it sometimes feels as if any new regulation, any new stakeholder demand is yet another burden on our business operations. It can feel daunting and weary. AND as world-renowned management guru Peter Senge reminds us in the statement above: We are not just working away burdensome paperwork and toward ever-new compliance standards, we are creating a better future for generations to come, and we are doing it together. If that is not an absolutely fantastic basis for audacious ambitions for each and every one of us, then I do not know what else could be.

Leon Seefeld is a co-founder of reframe.ventures, a consultancy firm specialized in helping SMEs to design and implement Regenerative Business Models. He has been working in social innovation and sustainability consulting for several years, among other things, advising on topics of Corporate Purpose, Sustainability Strategy, and Innovation, as well as the B Corp certification. Leon also worked on large-scale landscape restoration projects by weaving multistakeholder processes and social labs. Leon holds a Bachelor's degree in International Business Management and a Master's in Strategic Leadership toward Sustainability. He is now driven by the ambition to leverage innovative finance as a vehicle for systemic transformation. Website: www.reframe-rt.de. LinkedIn: https://www.linkedin.com/in/leon-seefeld/

9

Prometea: A Participative Way Toward Social Transformation

Iciar Montejo Romero

Caminante, son tus huellas el camino y nada más;
Caminante, no hay camino, se hace camino al andar.
Al andar se hace el camino, y al volver la vista atrás
se ve la senda que nunca se ha de volver a pisar.
Caminante no hay camino sino estelas en la mar.
Antonio Machado, 1875–1939
Wayfarer, only your footprints are the path, and nothing more;
wayfarer, there is no path, you create the path as you walk.
As you walk you create the path, and as you turn to glance behind
you see the trail that you never shall return to tread again.
Wayfarer, there is no path, only wake trails on the sea.
Antonio Machado, 1875–1939

On my path of personal discovery, each step taken has been guided by intuition, work, and creativity.

I. M. Romero (✉)
Prometea, Vitoria-Gasteiz, Spain
e-mail: iciar@prometeasc.com

Embracing Creativity on the Path to Social Transformation: My Story

I am Iciar. My journey with sustainability started in 1997 when I was 25 years old. Although I believe my connection with sustainability has deep roots in my childhood, it truly began to take shape at that pivotal moment. Since then, I have dedicated my efforts to issues related to sustainable development. In 2003, I founded my own company, Prometea, where this passion became my life's work.

My Childhood

I have always wondered what causes a person to possess a special affinity for nature, for the landscape, for biodiversity. In my case, the answer is clear: my connection with nature and the land was born in my childhood.

I grew up on a farm in a village of 50 inhabitants near my city, Vitoria-Gasteiz. My family worked and still works the land: they are enterprising farmers and ranchers. I spent my childhood days outdoors, surrounded by animals and tractors, very close to a mountain where I played among the native trees such as oaks, holm oaks, and beeches.

My family instilled in me a love for the land that produces food; I learned to look at the sky every day to know whether it was going to rain or if the weather was going to be pleasant. I understood the cycles of nature and learned to enjoy the starry nights. That was my childhood. Of course, I also made daily trips to school in the city, learned, and enjoyed spending time with my friends.

University: Finding My Way

In 1990, I began my university studies in Bilbao. I studied Economics and Business Administration with a specific goal in mind: I wanted to understand how "taxes" and "life" worked; I wanted to know how to file a tax return. In that regard, I succeeded.

On a poignant note, I would like to share with you that, in May 1991, my mother succumbed to cancer. She had taught me invaluable lessons about caring for the Earth, plants, and animals. Her teachings left a lasting legacy for my siblings and me.

Let's continue.

While I was in college, I realized, however, that I didn't want to spend my professional life behind a bank counter or in some company's accounting department. Something within me told me that this was not where belonged urging me to seek a different path.

Embarking on My Journey: Early Jobs and Continued Education

In 1995, with a business degree in hand, I started working in a family business as an accountant. Yes, it was precisely what I had hoped not to be doing!

At the same time, I continued my academic journey. I completed a postgraduate program in International Economics and Development Cooperation and took PhD courses. My heart found its calling in this field, especially during the Ecological Economics course taught by Professor Roberto Bermejo, a renowned professor in the field. It was during this time that I encountered profound concepts such as the Earth's carrying capacity, ecological footprints, and economic externalities. It was a revelation: beyond the teaching of Keynes, there was a branch of economics that embraced nature and the imperative of caring for our planet, Earth.

I also started looking into the 1987 Brundtland Report, the 1992 Rio Conference and Agenda 21, and the concept of sustainable development. This concept provided me with both a framework and the words to articulate what had resided in my heart and shaped my understanding since my childhood: the profound need to care for and protect our planet, our shared home, and all its inhabitants—from the smallest organism to the wisest elder.

1998–1999: A Turning Point in My Life

In the summer of 1998, I took a bold step and left my job as an accountant. It was not the obvious decision, but guided by the unmistakable whispers of my heart and my intuition, I knew that it was the right decision. My father did not try to dissuade me from abandoning the safe and conventional path but instead supported my choice to follow my passion.

I decided to take a break. I dedicated several months to intensive study, delving into how to bring sustainability to the grassroots, the local level. I immersed myself in the plans of cities and towns, eagerly absorbing all experiences.

At the beginning of 1999, I was offered an opportunity to work in a consultancy firm located in Vitoria-Gasteiz, in the Spanish Basque Country, specializing in locally based sustainable development. As a result, I started working on the system of sustainability indicators for Burgos, a city south of Vitoria-Gasteiz. It was my first project in this field, and it marked the beginning of a journey that led me to work on projects in other Spanish cities such as A Coruña, including in the regions of Bizkaia and Navarra.

Over 4 years, I collaborated with local authorities to shape their Agenda 21 and implement local action plans aimed at advancing sustainable development. I found immense purpose and fulfillment in this work, and my personal and professional commitment took root. However, something was not working. My life was out of balance: I was working 12-hour days, 7 days a week. Where was the sustainability of my own life? There was no point in crafting good sustainability plans for cities if my personal equilibrium was amiss.

Recognizing this, I decided to slightly deviate from my trajectory. A strong desire for entrepreneurship arose, compelling me to forge my own path step by step.

2003: The Birth of Prometea

On October 10, 2003, my partner Zorione and I gave birth to Prometea, our small yet ambitious company. We are a tandem of two, working closely together, with the shared vocation to guide and assist the cities and towns of Euskadi (Basque Country) in their move toward social, economic, and environmental sustainability. Seventeen years have passed, and we remain steadfast in this mission.

Throughout our journey, Prometea has served over 100 clients, mostly local authorities of towns and cities in the Basque Country. We have carried out and completed more than 600 projects.

Prometea is more than a company to me; it is another one of my babies.

Prometea: Our Sustainability Solution

Prometea is dedicated to guiding and accompanying organizations, towns, and cities through their transformative processes and facilitating the evolution of sustainability through active participation from all the people and agents involved.

Our guiding values at Prometea encompass sustainability, the common good, participation, collective creation, and social transformation and responsibility. Sustainability is a defining factor for every project we decide to undertake. Sustainability is woven into the fabric of our operations, our way of doing things, influencing our purchasing decisions as a company, our modes of transportation, i.e., how we move around, our daily choices, our collaborations, our working hours, and even the way we take care of ourselves.

Our Evolution and Growth

Since establishing Prometea, there has been an evolution, a subtle shift in how we offer our services to the market and contribute to society. Initially, our focus was collaboratively designing sustainable development strategies for towns, municipalities, and territories. We wanted to change the world, and that drive still burns within us. We aimed to influence public policies by designing and participating in planning strategies, developing sustainability plans, and launching programs and projects. These initiatives included sustainable mobility plans, Local Agenda 21, and landscape action plans, among others.

Today, while sustainability remains embedded in our DNA and serves as the foundation of our work and expression, our primary focus and contributions are centered on cocreation and active engagement with agents. Unconsciously, from the vast landscape of sustainable development within urban histories, our trajectory has gravitated toward a particular aspect—one that has emerged as a cornerstone: cocreation involving diverse agents, along with active community and citizen participation in the design and development of public policies. This evolution and the transformation of our company have been intuitive, shaped by our openness and keen interest in the needs of our clients and the broader society.

What Moves and Drives Us Today?

From our perspective, the integration of sustainability into the fabric of daily urban life, as well as within the realms of companies, associations, and individuals' lives, demands profound changes in the way we feel, think, act, and relate to each other.

To achieve this goal, beyond conveying scientific and technical knowledge, it is crucial to engage with, connect with and reach each and every individual—regardless of their role or position, guided by principles of equality and diversity. It is necessary to establish spaces of trust and foster public conversations to facilitate the creation of collective thinking and collaborative action. We need to start from specific individual interests and connect them to shared and collective interests because every person—along with all other living beings—shares and inhabits a common home: the Earth (Fig. 9.1).

At Prometea, our core mission is to create an appropriate atmosphere and an enabling environment where individuals can generate and contribute valuable content that advances sustainability. In other words, we are a tandem with a specialization in:

- Creating and sustaining environments of trust and opportunity
- Facilitating meaningful conversations and collective efforts among individuals, entities, and agents about a specific issue
- Providing visual and graphic documentation of the results and agreements reached, delivering substantial value (Fig. 9.2).

Fig. 9.1 Activating collective intelligence through group conversations; Project Donostia Lagunkoia, Prometea (Photograph by: Iñigo Ibáñez. All rights reserved)

Fig. 9.2 Our role: Generate environments of trust to activate and facilitate collective thinking and intelligence; Project Donostia Lagunkoia, Prometea (Photograph by: Iñigo Ibáñez. All rights reserved)

Prometea's Inspiring Sustainability Initiatives: Recent Projects in Complex Environments

In recent years, the projects we have participated in have become more complex. Our work has evolved to encompass projects in complex and chaotic environments, requiring extensive collaboration among various agents. Here are some examples:

- Participating in designing the Euskadi 2030 green procurement and contracting program
- Contributing to Donostia Lagunkoia, Donostia/San Sebastián's aging-friendly city plan
- Collaborating on the design of Gipuzkoa's anti-loneliness and relationship-building strategy
- Involvement in designing the Women's House in Portugalete
- Designing the Bizkaia Development Cooperation Strategy through multi-agent collaboration

Fig. 9.3 A citizen meeting to reflect on the future of the city; Project Donostia Lagunkoia, Prometea (Photograph by: Iñigo Ibáñez. All rights reserved)

- Integrating citizen participation into the new General Urban Planning Plan of Vitoria-Gasteiz
- Involvement in Bertatik bertara, the strategy for local food production and consumption in the Urola Garaia region in Gipuzkoa (Fig. 9.3).

Lessons Learned

Here are some lessons and reflections I have gathered on my sustainability journey:

- ***Choose and focus on an area of impact:*** Over time, I have come to realize that our effectiveness as a company is maximized when we identify a specific area of specialization and determine how we can best contribute to sustainability. In our case, that focus is on how to work with people on citizen participation.
- ***Beauty is a social value that connects us:*** Beauty holds the power to connect us. It serves as a significant tool in integrating artistic disciplines, captivating people, exciting them, and forging meaningful connections with them.

- ***Be the message:*** A responsible company places the sustainability of life at its core, even within economic activities. Living the message, based on a coherent concept of sustainability, is key. We need to dedicate time to ourselves and take care of ourselves so that we can offer our best to our personal, professional, and community spheres.
- ***Be present:*** Take a moment to stop and breathe, and be present in the here and now. We must develop our ability to listen and remain open to emerge possibilities at the personal, collective, and corporate levels. What is life asking of us? Keep an open mind. Set aside judgments and fears. An open heart can help.
- ***Innovate and invest in continuous training:*** How to create, add, and sustain value? We must continuously innovate and invest in our knowledge. Our knowledge is the raw material we offer to the market.
- ***Establish a daily connection to nature:*** Take the time to savor each sunrise and sunset. Appreciate the beauty of the trees, birds in flight, the vast sky, and the gentle warmth of sunlight. This daily connection not only links us to the cosmos but also grounds us, offering valuable perspectives.

To You

Thank you for taking the time to read my story. The knowledge that it will be a part of a collection of sustainability narratives, has inspired me to reflect on my own journey, learn from it, and share it with you.

> Wayfarer, there is no path. You create the path as you walk.

Iciar Montejo Romero, born in Vitoria-Gasteiz, Spain, followed an unconventional career path after studying economics. Her passion for interconnectedness emerged during specialized training and doctoral programs in international economics. The love for sustainability has shaped Iciar's professional journey, leading her to hold degrees in economics and business administration, as well as three master's degrees. Since 2003, she has been an engaged partner in a small business focusing on sustainability and community participation. Alongside her commitment to her child, Iciar continues to make choices influenced by her dedication to a holistic perspective on the world, nature, and diverse cultures. Website: www.prometeasc.com

10

Hanging on to a Dream

Franky De Cooman

In 1994, I worked for a start-up that is now a famous IT consultancy. As I have a tendency to look for the human being behind the "nerd," this company's management philosophy resonated with me as the CEO was into what one would now call Organizational Wellbeing of the employees. Their business model was likewise unusual, something that would these days be called "corporate social responsibility," or CSR. After some years, as that term became widely known, I decided to gain more insight into the subject, and I began academic research in CSR at Radboud University in the Netherlands. I realized then that very few studies explored the human aspect of CSR; most behaved as if institutions were making decisions, instead of the people within them. That is why I embarked upon my own research into what essentially drives leaders who have made a commitment to CSR. What began as a sideline soon took on a life of its own, leading to the 51 in-depth interviews that form the basis for this chapter. During this research, it emerged how important self-care is for those who take CSR seriously. All this, along with my own life's path, explains why I have specialized in self-care coaching for CSR leaders.

Some companies take their responsibility toward society seriously because their leaders believe it is the right thing to do (Waddock, 2006). Such organizations do not merely take on CSR as window dressing, where lofty claims are not reflected in decent acts (Kurucz et al., 2013). In contrast, these

---

F. De Cooman (✉)
MensJ, Lovenjoel, Belgium
e-mail: Franky@mensj.be

organizations distance themselves from the idea that business is about self-interest, competition, and using resources without ethical reflection (Freeman et al., 2007). Rather, taking responsibility for society is seen as the only normal and ethical thing to do (Jenkins, 2006; Waddock, 2006). CSR is for them a commitment (Crane & Matten, 2010), an ethical stance guided by what is thought to be fair, just, and beneficial for society (Carroll, 1991).

A commitment to CSR translates into a human obligation toward society (Baker & Roberts, 2012), and it becomes a leader's personal mission (Mostovicz et al., 2011). Taking responsibility becomes part of who one is (Pruzan, 2008; Rupp et al., 2010), an ambition in which one hopes to contribute to a better world (Pruzan, 2008; Rupp et al., 2010).

However, a leader authentically acting for CSR risks being criticized, opposed, and even ridiculed (Moody-Stuart, 2014). (S)he is not seen as a prophet of a new worldview, but as a problem, and hence, the leader risks becoming a target (Heifetz, 1994). Leaders committed to CSR (unwillingly) trigger feelings of discomfort (Nyborg, 2011) in those who think that the only social responsibility an executive has is to increase profits (Friedman, 1970).

For this reason, CSR-committed leaders risk being challenged by NGOs that label their efforts window-dressing (Whitehouse, 2006) or who criticize them for putting so much work into making changes that the cynics consider a mere drop in the bucket (Park, 2005). CSR leaders can be seen as threats because they show the feasibility of doing business in an ethical way. It is no wonder that less socially committed leaders often try to disparage CSR-committed leaders (Heifetz, 1994).

Therefore, a commitment to CSR creates a genuine leadership challenge (Benn et al., 2010; Maak & Pless, 2006; Waldman & Siegel, 2008), as executives must have strong characters to sustain their commitment (Rest, 1986) in the face of harsh criticism. However, such confrontations should not mean game-over, even when they result in a leader's personal distress (Mendonca, 2001).

To gain insight into the effects of such confrontations, leaders in a variety of organizational sectors, with differing levels of responsibility, were interviewed for an inductive study in accordance with the Grounded Theory methodology (Bryant & Charmaz, 2007; Corbin & Strauss, 2008; Glaser & Strauss, 1967), setting off with "general wonderment" (Glaser, 1992) to gain an unbiased understanding (Edmondson & McManus, 2007) on *why* and *how* leaders respond to societal issues. Interviewees were selected as the business model of their organization was based upon product stewardship, i.e., providing products and services that take the welfare of society into consideration as much as possible (Hart, 1995) or because they behaved in a manner not conforming to institutional simplicity (Miller, 1993), e.g., a fast-food company working on a permanent basis with an animal rights organization to improve animal welfare or a police superintendent writing a sustainability report for his district. It is a common belief that CSR is only applicable to for-profit organizations; however, because all types of organizations should be vigilant not to ill-treat employees, the environment, and other stakeholders (Acar et al., 2001; Bouckaert & Vandenhove, 1998; Phillips et al., 2003), our sample contains a blend of commercial, nonprofit, and governmental organizations (Griffin & Prakash, 2014).

The conclusions of the study led to the proposal of a *theoretical model* that reveals the mechanisms supporting the ethical decision-making process of responsible leaders against confrontation (Fig. 10.1). Confrontations are those provoking moments making people wonder "who am I, and who do I want to be?" (Weick, 1995). The mechanisms behind the ethical decision-making process of those feeling the internal urge of adhering to the commitment of living an ethical life yield the necessary insights for comprehending their CSR commitment.

The model was submitted to 16 of the respondents for validation (Corbin & Strauss, 2008), and all the consulted interviewees could recognize themselves in it and started elaborating on its content. As a final step, the model was submitted to 20 individuals, all of whom agreed with the proposal. As a self-care coach, I regularly put the model into practice with beneficent results.

The theoretical model highlights two parallel processes that arise after such a confrontation takes place: the "probing process" and the "coping process." As will be demonstrated, each of the processes exhibits distinct functionalities: the probing process helps when constructing and justifying an ethical answer, whereas the coping process serves as a support for building and maintaining moral character by empowering the incited emotions (Weick & Putnam, 2006).

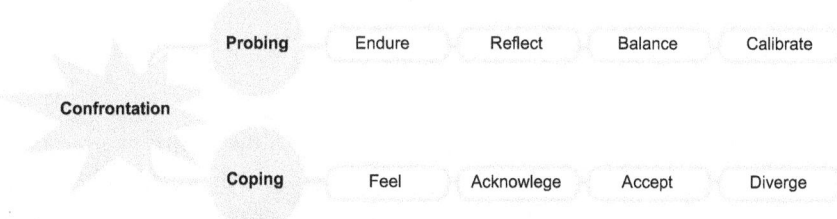

Fig. 10.1 The theoretical model of the probing and coping process (Image by: Danny Juchtmans. All rights reserved)

The Probing Process

The probing process is divisible into four stages—endure, reflect, balance, and calibrate—that I will hereafter explain and illustrate with quotes from my interviewees and documents. By the completion of the fourth stage, it should be obvious to the leader how to respond to the confrontation and the reason for doing so.

Endure

At first, the respondents seem unaffected.

> One of the statements I was confronted with was, "To do business, you shouldn't be too honest." I did not react immediately. However, this went against the ideals that I had developed throughout my education, which I had adopted for my business (Chairman, paint manufacturing company).

Enduring is something that people can (or even should?) learn, as indicated by the person guiding stakeholder dialogs when proposing him the constructed model for validation.

> It is interesting to observe stakeholder dialogs. An organization volunteers to openly show how they take responsibility. Rapidly, they get criticized, and the ambience soon turns sour when one starts defending oneself. One should avoid reacting defensively, which is not easy. As soon as one takes a silent, nondefensive position, the atmosphere improves" (Fellow, Trainer, Researcher Sustainability/Transnational Public Organization).

They are bewildered, but they realize that self-defense is useless. Enduring is not considered an indication of weakness. In contrast, like martial arts, it aims to redirect energy toward more worthy pursuits (Puka, 2011).

Reflect

Confrontations are moments in which one tries to determine the reason for the attack (Weick, 1995). The quest starts when an individual's self-image as an ethical person—the immediate cause of the confrontation—originates (Weick, 1995).

People realize that confrontation is the result of human beings adhering to dissimilar moral norms that conflict. As ethical behavior is not predefined when remaining within the boundaries of hypernorms—the international, general understanding of moral minima (Husted, 1999)—in which moral free space is available, i.e., the personal/organizational choice to what comprises ethical behavior (Donaldson & Dunfee, 1999). Our interviewees utilized this free space for taking responsibility toward society (De George, 1993; Donaldson, 2000; Verbos et al., 2007), whereas others may employ it to do only the moral minimum.

> It is an ethical discussion, how do we define our norms and values with respect to one another, with respect to society? People start connecting to this idea; for some, it even becomes a new kind of religion. There are indeed similarities with religion, and doing good toward your fellow human beings is certainly part of it (CTO and Sustainability Director/Sustainable Chemistry Company).

Realizing that a specific ethical stance must be made entails reflecting on the origins of this stance when filling moral free space with a specific bias for taking responsibility toward society. A quest begins that attempts to determine from where this ethical vision of the individual self—being the immediate cause of the confrontation—originates (Weick, 1995).

This reflection reveals the confrontation to be the most recent in a series of events. It is realized then that ethical behavior is not actually that common, and with that, ethical behavior evolves from a naïve perspective—isn't everybody just ethical?—into an explicit attitude.

> It's just like a child being born, then starting to crawl, then to walk, then to run. How long does it take for a tsunami to manifest? A tsunami is building for a decent amount of time before it is evident. How long is the process of preparing itself before it becomes visible? (CEO, architectural firm).

The first steps toward CSR are not judged to be deliberate (Jonker et al., 2003) and are, retrospectively, considered simply logical (Jenkins, 2004) due to these managers' self-perceptions and the manner in which their lives have evolved.

One finds that ethical behavior is deeply ingrained (Blasi, 2005; Pruzan, 2008) and results in the construction of an ethical narrative. CSR is discovered to be a manifestation of one's worldview (Wray-Lake & Syvertsen, 2011), initiated from deep within (Jonker et al., 2003).

> The founding father of our company did not need a sustainability report back in 1954 to do what he deemed important (Introduction to a sustainability report, paint manufacturer).

Balance

Realizing that ethical behavior is individually ingrained is only a first step. Composing ethical answers, even in difficult situations, is a more challenging step (Rest, 1986). The confrontation transforms into a balancing act between individual, inward, and dissimilar moral norms.

To construct the best possible outcome, issues are examined from different perspectives (Hartman, 2009) with the awareness that no solution is perfectly ethical.

> Just like in the Tour de France, one needs short-time objectives … but eventually, the tour is won in 25 rides. It might be the case that, some days, you don't sprint. You don't need to act on all challenges in your path. You must make sure to score in the long run" (CEO, advertising agency).

The challenge is to find balance by deriving answers in accordance with one's narrative.

Calibrate

Confrontations serve as occasions to calibrate one's ethical compass. CSR is "continually becoming" (Freeman & Harris, 2009; McShane & Cunningham, 2011), i.e., it is a process with a continuous challenge to improve (Woermann, 2013).

> I have been very demanding in my desire to make a beautiful magazine. I can see my mistakes (or as I call them, my learning processes), and I show them to my readers. The first magazines were on glossy paper with gold print. In the beginning, I did not realize that this has an impact on the environment. Since the moment I realized this, my readers can follow, via my editorial, the steps we are taking to minimize environmental impact (CEO, publishing house).

In short, the probing process ensures the formulation of a clear response to confrontation. However, a distinction exists between knowing what should be done and actually doing it (Nijhof & Jeurissen, 2006; Rest, 1986). The coping process, explained below, plays a crucial role in that commitment.

The Coping Process

The coping process is an emotional one and consists of four phases: feel, acknowledge, accept, and diverge.

Feel

The first reaction immediately following a confrontation is the sensation that something is amiss.

> When you are a good manager, (ideas) seize you by the throat, even if you cannot do anything about them" (Head of Corporate Relations, Urban Mining Company).

Negative emotions are a signal that something is "not right" (Salvador & Folger, 2009) and are a crucial step in the process as they function as a stimulant to investigate further as to what is occurring (Weick, 1995).

Acknowledge

Emotions are then acknowledged in a nonjudgmental manner, as they teach us something about ourselves and what we consider important (Puka, 2011).

> *One should learn to accept things the way they are, to accept emotions, and to name them. This is not an obvious skill. If you can access your emotions and voice them, you have come a long way (CEO, brewery).*

Not taking the time to acknowledge emotions might be fruitful at first; however, it is counterproductive for the forthcoming future. Due to acknowledging emotions, executives realize that their moral character induces difficult situations. This leads to the observation that it is necessary to reserve sufficient time to just take care of oneself.

Accept

After acknowledging the emotions, one completely accepts by not resisting feelings of pain and fear. This translates into living fully in the moment, not thinking of possible action (Weick, 2001). These emotions should be taken seriously because if they are not accepted, they might paralyze one's ability to think rationally (Lord & Kanfer, 2002).

> I thought I would explode, that I could not see it through. But something inside of me asked: "Do you believe?" My answer was, Yes. Then, it was a matter of not giving up. And just before you hit bottom, you feel a breakthrough. But this also takes a certain amount of time, time in which you need persistence (CEO, architectural firm).

Accepting signifies not fighting the emotions but bearing them as such. One accepts the inability to control the situation and pushes aside long-term ethical commitment in favor of just taking care of oneself. In this respect, the moment of being introduced into a new setting is fully experienced (Weick & Putnam, 2006), and there is acceptance of the inability to manage the situation. The affirmation of the realization of this inability begins a transition process (Cunha et al., 2010) where for the time being, normal order is disregarded (Turner, 1969). This moment of surrender where vulnerability is recognized and accepted is the critical stage that will afford the opportunity to overcome the situation.

Diverge

After full acceptance, the situation reaches a juncture where the first glimpse of positive energy reappears. Negative emotions tend to disappear after being fully accepted, and as a result, room is set free for positive emotions when they start slipping in. These positive emotions then further counter the negative emotions (Wegner, 1994), and the necessary energy to commit to action emerges.

> Everything appears simple and clear. You can throw away a lot of your baggage. This leads to an energetic good feeling, profound restfulness (Owner, organic and fair trade wine wholesaler).

At this stage, people regain the courage and the energy to be who they aspire to be (Harbour & Kisfalvi, 2013; Tillich, 1952) and recapture the energy to act (Harbour & Kisfalvi, 2013). It is as if the crisis of the confrontation is diverging into an opportunity (Kegan, 1982) to proceed one step closer to individual ideals.

True CSR commitment is the result of being knocked down and getting up, again and again. Confrontations can result in an escalation in commitment (Sleesman et al., 2012; Staw, 1976), i.e., an increase in the effort to create one's dream of a better world.

Key Takeaways for Business Leaders

With this research, I hope I have shown how leaders can take up (again) their sense of responsibility (Deslandes, 2012) without "frying their circuits" after being seriously challenged (Senge et al., 2008).

As the ways of understanding and acting on CSR are unique to each individual, I advise that a CSR-committed person study the origins of that commitment in him/herself, that is, determine how such personal dedication came into being (Nijhof & Jeurissen, 2006). To facilitate this process, a narrative can be constructed with those elements from the past that enable actions for the future (Weick, 1995). These narratives can even employ experiences from the remote past, as a person's roots in ethical decision-making emanate from one's life experiences (Hegarty & Sims, 1978). The way that a person dealt with ethical dilemmas in the past becomes the template by which judgments are made in the present (Shamir & Eilam, 2005; Treviño & Nelson, 2011).

This narrative construction process is crucial. Confrontations can generate a substantial loss of sense of self, generating emotions, which the narrative helps to address by recalling how one has dealt with them in the past (Weick et al., 2005). Emotions are difficult to regulate, and leaders should learn how to cope with them, as emotions—unwittingly or otherwise—influence the decision-making process (Lord & Hall, 2005). Leaders who do not know how to deal with emotions may decide that it would be easier to just scrap the commitment, take care of oneself (Baker & Roberts, 2012) and accept the path that society is currently on (Benn & Dunphy, 2009).

Dealing with emotions is rather scary. For this reason, I suggest learning—as Kierkegaard suggested—the lessons of anxiety. One should learn to work with emotions by looking at the anxiety doing so entails.

Not taking the time, for whatever reason, to work through emotions might seem more manageable at first, but it is counterproductive for the future. When neglected, emotions impact one's rational thinking (Lord & Harvey, 2002), thus increasing the risk of one being held hostage by one's own negative thoughts.

References

Acar, W., Aupperle, K. E., & Lowy, R. M. (2001). An empirical exploration of measures of social responsibility across the spectrum of organizational types. *The International Journal of Organizational Analysis, 9*(1), 26–57.

Baker, M., & Roberts, J. (2012). All in the mind? Ethical identity and the allure of corporate responsibility. *Journal of Business Ethics, 101*(S1), 5–15. https://doi.org/10.1007/s10551-011-1171-8

Benn, S., & Dunphy, D. (2009). Leadership for sustainability. In R. Staib (Ed.), *Business management & environmental stewardship* (pp. 56–75). Palgrave Macmillan.

Benn, S., Todd, L. R., & Pendleton, J. (2010). Public relations leadership in corporate social responsibility. *Journal of Business Ethics, 96*(3), 403–423. https://doi.org/10.1007/s10551-010-0474-5

Blasi, A. (2005). Moral character: A psychological approach. In D. K. Lapsley & F. C. Power (Eds.), *Character psychology and character education* (pp. 67–100). University of Notre Dame Press.

Bouckaert, L., & Vandenhove, J. (1998). Business ethics and the management of non-profit institutions. *Journal of Business Ethics, 17*, 1073–1081.

Bryant, A., & Charmaz, K. (2007). Grounded theory research: methods and practices. In A. Bryant & K. Charmaz (Eds.), *The SAGE handbook of grounded theory* (pp. 1–28). Sage.

Carroll, A. B. (1991). The pyramid of corporate social responsibility: Toward the moral management of organizational stakeholders. *Business Horizons, 34*(4), 39–48. https://doi.org/10.1016/0007-6813(91)90005-G

Corbin, J., & Strauss, A. L. (2008). *Basics of qualitative research* (3rd ed.). Sage.

Crane, A., & Matten, D. (2010). *Business ethics: Managing corporate citizenship and sustainability in the age of globalization* (3rd ed.). Oxford University Press.

Cunha, M. P., Guimarães-Costa, N., Rego, A., & Clegg, S. R. (2010). Leading and following (un)ethically in Limen. *Journal of Business Ethics, 97*(2), 189–206. https://doi.org/10.1007/s10551-010-0504-3

Deslandes, G. (2012). In search of individual responsibility: The dark side of organizations in the light of Jansenist ethics. *Journal of Business Ethics, 101*(S1), 61–70. https://doi.org/10.1007/s10551-011-1173-6

De George, R. T. (1993). *Competing with integrity in international business*. Oxford University Press.

Donaldson, T. (2000). Are business managers "professionals"? *Business Ethics Quarterly, 10*(1), 83–94.

Donaldson, T., & Dunfee, T. W. (1999). *Ties that bind: a social contracts approach to business ethics*. Harvard Business School Press.

Edmondson, A. C., & McManus, S. E. (2007). Methodological fit in management field research. *Academy of Management Review, 32*(4), 1155–1179.

Freeman, R. E., & Harris, J. D. (2009). Creating ties that bind. *Journal of Business Ethics, 88*(S4), 685–692. https://doi.org/10.1007/s10551-009-0333-4

Freeman, R. E., Martin, K., & Parmar, B. (2007). Stakeholder capitalism. *Journal of Business Ethics, 74*(4), 303–314. https://doi.org/10.1007/s10551-007-9517-y

Friedman, M. (1970). The social responsibility of business is to increase its profits. *New York Times*, (September 13), 122–126.

Glaser, B. G. (1992). *Basics of grounded theory analysis: emergence vs forcing*. Sociology Press.

Glaser, B. G., & Strauss, A. L. (1967). *The discovery of Grounded Theory: strategies for qualitative research*. AldineTransaction.

Griffin, J. J., & Prakash, A. (2014). Corporate responsibility: initiatives and mechanisms. *Business and Society, 53*(4), 465–482. https://doi.org/10.1177/0007650313478975

Harbour, M., & Kisfalvi, V. (2013). In the eye of the beholder: An exploration of managerial courage. *Journal of Business Ethics, 119*(4), 493–515. https://doi.org/10.1007/s10551-013-1835-7

Hart, S. L. (1995). A natural-resource-based view of the firm. *Academy of Management Review, 20*(4), 986–1014.

Hartman, E. M. (2009). Principles and hypernorms. *Journal of Business Ethics, 88*(S4), 707–716. https://doi.org/10.1007/s10551-009-0331-6

Hegarty, W. H., & Sims, H. P. J. (1978). Some determinants of unethical decision behavior: An experiment. *Journal of Applied Psychology, 63*(4), 451–457. https://doi.org/10.1037//0021-9010.63.4.451

Heifetz, R. A. (1994). *Leadership without easy answers*. Harvard University Press.

Husted, B. W. (1999). A critique of the empirical methods of integrative social contracts theory. *Journal of Business Ethics, 20*, 227–235.

Jenkins, H. (2004). A critique of conventional CSR theory: an SME perspective. *Journal of General Management, 29*(4), 37–57.

Jenkins, H. (2006). Small business champions for corporate social responsibility. *Journal of Business Ethics, 67*(3), 241–256. https://doi.org/10.1007/s10551-006-9182-6

Jonker, J., Cramer, J., & van der Heijden, A. (2003). *Developing meaning in action: (Re) constructing the process of embedding corporate social responsibility (CSR) in companies (No. 16)*. Nottingham.

Kegan, R. (1982). *The evolving self: Problem and process in human development*. Harvard University Press.

Kurucz, E., Colbert, B., & Wheeler, D. (2013). *Reconstructing value: Leadership skills for a sustainable world*. University of Toronto Press.

Lord, R. G., & Hall, R. J. (2005). Identity, deep structure and the development of leadership skill. *The Leadership Quarterly, 16*, 591–615. https://doi.org/10.1016/j.leaqua.2005.06.003

Lord, R. G., & Harvey, J. L. (2002). An information processing framework for emotional regulation. In R. G. Lord, R. J. Klimoski, & K. Ruth (Eds.), *Emotions in the workplace: Understanding the structures and role of emotions in organizational behavior* (pp. 115–146). Jossey-Bass.

Lord, R. G., & Kanfer, R. (2002). Emotions and organizational behavior. In R. G. Lord, R. J. Klimoski, & K. Ruth (Eds.), *Emotions in the workplace: Understanding the structures and role of emotions in organizational behavior* (pp. 5–19). Jossey-Bass.

Maak, T., & Pless, N. M. (2006). Responsible leadership: A relational approach. In T. Maak & N. Pless (Eds.), *Responsible leadership* (pp. 33–53). Routledge.

McShane, L., & Cunningham, P. (2011). To thine own self be true? Employees' judgments of the authenticity of their organization's corporate social responsibility program. *Journal of Business Ethics, 108*(1), 81–100. https://doi.org/10.1007/s10551-011-1064-x

Mendonca, M. (2001). Preparing for ethical leadership in organizations. *Canadian Journal of Administrative Sciences, 18*(4), 266–276.

Miller, D. (1993). The architecture of simplicity. *Academy of Management Review, 18*(1), 116–138.

Moody-Stuart, M. (2014). *Responsible leadership: Lessons from the front line of sustainability and ethics*. Greenleaf Publishing.

Mostovicz, E. I., Kakabadse, A., & Kakabadse, N. K. (2011). The four pillars of corporate responsibility: Ethics, leadership, personal responsibility and trust. *Corporate Governance, 11*(4), 489–500. https://doi.org/10.1108/14720701111159307

Nijhof, A., & Jeurissen, R. (2006). Editorial: A sensemaking perspective on corporate social responsibility: Introduction to the special issue. *Business Ethics: A European Review, 15*(4), 316–322. https://doi.org/10.1111/j.1467-8608.2006.00455.x

Nyborg, K. (2011). I don't want to hear about it: Rational ignorance among duty-oriented consumers. *Journal of Economic Behavior & Organization, 79*(3), 263–274.

Park, H. (2005). The role of idealism and relativism as dispositional characteristics in the socially responsible decision-making process. *Journal of Business Ethics, 56*(1), 81–98. https://doi.org/10.1007/s10551-004-3239-1

Phillips, R., Freeman, R. E., & Wicks, A. C. (2003). What stakeholder theory is not. *Business Ethics Quarterly, 13*(4), 479–502.

Pruzan, P. (2008). Spirituality as a firm basis for corporate social responsibility. In A. Crane, A. McWilliams, D. Matten, J. Moon, & D. Siegel (Eds.), *The Oxford handbook of corporate social responsibility* (pp. 552–559). Oxford University Press.

Puka, B. (2011). Taking CARE OF BUSINESS: Caring in COMPETITIVE CORPORATE STRUCTURES. In M. Hamington & M. Sander-Staudt (Eds.), *Applying care ethics to business. Issues in business ethics* (Vol. 34, pp. 175–199). Springer. https://doi.org/10.1007/978-90-481-9307-3_10

Rest, J. R. (1986). *Moral development: Advances in research and theory*. Greenwood Press.
Rupp, D. E., Williams, C. A., & Aguilera, R. V. (2010). Increasing corporate social responsibility through stakeholder value internalization (and the catalyzing effect of new governance): An application of organizational justice, self-determination, and social influence theories. In M. Schminke (Ed.), *Managerial ethics: Managing the psychology of morality* (pp. 69–88). Routledge Academic.
Salvador, R., & Folger, R. G. (2009). Business ethics and the brain. *Business Ethics Quarterly, 1*(January), 1–31.
Senge, P., Smith, B., Kruschwitz, N., Laur, J., & Schley, S. (2008). *The necessary revolution: How individuals and organizations are working together to create a sustainable world*. Doubleday.
Shamir, B., & Eilam, G. (2005). "What's your story?" A life-stories approach to authentic leadership development. *The Leadership Quarterly, 16*(3), 395–417. https://doi.org/10.1016/j.leaqua.2005.03.005
Sleesman, D. J., Conlon, D. E., McNamara, G., & Miles, J. E. (2012). Cleaning up the big muddy: A meta-analytic review of the determinants of escalation of commitment. *Academy of Management Journal, 55*(3), 541–562. https://doi.org/10.5465/amj.2010.0696
Staw, B. M. (1976). Knee-deep in the big muddy: A study of escalating commitment to a chosen course of action. *Organizational Behavior and Human Performance, 16*(1), 27–44. https://doi.org/10.1016/0030-5073(76)90005-2
Tillich, P. (1952). *The courage to be (2000)* (2nd ed.). Yale University Press.
Treviño, L. K., & Nelson, K. A. (2011). *Managing business ethics: Straight talk about how to do it right* (5th ed.). Wiley.
Turner, V. (1969). *The ritual process: Structure and anti-structure*. Aldine de Gruyter.
Verbos, A. K., Gerard, J. A., Forshey, P. R., Harding, C. S., & Miller, J. S. (2007). The positive ethical organization: Enacting a living code of ethics and ethical organizational identity. *Journal of Business Ethics, 76*(1), 17–33. https://doi.org/10.1007/s10551-006-9275-2
Waddock, S. (2006). *Leading corporate citizens: Vision, values, value added*. McGraw-Hill.
Waldman, D. A., & Siegel, D. S. (2008). Defining the socially responsible leader. *The Leadership Quarterly, 19*(1), 117–131. https://doi.org/10.1016/j.leaqua.2007.12.008
Wegner, D. M. (1994). Ironic processes of mental control. *Psychological Review*.
Weick, K. E. (1995). *Sensemaking in organizations*. Sage Publications.
Weick, K. E. (2001). Leadership as the legitimation of doubt. In W. Bennis, G. M. Spreitzer, & T. G. Cummings (Eds.), *The future of leadership: Today's top thinkers on leadership speak to the next generation* (pp. 91–102). Jossey-Bass.
Weick, K. E., Sutcliffe, K. M., & Obstfeld, D. (2005). Organization science and the process of sensemaking. (Paul C Nutt & David C Wilson, Eds.). *Organization Science, 16*(4), 409–421. https://doi.org/10.1287/orsc.1050.0133

Weick, K. E., & Putnam, T. (2006). Organizing for mindfulness: Eastern wisdom and western knowledge. *Journal of Management Inquiry, 15*(3), 275–287. https://doi.org/10.1177/1056492606291202

Whitehouse, L. (2006). Corporate social responsibility: Views from the frontline. *Journal of Business Ethics, 63*(3), 279–296.

Woermann, M. (2013). *On the (im)possibility of business ethics: Critical complexity, deconstruction, and implications for understanding the ethics of business.* Springer.

Wray-Lake, L., & Syvertsen, A. K. (2011). The developmental roots of social responsibility in childhood and adolescence. In *New directions for child and adolescent development* (pp. 11–25). https://doi.org/10.1002/cd.308

Franky De Cooman was in 1994 at the cradle of a, now famous, consultancy company in IT. Seeking to understand the person behind the "nerd" stereotype, he explored coaching with neurolinguistic programming. The business operations of his management area would now fall under the umbrella of "corporate social responsibility" (CSR). Motivated by a desire for greater insight, Franky pursued a Master's class in CSR at Radboud University. During his studies, he discovered a lack of knowledge concerning the human aspect of CSR, with companies seemingly making decisions instead of individuals. This prompted him to conduct his own research to understand the driving forces behind committed CSR leaders. This endeavor resulted in 51 in-depth interviews, forming the basis of this chapter. It sheds light on the critical role of self-care for dedicated CSR leaders. Inspired by his own journey, Franky has specialized in self-care coaching for servant leaders. Since 2021, he has been a part-time student in Psychology at Open University. The other part-time of him is filled with being a spouse, (grand)father, coaching servant leaders in their self-care endeavor and people with a distance from the labor market and helping to install psychological safety in teams. Website: https://www.mensj.be. LinkedIn: https://www.linkedin.com/in/frankydecooman/

11

Sustainability Professionals as Ambassadors for Change: Redefining Communication

Stella Blohmke

I believe that in this complex and interconnected world, in which only proper systemic change can prevent an environmental collapse, it is time for business managers and business leaders, in general, to start thinking about the world we all want to live in and promote a more global, a more inclusive, and a more sustainable vision of doing business.

At the Roots of My Sustainability Story: Easter Island!

Looking back at the moment in my life when sustainability started to grab me, I know exactly when the cornerstone of my "sustainability story" was placed. It was the story of Easter Island that hugely impressed me as a young student in 2006, and, years later, when teaching courses on sustainability management, my students were equally fascinated by the same story. Some of them now work in the field of sustainability.

S. Blohmke (✉)
KYBELE, Hamburg, Germany
e-mail: stella@thinkkybele.de

Easter Island is one of the world's most isolated scraps of habitable land. The island has an area of only 64 square miles and is known for its remarkable collapse in the 1860s: "In just a few centuries, the people of Easter Island wiped out their forest, drove their plants and animals to extinction, and saw their complex society spiral into chaos and cannibalism" (Diamond, 1995, 2005).

The study of Easter Island provides much insight into current global environmental challenges: it is the story of our planet in a nutshell. The most striking difference is, of course, that because they lived on a small island, the inhabitants of Easter Island were direct spectators to their own decline or, as Jared Diamond put it, "What were they thinking when they cut down the last palm tree?" (1995). It is remarkable that even though they were direct witnesses to the destruction of their environment, they did not counteract that development.

Working as a consultant and interacting with my clients, I often think about that same Easter Island story, and I wonder: do my clients know it, too? What is their personal motivation (if they have one) in the sustainability sphere, and when was it triggered? Rarely have I asked or talked about this with any of them at such a personal level.

While it seems there is a growing number of motivated sustainability pioneers in the business world, in many business environments, the concept of sustainability is approached as a regulatory issue to deal with or just another task on their long to-do lists. At the same time, due to the tremendous media attention in recent years, the average person's knowledge about the environmental crisis we face has increased fundamentally, and it has become a popular *Stammtisch*[1] topic. However, I tend to believe that the dramatic consequences of failing to meet environmental and climate goals that have been set (and those that urgently still need to be set) have still not entered many people's heads or face the classic knowledge-behaviour gap.

A Business Language for Sustainability?

In regard to sustainability management for businesses, what I have learned—both from an academic and a business standpoint—can be boiled down to the following: sustainability is a business issue, and we need to make company

---

[1] In the German tradition, a *Stammtisch* is an informal group meeting held on a regular basis, generally in a bar, where members (artists, journalists, politicians, etc.) discuss specific topics. It is the equivalent to the "tertulia" and the "salon," respectively, in the Spanish and the French culture.

leaders understand that there are business risks and opportunities in the sphere of sustainability. We must speak their language to get the message across. Full stop.

Is that truly enough to solve a crisis of such proportions? Take the example of the climate crisis: in its World Energy Outlook, 2020, the Energy Information Administration (EIA) writes that, to achieve net-zero emissions by 2050, primary energy demand in 2030 needs to be on a level similar to 2006, even though the economy will be twice as large. Electrification, energy efficiency gains, and behavioral change are central to achieving this, according to the EIA. If behavioral change is necessarily part of this equation, the climate goals—apart from living in a planned economy—can only be achieved through education.

With only a few years left to meet the requirements of carbon reduction, the goal of which is to decrease the rate of global warming rise, my rebellion against our (my own) business language is growing—it is a language that wraps sustainability up in little boxes that can be "sold" like "just another service." Other than selling their services, sustainability professionals should consider using their voices in a more energetic way. Just because we think we are already "doing good" because we are working in the field of sustainability—in my view, this is not enough. What is more, implementing all these brilliant strategies, measures, and targets in business, a deeper understanding of the issues at stake should get more space in our discussions with clients and the business world in general. I think we must all become ambassadors of change with a clear mission: save this beautiful planet.

Given that we are not activists and do not work for nongovernmental organizations, we usually think we must be "more professional" and wrap the sustainability "issue" in small, handy packages that are labeled Carbon Accounting, Sustainable Development Goal (SDG) Mapping, or Climate-Risk Analysis. Don't get me wrong: this work is of tremendous importance and highly valued. However, I argue that the success story of sustainability will also depend on bridging technical knowledge and strategy consulting with a broader understanding of the actual consequences and a vision of the world we all want to live in, which is where it all gets personal.

Sustainability issues, such as the climate crisis or the loss of biodiversity, are not just another form of regulatory requirement that companies need to meet. You cannot equate them with a new tax regulation. They are a race against time. In addition, a race for a future that is livable for generations to come. Climate activists and scientists have long said these things—but anyone can find this in the media. However, too often, the business world is disconnected from these discussions. In my view, these discussions should be reflected in the language we use when talking about these issues, particularly in a business context.

A Plea for Changing the Rhetoric in Sustainability Management

The business case for sustainability is most likely not suited to fixing any of the global environmental crises we face, as the issues are too complex and too global. In addition, by doing good, by doing things right, or by engaging in sustainable practices for the public good (e.g., use fewer land resources), a company will always incite other competitors or any other stakeholder to act as free riders[2] (Olson, 1965; Ostrom, 1990). Every single global sustainability challenge can be seen as a "tragedy of the commons" (Hardin, 1968): individual actors (e.g., businesses) use common resources (land, air, water) in a way contrary to the common good of all users. Although we have seen many positive examples of cooperation toward preserving common resources (Ostrom, 1990), the tragedy of the commons remains problematic whenever the political will is too weak, and thus, regulation falls short.

In sum, I believe that in this complex and interconnected world, in which only proper systemic change can prevent an environmental collapse, it is time for business managers and business leaders, in general, to start thinking about the world we all want to live in and promote a more global, a more inclusive, and a more sustainable vision of doing business.

This is a plea directed at all professionals who work at the interface between business and the goal of a sustainable future. I strongly encourage sustainability professionals to start using stronger language and engaging with a variety of channels that might address action at another level. We are the visible translators of sustainability issues in business. We can continue to argue on behalf of business interests, but that should not prevent us from becoming intermediaries for change.

You can doubtless say that it is easier to inspire other people when you play with images in their minds when you tell simplified and exemplifying stories that they can relate to. Although I think the pure facts about the environmental crisis are already impressive enough, they easily get lost on businesses when they are put in terms of risk, efficiency, or competitiveness.

---

[2] Broadly speaking, a free rider is someone who receives a benefit without contributing toward the cost of its production. Source: Stanford Encyclopedia of philosophy, https://plato.stanford.edu/entries/free-rider/, retrieved March 3, 2021.

A discussion that expands the sustainability discourse by including the bigger picture and creating a feeling of urgency could help where companies demand even more regulation from governments to create a level playing field. In my view, while many companies are now engaged in seriously tackling sustainability challenges, the described "tragedy of the commons" is unresolved, which means that the only solution can be regulation. For that purpose, political will with regard to stronger regulations on environmental and social issues needs to be challenged and strengthened by informed and determined business leaders: if they lobby for sustainability, politicians will hopefully deliver quick results.

However, how do we get business leaders to become proactive? More precisely, how can sustainability professionals contribute? In my view, strong communication is a starting point. There are multiple ways of starting a new conversation on sustainability in business. As a first measure, I propose that anyone who is keen on joining this vision think about his or her own motivation for sustainability and when, where, and by whom it was triggered. Maybe you can talk about this personal experience in more informal moments of interaction. Another approach would be to enrich the content of a presentation with broader insights into the issue at stake. Ask people in the business about their opinions! Ask concise questions, such as whether or not they believe that the Paris Agreement can still be met.

Dare to be drastic! Yes, we still need to sell the concept of sustainability to businesses, yet if we impart the feeling that we are living in historic times, and that we are part of a bigger movement, then true systemic change might be possible.

References

Diamond, J. M. Easter Island's end. *Discover* (August 1995).
Diamond, J. M. (2005). *Collapse: How societies choose to fail or succeed*. Viking.
Hardin, G. (1968). The tragedy of the commons. *Science, 162*, 1243–1248.
Olson, M. (1965). *The logic of collective action: Public goods and the theory of groups*. Harvard University Press.
Ostrom, E. (1990). *Governing the commons: The evolution of institutions for collective action*. Cambridge University Press.

Stella Blohmke after interdisciplinary studies in humanities and social sciences at University College Maastricht and a specialization in economic history at the London School of Economics, Stella started her career in the field of sustainability at oekom research AG (today ISS oekom) in 2012. For several years, she worked as a lecturer and researcher in sustainability management at Nürnberg University. After that, she worked for a couple of years as a sustainability consultant at the global consultancies PricewaterhouseCoopers GmbH and Ramboll Management Consulting. In 2023, she founded KYBELE together with Valéa Vadaleau. KYBELE is a sustainability consulting boutique with a special focus on the textile industry, consumer goods and other industries with complex supply chains. Website: www.thinkkybele.de/en. LinkedIn: https://de.linkedin.com/in/stella-blohmke-953674a1

12

The Ten Essentials of Responsible Business Conduct

Brigitte Bernard-Rau

In the past, companies engaged in mere philanthropy, addressing the needs of a variety of communities via the projects they had selected. Today, in addition to their philanthropic initiatives, these same companies undertake activities that address the concerns of their key stakeholders. In fact, an increasing number of stakeholders, including shareholders, consumers, employees, suppliers, governments, NGOs, and investors, among others, are becoming more concerned about companies' activities and their environmental and social impact. As a result, an increasing number of businesses are feeling compelled to enhance cooperation with their stakeholders. To succeed, their initial steps should involve developing a corporate social responsibility (CSR) strategy and a sustainability policy, with the ultimate goal being the creation of shared value solutions.

Sustainability and Business Are Two Sides of the Same Coin

Long before the UN Sustainable Development Goals (SDGs) made their universal call to action to end poverty, protect the planet, and ensure peace and prosperity in 2015, and long before investors took an interest in investments aimed at contributing to the realization of these 17 goals, the OECD and the

---

B. Bernard-Rau (✉)
University of Hamburg, Hamburg, Germany
e-mail: info@thesustainabilitystories.com

© The Author(s), under exclusive license to Springer Nature Switzerland AG 2024
B. Bernard-Rau (ed.), *Sustainability Stories*, https://doi.org/10.1007/978-3-031-52300-7_12

European Commission had set up principles and a strategy for CSR, firmly establishing the relationship between sustainability and business.

In its communication on a renewed EU strategy 2011–2014, the European Commission offered a definition of CSR as "the responsibility of enterprises for their impact on society," suggesting that CSR should be, first and foremost, a company's affair. This responsibility implies that to become socially responsible, companies should comply with laws and regulations. Moreover, they should put in place a process to integrate societal concerns (social, environmental, ethical, consumer, and human rights) into their core strategy and business operations in close collaboration with their stakeholders. In a statement published on the website for its Internal Market, Industry, Entrepreneurship, and SMEs[1] General Directorate (DG GROW, for the insiders), the European Commission underlines that "companies' actions have significant impacts on the lives of citizens in the EU and around the world. Not just in terms of the products and services they offer or the jobs and opportunities they create but also in terms of working conditions, human rights, health, the environment, innovation, education, and training." With these responsibilities in mind, companies should maximize the creation of shared value for their owners, shareholders, other stakeholders, and society at large by identifying, preventing, and mitigating possible adverse impacts of their activities.

Since the first Intergovernmental Panel on Climate Change (IPCC) assessment report in 1990, the debate around the notion of responsible business conduct has focused mainly on measures tackling climate change and environmental issues in general. Today, there is an increasing trend toward shedding light on social issues such as health, human rights, gender equality, social justice, and working conditions. This more recent focus uses as one of its frameworks the UN Guiding Principles on Business and Human Rights, with its three main pillars—the state's duty to ensure the continued protection and respect of the human rights of its citizens; the corporate responsibility to protect and uphold those rights; and the need to provide for appropriate and effective remedies when human rights are breached, which includes preventing and addressing the human rights abuses committed in business operations.[2]

With this increasing external institutional pressure, businesses are forced to change their dynamics. They are expected not only to focus on maximizing

---

[1] https://ec.europa.eu/growth/industry/sustainability/corporate-social-responsibility_en. Retrieved on March 25, 2021.

[2] https://www.ohchr.org/Documents/Publications/GuidingPrinciplesBusinessHR_EN.pdf; https://www.ohchr.org/Documents/Issues/Business/Intro_Guiding_PrinciplesBusinessHR.pdf. Retrieved on March 25, 2021.

their profit but also on creating a specific value that can benefit both business and society, ideally in a long-term and sustainable way.

Therefore, many companies, regardless of their size, industry, or geographical scope, are now grappling with two crucial questions: (1) Are there overarching principles for conducting responsible business? and (2) To whom can they turn for guidance on sustainable and responsible business practices?

In the following, I will present a "backpack" containing 10 essential tools that are easy to understand and implement for any business manager, along with an example of responsible business conduct from a well-regarded company in regard to its engagement in sustainability and how it translates the concept into action over time.

The "Ten Essentials" of Responsible Business Conduct

No matter how large or small a company is, no matter its business activities and where its operations are located, here are the 10 overarching elements that favor an authentic approach to conducting one's business responsibly:

1. A long-term vision by the company's leadership.
2. A determination to shift that vision toward more sustainable development strategies and to innovate in sustainable products and services.
3. A code of conduct that contains, among other things, a clear commitment to sustainability and ethical values—business ethics, basic rights, and freedoms under international standards—that is a "living reality" for the company.
4. An integration of sustainability values (economic, environmental, and social) into the business strategy and into its execution.
5. A clear and systematic way to identify social and environmental issues connected to the company's business activities.
6. A transparent and informative reporting system, integrating financial and nonfinancial information.
7. A firm commitment to the continuous monitoring and evaluation of CSR and sustainability initiatives.
8. A comprehensive environmental and social risk management system, including compliance policies, due diligence processes, impact assessments, and grievance mechanisms.
9. A responsible supply chain management.
10. An effective multistakeholder dialog.

Of these "Ten Essentials," I consider #6, a transparent and informative reporting of nonfinancial information, to be a tool that companies, across sectors and geographical regions, should use for communicating with their stakeholders and demonstrating accountability. The following case of Natura & Co shall exemplifies the detailed reporting on specific social and environmental within the cosmetics and personal care industry.[3]

Natura & Co.: Embedding Sustainability in its Core Business

Natura & Co. (Natura), a certified B corporation[4] with headquarters in Brazil, operates in the cosmetics and personal care industry. The company's product line includes deodorants, sunscreens, lotions, creams, lipsticks, and perfumes that are sold through more than 450,000 door-to-door salespeople (whom the company calls "consultants") working on commission. Natura uses essentially sustainable ingredients from special reserves in remote Brazilian areas and strives to combine business success with aid to community development in these areas.

With a strong presence in Latin America, a production in France, and recent acquisitions that include cosmetics brands such as The Body Shop, Avon and the Australian Aesop, Natura is today the world's fourth-largest beauty group.

From a profit-oriented perspective, the company is a real success story.[5] At the same time, as industry and financial reports,[6] academic papers,[7] and data

---

[3] According to the annual global 2020 Leaders Survey by GlobeScan and SustainAbility, Natura &Co is—together with Unilever, Patagonia, Ikea, and Interface—one of the most recognized sustainability leaders. https://globescan.com/unilever-patagonia-ikea-interface-top-sustainability-leaders-2020/. Retrieved on March 26, 2021.

[4] Certified B Corporations are businesses that meet the highest standards of verified social and environmental performance, public transparency, and legal accountability to balance profit and purpose. https://bcorporation.net/directory/natura-co. Retrieved on March 26, 2021.

[5] The group has an annual gross revenues of over US$10 billion, more than 40,000 employees, and a global footprint in over 100 countries. Source: https://www.premiumbeautynews.com/en/brazil-s-natura-closes-acquisition,15999. Retrieved on March 25, 2021.

[6] V.E. (Moody's ESG Solutions (2021). Second Party Opinion on Natura Cosméticos' Sustainability-Linked Bond Framework. spo-20210419-slb-spo-natura.pdf (moodys.com). Retrieved on October 03, 2023.

[7] Cheng, J. (2021) Analysis of Integrated Report Adoption for Natura Cosmeticos. *Open Journal of Business and Management*, 9, 489–495. doi: https://doi.org/10.4236/ojbm.2021.92026; Giraldi, J.M.E; Borini, F.M.; Mac Lennan, MLF; Crescitelli, E.; (2018) In search of tools for the use of country image (CI) in the brand. *Journal of Brand Management*, 25(2), 119–132; Simões-Coelho, M., Figueira, A.R. & Russo, E. (2023). Motivations for a sustainable ethos: evidence from the globally present Brazilian mul-

available on the company's website[8] show, one of the keys to this success is a strong sustainable development perspective taken by the company's management ever since it was founded in 1969. The company has been implementing its own strategic approach to CSR and claims that, beyond well-intended words, sustainability is part of its DNA and its day-to-day activities. Natura's strategy, "The Triple Bottom Line," concentrating on improved financial, social, and environmental performance,[9] is evidence of that.

Among the major social and environmental issues in the cosmetics and personal care industry, Natura shows a particular commitment to the impact of ingredients and final products on the environment and human health, specifically with regard to renewable raw materials and product safety.

Promoting the use of sustainable renewable raw materials in products Natura has established a policy for the sustainable use of biodiversity and traditional knowledge that seeks to comply with the precepts of the Convention on Biological Diversity.[10] The policy regulates the use of biodiversity and traditional knowledge as elements of local and global socioenvironmental sustainability, minimizing impact through sustainable handling, ecological models of plant production, and certification.

The substitution of raw mineral materials or animal products with renewable raw materials in its products has proven to be a competitive advantage in the industry. Natura has reported the complete substitution of animal fats with vegetable oils in their line of soaps and the substitution of mineral oils with vegetable oils in body oils. In 2020, over 80 percent of the raw materials used in Natura's products came from renewable sources.

To secure the supply of renewable raw materials, Natura opened a factory in a northern Brazilian state for the extraction and development of their supply chain of vegetable oils. In addition, a program for the certification of raw plant materials is being implemented. It promotes sustainable cultivation and handling by certifying plantation areas and native forests managed by local farmer families and traditional communities.

---

tinational Natura &Co. *Environment Systems and Decisions* 43, 321–336. https://doi.org/10.1007/s10669-022-09890-y

[8] Natura Sustainability - 2050 Vision. Available at: Vision 2050 - Natura (naturabrasil.com).

[9] Eccles, R.G., Serafeim, G., & Heffernan, J. (2011). Natura Cosmeticos, S.A. Harvard Business School Accounting & Management Unit Case No. 412–052, Available at SSRN: https://ssrn.com/abstract=1998220

[10] United Nations (1992). Convention on Biological Diversity. https://www.cbd.int/doc/legal/cbd-en.pdf. Retrieved on March 26, 2021.

Life cycle assessment: the monitoring of adverse effects Natura uses life cycle assessments to quantify the environmental impact of products in the stages of extraction of raw materials, production, use, and final disposal. The safety analysis of its products even extends to the after-sales phase through a product-vigilance system that aims to monitor adverse effects possibly related to the use of Natura's products and to provide feedback from the safety process. In this context, the company has established different contact channels for consumers, such as online forms, chats, email, and toll-free telephone numbers. Natura also publicizes its positions regarding controversial substances. It has already prohibited the use of diethyl phthalate and triclosan in new products, is phasing out parabens, and is working on new bactericides that are less aggressive to the environment.

Animal testing Natura assesses the safety of its products to comply with the precautionary principle and with respect to the ethical principles of research involving humans as per the Helsinki Declaration.[11] The use of animals for scientific and cosmetic research has contributed to much controversy around the globe, and it is often hard to justify the suffering of animals in conducting analyses and tests to develop cosmetic products so that humans can advance their beauty technology. When, in 2006, the question of animal testing was discussed at Natura, the company decided to ban the practice and replace it with an alternative research platform of in vitro testing. Therefore, today, all new ingredients and formulas are analyzed by health and safety specialists and subjected to tests conducted on humans to verify the compatibility, acceptability, and benefits of Natura products.

Managing product safety The cosmetics company has also established a product safety committee that is responsible for formulating strategies and guidelines regarding the safety of the ingredients used in cosmetics as well as in finished products.

Lessons to Learn

The example of Natura shows the systematic integration of environmental and social concerns into business strategy and operations. Together with financial information, sustainability policies, and practices are reflected in

---

[11] The World Medical Association (WMA) has developed the *Declaration* of *Helsinki* as a statement of ethical principles for medical research involving human subjects, including research on identifiable human material and data. https://www.wma.net/policies-post/wma-declaration-of-helsinki-ethical--principles-for-medical-research-involving-human-subjects/ Retrieved on March 26, 2021.

integrated reports with the objective of addressing the vast majority of stakeholders' interests and concerns. The materiality topics that have been identified reflect not only the organizations' economic objectives but also the environmental and social impacts of the company on its internal and external stakeholders.

All companies, regarding of their size, industry, or geographical scope, should take the above "Ten Essentials" to heart. They should also publicly report on their sustainability goals and results to show true accountability. Transparent and informative sustainability reporting is only one of the "Ten Essentials" of the sustainability backpack. However, together with a clear long-term vision by the leadership, a business aligned on key social and environmental priorities and an effective multi-stakeholder dialogue forms the backbone of a company's responsible business conduct, now and into the future.

Brigitte Bernard-Rau is a lecturer and researcher at the Faculty of Business, Economics and Social Sciences at Hamburg University, Germany. She holds a PhD in Management Sciences from Radboud University in the Netherlands and specializes in sustainable finance with a focus on impact investing, environmental, social, and governance (ESG) issues, and corporate social responsibility (CSR). Brigitte gained deep insights into these areas during her tenure as an ESG analyst at oekom research AG (now ISS-ESG) in Munich, Germany. Before that, Brigitte worked in international business development roles in Paris and Madrid and served as a public procurement officer at the European Commission in Brussels, handling contracts and financing for Latin America. She holds a graduate business degree from Novancia Business School in Paris and an LLM in European and Comparative Law from the University Carlos III in Madrid. A French native, Brigitte's other languages include English, Spanish, and German. LinkedIn: https://www.linkedin.com/in/brigitte-bernard-rau-phd-ll-m-a457964/

13

Synergies for Hope: Partnering for Sustainable Development in Kenya

Janine Kaiser and Peter Wanderi

This story centers around partnerships that have a transformative impact on society, referred to as "synergies for hope." Within this story, two colleagues, Peter from Kenya and Janine from Germany, share the origins of their collaboration and the valuable lessons learned from the partnerships of their respective universities.

Our collaboration started in 2017 when an entrepreneurial training initiative was initiated through the partnership between Leuphana University in Germany and Mount Kenya University in Thika, Kenya. Peter was the coordinator for Mount Kenya University (MKU), while Janine served as the coordinator for Leuphana University.

Let's start with a glimpse back in time from Janine...

Janine recollects: It's 2017, and I am attending the "Start-up Africa" conference in Bonn,[1] representing a university project known as STEP, which stands for Student Training for Entrepreneurial Promotion. In my role as a research coordinator, I am here to promote this initiative. STEP, as the name

---

[1] Bonn was the federal capital of Western Germany until 1990 and the seat of government of reunited Germany until 1999.

J. Kaiser (✉)
University of Hamburg, Hamburg, Germany

P. Wanderi
Mount Kenya University (MKU), Thika, Kenya
e-mail: pwanderi@mku.ac.ke

suggests, focuses on providing training in several East African countries aimed at promoting entrepreneurship among students, empowering them to become job creators. I take immense pride in my involvement with this project, fully aware of the profound impact it has on the students. Back then, many graduate students ended up jobless after school or university, and our training program offered them alternative career paths.

So, I am at the conference, listening to representatives of major corporations sharing the floor with a large German industry association), all in pursuit of fostering cooperation with Africa. They are talking about big business, big profits, and have big plans. I can't help but feel a little bit out of place, as if I was sitting in the wrong room. Wasn't the conference supposed to focus on start-ups? The name "**start-up**" implies to me that we are supposed to talk about those starting—those emerging—those taking root from the ground up. What do the other participants think entrepreneurship and start-ups in Africa look like?

I raise my hand to steer the conversation in another direction. "Well," I begin, "I think we are on the wrong track here. You are talking about large companies going to Africa, to do their business-as-usual. But you haven't really talked about the conference's topic: emerging start-ups, African businesses, and the people behind them: SMALL entrepreneurs. Let's start thinking about partnerships with them, support people from the bottom-up."

To my surprise, the room erupted in applause, and investors quickly surrounded me, eager to connect with these small entrepreneurs. It was a hot topic that had struck a chord with the audience.

As this scenario illustrates, investors truly want to establish meaningful connections with small-scale entrepreneurs. However, the challenge lies in finding the right platform for these connections. The root of this challenge, we posit, lies in a missing link: Establishing synergies and mutually beneficial North–South partnerships often requires extra effort and the identification of suitable platforms to bring them to fruition.

The platform we propose as a pivotal driver for these connections is university partnerships. These connections turned into alliances and can serve as catalysts. Universities can become a space for knowledge exchange. In the context of (research) conferences, academic researchers, practitioners (investors), and students (future entrepreneurs) from various countries can come together to initiate contact and establish project or research groups. Seminars conducted in cooperation with practitioners can lead to fruitful partnerships, while resources and insights can be shared among all stakeholders. After all, universities are "start-hubs," acting as physical spaces, where innovations originate, where prototypes of various kinds can be tested, and where "experiencing failures" is allowed. Moreover, failures are not only permitted but also encouraged as they are often a necessary step in the process of iterative growth. In addition, universities play an important role in contributing to bigger objectives, such as the achievement of the Sustainable Development Goals (SDGs) for 2030 or the Global Goals.

Challenges Ahead: Achieving the Sustainable Development Goals

In response to the pressing global challenges we face, the United Nations member states unanimously adopted the 17 Sustainable Development Goals (SDGs) in 2015. These 17 goals, comprising 169 sub-targets and measurable actions, are meant to be achieved by 2030. However, as we find ourselves with only six and a half years remaining, a recent preliminary progress report by the General Assembly Economic and Social Council reveals a stark reality: merely 12% of these targets are currently on track. The report unequivocally states that "it's time to sound the alarm."[2] Certainly, most investors are motivated by the prospect of generating profits through rather large and highly profitable ventures. However, in the year 2023, we must decide whether we are serious about safeguarding our world. Do we want to realize the SDGs by 2030, those SDGs that we so proudly introduced in 2015? This is a critical question we should address.

Underinvestment: A Key Factor for Underachieving the SDGs

All targets, whether they pertain to the preservation of biodiversity, access to clean energy, climate action, or the promotion of peace, justice, and strong institutions, can only be realized with adequate financial support. Currently, the average funding gap for achieving the SDGs in developing countries is estimated to exceed USD 4 trillion annually. This represents an increase of up to 1.5 trillion compared to previous years.[3] One of the main reasons for this gap is underinvestment.

Yet, there is hope: Over the last couple of years, investing has been steering in a new direction. A group of investors, called impact investors, increasingly invest in assets that specifically address and solve pressing social and

---

[2] Report of the Secretary-General, General Assembly Economic and Social Council, 2023, p. 12; https://sdgs.un.org/sites/default/files/2023-04/SDG_Progress_Report_Special_Edition_2023_ADVANCE_UNEDITED_VERSION.pdf

[3] United Nations Conference on Trade and Development [UNCTAD], 2023.

environmental challenges. And they intend to do more. What sets them apart is their commitment to measuring and transparently reporting the social and/or environmental consequences their investments have on the people and the planet. In other words, they ask themselves the following questions: Does the money I invest in this specific project truly benefit the village? What might the outcome be in 10 years' time? Recent reports, such as the one from Bundesinitiative Impact Investing, which evaluates the German impact investing market, indicate that impact investments not only generate a positive impact on society but also yield financial returns. In fact, many impact investors have made it their mission to align their strategies with the SDGs, underlying their commitment to achieving positive, measurable impacts.[4]

Missing Synergies and Missing Mutual Partnerships: A Reason for Underinvestment?

In our opinion, underinvestment can stem from a lack of partnerships between the public and the private sector addressing the SDGs. We believe one reason for underinvestment is a missing link: synergies and mutual North–South partnerships between investors and small entrepreneurs are often hard to find.

Synergies and mutual partnerships entail a collaborative effort where both sides contribute equally and derive equal benefits. Common purpose is of particular importance. Both Leuphana University and Mount Kenya University (MKU) are certified higher education institutions. Mount Kenya University's 2020–2029 Strategic Plan entails a commitment to work with partners to fulfill three main roles: teaching, research, and community outreach. This aligns with the United Nations' goals set in 2015 for worldwide development, especially Goal No. 17, which emphasizes teamwork.

The Project "STEP"[5] (Student Training for Entrepreneurial Promotion) has always been based on synergies and mutual partnerships. Long before our mutual journey started, researchers from Germany and East African Institutions worked together to develop a training concept for young students. It was highly important for them to develop the training material together, which also led to several joint publications (Gielnik et al., 2015, 2016) and STEP research conferences organized, for example, in Kampala, Uganda or in Lueneburg, Germany. This resulted in many north-south and south–south partnerships between various countries, for instance, Uganda,

---

[4] Bernard-Rau et al. (2022) Impact Investing in Deutschland: Marktstudie 2022. https://bundesinitiative-impact-investing.de/wp-content/uploads/2023/05/BIII-Marktstudie_Impact-Investing-in-Deutschland-2022_single-pages-1.pdf

[5] www.step-training.com

Rwanda, Tanzania, Kenya, and Germany. Looking ahead to the present day, initiatives such as STEP have had an impact on the African continent. They are aligned with the spirit of entrepreneurship and the overarching objectives of the United Nations Sustainable Development Goals (SDGs). For example, SDG Number 8, which focuses on Decent Work and Economic Growth, and Number 17, which emphasizes Partnerships, stand out as key areas of impact. In total, 150 students successfully finished the training in 2017. To see whether the training impacts job and business creation, the students, as well as a control group, take part in frequent evaluations. At the closing ceremony, many of the beneficiaries were motivated to embrace the future as entrepreneurs.

In the monitoring and evaluation exercises conducted by the Kenyan author of this paper before the onset of COVID-19, the training was found to have been very effective, with several of the students having started their own businesses.

Fast Forward to Today

A third case of effective use of STEP was witnessed between March and July 2023 when the program was successfully administered to a group of 50 combined adolescents and adults, of whom a majority were recovering from alcoholic addiction. This initiative was a grand partnership of many organizations, including the Murang'a County Government, the Catholic Diocese of Murang'a represented by the Sisters of Emmanuel who put together the trainees, Gatanga Catholic Parish, Mount Kenya University as the program coordinators, and the Leuphana University of Germany as the sponsoring institution, the Mulli Children Family (MCF), Conscious Work Consultants, the National Authority for the Campaign Against Alcohol and Drug Abuse (NACADA), LIONS International Thika—Kilimambogo Club, Association of Pentecostal and Evangelical Clergy of Kenya (APECK), among others. The training saw the beneficiaries start new businesses in different groups. The businesses started included livestock rearing, agroforestry, sports and entertainment teams and dairying. The beneficiaries of this STEP project registered a business group under the name of the Emmanuel Youth Group. In addition to the small businesses created, the impact of the STEP training on the Emmanuel Youth Group has led to total abstinence from alcohol of a steadily rising number of former addicts who have taken a vow in the Catholic Church for total alcoholic abstinence. Additionally, some were also able to get new jobs, or others returned to their previous jobs, which they had lost due to alcoholism.

The mutual partnership between several small organizations ultimately led to several positive effects. The creation of new jobs and the reduction of drug addiction had direct positive effects on the people who participated in the training and led to positive developments within the communities. This is what we call synergies of hope.

The United Nations Academic Impact (UNAI) Platform

Another example of a partnership with scaling effects is the collaboration of universities through the United Nations Academic Impact (UNAI) platform. Since 2015, when the UN introduced the SDGs 2030, many efforts worldwide have started to create partnerships that help toward the achievement of these goals or Global Goals.

The UNAI platform gathers hundreds of universities worldwide. "Mount Kenya University is part of this group, and we send an annual report to the UNAI office. The report contains the activities we do every year to help achieve the SDGs 2030", says Peter, the co-author of this chapter, who served as MKU's platform overseer. The United Nations Academic Impact (UNAI) platform aligns the efforts of higher education institutions with those of the United Nations in a mutually supportive way that contributes to achieving the goals and mandates of both the UNAI member universities and the UN. "You can see how our partnership with UNAI makes a difference when you read the yearly reports on all the global activities."[6]

In summary, United Nations Academic Impact (UNAI) partnerships have a significant impact on the global community in different ways including the following two major areas among others.

Exchange of Information and Benchmarking

UNAI member universities, including MKU, exchange information and learn from each other. For example, the UNAI office in New York organizes webinars where universities can participate. This creates a global network of universities working toward promoting the SDGs.

---

[6] You can learn about the reports here: https://www.un.org/en/articles-by-property-local-category/59098/9319?page=5

UNAI Hub Universities

Some universities are chosen to be UNAI Hub Universities for a renewable period of 3 years, where they champion all the SDGs 2030 goals, with a special focus on one specific goal per university. In fact, there are 17 UNAI hubs, and MKU served primarily as the UNAI SDG Hub for SDG number 10 on Reduced Inequalities for a term of three years (1st June 2021 until 31st May 2024). As a Hub University, MKU's teams have either traveled or held online interactions/meetings hosted by universities in various countries, namely, Tanzania, Uganda, Scotland, Estonia, Nigeria, and Ethiopia all in promotion of the SDGs. Other meetings for the promotion of the SDGs that involved Mount Kenya University took place at universities in Japan, Zanzibar, the USA, and Saudi Arabia between November 2023 and January 2024.

It is important to talk about these partnerships, as they provide valuable learning opportunities for the participants. Furthermore, recognizing the significance of this high-level international dialog has the potential to facilitate the establishment of additional partnerships and the successful implementation of broader-scale initiatives.

Four Key Takeaways

In the end, you may wonder what our own takeaways for a mutual partnership are. Here are four key takeaways that help partners strive together:

1. ***Identify your common purpose and keep it close to your heart and agenda***
   Whether you are striving for positive impact, a commitment to change, or both, partnerships with aligned goals are the catalyst for meaningful transformation. The key is to identify your common purpose, and make your goals and subgoals crystal clear to everyone involved. Address the following question: How can both sides reap the benefit of a successful collaboration?
2. ***Communication is not a one-way traffic***
   Whenever you give feedback, be keen on receiving feedback. The feedback loops may work differently, depending on the culture. Germans often provide direct and candid feedback, while the approach may be more nuanced and gentler in other cultures. Regardless of the cultural context, valuing and showing appreciation for feedback is essential. Furthermore,

proactive communication, where expectations and intentions are clearly expressed beforehand, can improve collaboration.

3. ***Be ready for a mind- and perspective-shift***

As previously mentioned, cultural differences exist, and they should be acknowledged and appreciated. Celebrate the difference as you will learn, adapt, grow, learn, and grow again. Embrace a mindset and perspective that welcomes diversity. When faced with challenges or misunderstandings, take the initiative to seek the perspective of others. Understanding their viewpoint can bridge communication gaps and foster mutual understanding.

4. ***Be open to new and unexpected partnerships***

This takeaway stems from another historical reflection, this time from Peter …

Peter recollects The partnership with the Mulli Children Family (MCF) represents a crucial aspect of our commitment to partnerships at Mount Kenya University (MKU). Our introduction to Evangelist Prof. Dr. Charles Mulli, the CEO and Founder of MCF, took place during a conference held at the Hochschule Bonn Rhein Sieg University (H-BRSU) of Applied Sciences in 2017. Although MKU had no prior knowledge of MCF, fate connected us on a shared path, much like our collaborations with STEP and UNAI.

Upon witnessing Dr. Mulli's presentation, which began with a documentary titled "The Mulli Children Family," I felt an immediate connection. I pledged to be an ambassador for MCF. This commitment remains steadfast to this day. Understanding the remarkable impact of MCF on humanity, including hosting, feeding, and educating over 4500 former street children on a daily basis across five camps in Kenya and Tanzania, has only strengthened my resolve.

MCF engagement spans various sectors: formal education, vocational training in different areas including wielding, hospitality, and tourism management. MCF has also invested heavily in agribusiness, reforestation, and climate change mitigation programs. Their products are sold locally and find their way to international markets, including the Netherlands. In 2019, MKU and MCF formalized their partnership, leading to a series of successful joint initiatives, such as mentoring the youth, participating in conferences and workshops, developing funding proposals, and launching climate change campaigns.

Plans are underway to expand our collaborative efforts, aiming to reach more street children in local towns and to enhance environmental sustainability in neighboring communities. Together, through partnerships with

STEP, UNAI, and MCF, we are making strides toward a brighter future, proving that collective action can indeed create positive change for all partners.

Conclusion

The journey, which started in that conference room in 2017, and which led us to the impactful partnerships forged until today, underscores the fact that in mutual partnerships, everyone strives. Now, imagine we find ourselves once again in a conference room with our fellow investors, what insights would we want to share with them today?

Recognize the Power of Small Entrepreneurs

Small entrepreneurs create jobs for their communities, which leads to prosperity and development within the communities. Investors should not forget that (1) small entrepreneurs can already be found and supported at an early stage (at universities) and (2) these small businesses can drive innovation and sustainable development, making them attractive investment opportunities.

Invest with Purpose Is Also Financially Attractive

There is a shift toward investments focusing on measurable social and environmental returns alongside financial gains. More investors need to know that aligning investments with the Sustainable Development Goals (SDGs) can create both positive impact and profits.

Seek Diverse Partnerships—Find Connections Beyond Your Nose

Universities, nonprofit organizations, and local communities are drivers of change. Diverse teams and partnerships bring unique insights and solutions, ultimately leading to more successful and impactful investments. Our story highlights the role of universities and organizations such as the United Nations Academic Impact (UNAI) in promoting the SDGs. However, to achieve our diverse objectives, we strive to work with partners of different levels "leaving-no-one-behind" in what is popularly referred to as a

Quadruple Helix collaboration model. Investors should explore such partnerships to access (large) networks and (small) initiatives aligned with their goals with enormous impact.

Embrace Cultural Differences

Understanding and respecting cultural differences is crucial in building successful partnerships. Investors can learn that cultural sensitivity and adaptability are key to effective collaboration in global contexts.

Explore Unexpected Opportunities

The partnership with the Mulli Children Family (MCF) serves as an example of how unexpected opportunities can lead to impactful collaborations. Investors can learn to be open to unexpected encounters and seize opportunities that align with their values and goals.

Focus on Long-Term Impact

Investors should be willing to commit to partnerships and initiatives that may take time to yield results but can ultimately create lasting positive change.

Measure Impact

Student Training for Entrepreneurial Promotion (STEP) is an example of a project that developed a rigorous evaluation procedure. Investors can learn from such projects and adapt their own evaluation procedures.

Foster Collective Action for All SDGs

Finally, investors can learn that collective action and collaboration among various stakeholders, including businesses, universities, governments, and local communities, including nonprofits, can be powerful in addressing global challenges and advancing the SDGs.

Mutual partnerships with clear goals and outcomes can and will drive positive change—it is our responsibility to share these stories.

References

Gielnik, M. M., Frese, M., Kahara-Kawuki, A., Wasswa Katono, I., Kyejjusa, S., Ngoma, M., Munene, J., Namatovu-Dawa, R., Nansubuga, F., Orobia, L., Oyugi, J., Sejjaaka, S., Sserwanga, A., Walter, T., Bischoff, K. M., & Dlugosch, T. J. (2015). Action and action-regulation in entrepreneurship: Evaluating a student training for promoting entrepreneurship. *Academy of Management Learning & Education, 14*(1), 69–94. https://doi.org/10.5465/amle.2012.0107

Gielnik, M. M., Frese, M., Bischoff, K. M., Muhangi, G., & Omoo, F. (2016). Positive impact of entrepreneurship training on entrepreneurial behavior in a vocational training setting. *Africa Journal of Management, 2*(3), 330–348. https://doi.org/10.1080/23322373.2016.1206804

Janine Kaiser is a certified Environmental, Social and Governance (ESG) Analyst with a Master's degree in Innovation, Business and Sustainability from the University of Hamburg. She also holds a Bachelor of Science degree in Business Psychology from Leuphana University in Lüneburg. Her academic interests and expertise lie in the fields of Psychology, Sustainability, Entrepreneurship and Sustainable Finance. Prior to her master's studies, Janine worked at the Institute for Management and Organization in Lüneburg from 2014 to 2019, where she coordinated two Kenyan projects funded by the Federal Ministry of Education and Research (BMBF). Janine's international experience also include a period of over one year in Russia, during which she immersed herself in the culture and language, significantly advancing her language skills. She is fluent in German, English, and Russian. Janine currently resides in Hamburg, Germany, with her partner and two children. LinkedIn: https://www.linkedin.com/in/kaiser-janine/

Mwangi Peter Wanderi is a distinguished educator, researcher, grant writer, project manager, and administrator with over 30 years of experience. His focus on policy, research and training has led to a remarkable career in teaching, overseeing externally funded research endeavors, and empowering youth through education and sports entrepreneurship programs. Since 2012, he has contributed to Leuphana University's Student Training for Entrepreneurial Promotion (STEP) program by pioneering its introduction in Kenya through Kenyatta University in 2012 and later on at Mount Kenya University in Thika, Kenya. Additionally, he has been instrumental in establishing and supervising the United Nations Academic Impact (UNAI) SDG 10 hub on Reduced Inequalities at his university, Mount Kenya University (MKU). LinkedIn: https://www.linkedin.com/in/prof-peter-wanderi-887039b9/

14

The Power of Fellowships

Claire Coletti

> *Three Rings for the Elven-kings under the sky, Seven for the Dwarf-lords in their halls of stone, Nine for Mortal Men, doomed to die, One for the Dark Lord on his dark throne In the Land of Mordor where the Shadows lie. One Ring to rule them all, One Ring to find them, One Ring to bring them all and in the darkness bind them. In the Land of Mordor where the Shadows lie.*
> —*The Fellowship of the Ring*
> by J.R.R. Tolkien

This is the Ring Verse, a poetic description of the Rings of Power, and a recurring motif within J.R.R. Tolkien's acclaimed fantasy series initially published in 1954 under the title "The Lord of the Rings." It consists of three novels: "The Fellowship of the Ring," "The Two Towers," and "The Return of the King."

Everybody knows the story. "The Dark Lord Sauron has gathered to him all the Rings of Power, the means by which he intends to rule Middle-earth. All he lacks in his plan for dominion is the One Ring—the ring that rules them all—which has fallen into the hands of the hobbit Bilbo Baggins. In a sleepy village in the Shire, young Frodo Baggins finds himself faced with an immense task when his elderly cousin Bilbo entrusts the One Ring to his care. Frodo must leave his home and make a perilous journey across Middle-earth to the Cracks of Doom, there to

---

C. Coletti (✉)
Ecodesign, Neuilly-Plaisance, France

destroy the Ring and foil the Dark Lord in his evil purpose." In the beginning, he leaves the Shire with three fellow hobbits, hoping that he will reach the lands of Sauron unnoticed. Very soon he realizes that he will not be able to achieve his task without the help of a fellowship coming from the four corners of Middle-earth, a fellowship that includes elves, humans, and dwarves. Despite their differences of opinion, which date back to the beginning of their history, they all decide to join forces against the common threat. Although they were all unable to physically carry Frodo's burden, it was through their support and fighting ability that Frodo managed to make it across Middle-earth.

What can we learn from this story, rooted in the archetype of the battle between good and evil, selfishness and solidarity, and ultimately serving as an allegory for hope and perseverance?

I think three main lessons emerge from this story:

1. *The power of the utopian ideal*: A strong belief, a goal greater than the will of a single person, can enable one to do things that had been considered impossible at first. A utopian ideal is beyond words and is instead experienced emotionally. It is, most of the time, the driver of outstanding actions.
2. *The power of fellowship:* Creating communities united by a common goal and motivated by common goodwill.
3. *The power of action*: There is no genuine achievement without many actions. The success of an action reinforces the driver's legitimacy and thus motivates the driver to initiate further actions. It is a virtuous circle.

Of these three powers, the power of fellowship is above all. The utopian ideal is a great driver but remains theoretical if it is not appropriated by an individual into her/his own story and choices in life. Indeed, it is when people gather through common interests that they create more leverage to implement actions and make them successful.

This is what I experienced when I joined a French retail group in clothing and accessories.

Beginning the corporate social responsibility (CSR) journey of this company as a sustainability manager was a rather difficult task. First, it is only recently that the fashion industry and its customers have become aware of its social and environmental impact. The main driver in the fashion industry is "fast fashion." Fast fashion is a concept based on offering new products continuously at affordable prices and therefore lower quality so that the consumer is tempted to buy new items at a frequent pace and discard the old ones. Over the past three decades, the concept of fast fashion has been the most successful business model for lower to medium-price-range garments.

The scheme constantly introduces new trends and appealing new looks, which are mostly copied from designers' runways, leading to premature product replacement and fashion obsolescence. To offer affordable prices, relocating production to developing countries has become the prevalent choice due to the low-cost labor there and less stringent social standards and regulations.

The CEO I was working with was no exception. Despite being aware of the social impact of poor working conditions, long hours, low wages, child labor, and health/safety issues, he did not sponsor any initiatives outside of social audits in a limited number of factories.

Environmental impact was not a matter of his concern, although alarming data were presented to him, such as the fact that the fashion sector comprises 10% of total global carbon emissions, as much as the entire European Union. Numerous studies have underscored the fact that the textile industry dries up water sources, pollutes rivers and streams, and produces massive waste, with 85% of all textiles discarded each year.

My roadmap to CSR was almost blank, but the company had created my position. One might wonder how I could have proceeded under such circumstances.

Identifying Utopias Within the Company

I was convinced that my task was to mitigate the social and environmental impact at every stage of the value chain of the company and to convert the business model to a more sustainable one through codesigned innovations with our stakeholders.

That was my utopian ideal. However, I soon realized that it had to be shared by people whose jobs had real leverage. A CSR manager may have many ideas for projects, but most of the time, she/he does not have the power to implement the actions she/he recommends, which impacts the entire value chain. Working alone, I had limited power to change things. My objective was therefore to identify the right people and involve them.

After informal discussions with some colleagues, I discovered that the level of knowledge on sustainability was quite low and that there were some prejudices regarding the sustainability of some fabrics (organic cotton, polyester, etc.). It became obvious to me that training would be a good solution to meet with people and change their work processes to more sustainable ones.

One of the paths to more sustainable fashion is to develop eco-designed collections. Therefore, I designed a program to train more than 100 people with different profiles—stylists, buyers, and merchandisers. I organized several workshops to brainstorm on actions that could be taken.

Beyond the great ideas that emerged from these sessions, the most valuable outcomes, I thought, came from the informal discussions. I discovered that a lot of employees were deeply concerned about climate change and pollution and that they had taken many actions to combat these in their daily lives. They often struggled to connect this personal involvement with their jobs, and the training enabled them to bridge the gap. However, these discussions also made me realize that changing work processes and habits (which are the main pull factors for sustainability in a company) would not be deeply accepted if the working environment of the staff was not itself environmentally friendly. Thus, discussions elaborated on actions that I would consider minor (distributing reusable bottles and cups, collecting sock samples, etc.) to support a more sustainable mindset.

Discussing matters with my colleagues made me aware of their personal drivers and priorities on sustainability matters: one colleague dreamed of a zero-plastic world, the other was all about second-hand consumption, etc. Do these projects not sound idealistic, or utopian?

I must confess that I would have preferred to put in place a single driving vision for sustainability, a utopian ideal/purpose that was shared by all employees and management. However, as top management was not convinced of the value of such, I had to be satisfied with numerous, smaller projects for the next steps along the company's CSR journey. They were a great help, as it turned out.

Creating Fellowships

The banishment of single-use plastic in the supply chain has been suggested at different levels for several reasons:

- At the warehouse, many used plastic bags were thrown away in the reception area.
- Operators complained that some oversized plastic bags blocked the automatic distribution system.
- In the stores, many salespeople complained about the time spent every day unpacking all the cartons.
- Finance, audit, and management control had launched a cost-saving program.

Thus, I gathered a team, mixing top managers and technicians, who had the same objective—ban the use of plastic bags—but for various individual reasons. From my experience, a successful project in sustainable development must combine three dimensions: environmental, social, and economic. It must also gather managers with the ability and position to make decisions effectively and technicians to provide tangible and effective solutions based on their everyday experience.

In addition, in the case of transport plastic bags, the project team gathered together:

- The sales director is in charge of all retail staff
- The person in charge of cutting costs
- The warehouse manager
- The quality manager
- Myself.

The first step was to make an inventory of all plastics used and then decide which plastics could be eliminated without damaging the quality of the final products. Finally, the decision to keep or ban a plastic bag per product category was monetized and estimated in terms of the time needed to remove them from stores.

The inventory phase was long, and the quality manager played a crucial role in defining which products were worth packaging or not.

In the end, we estimated that 23% of the garments were overpacked for winter collections and 32% for summer collections. The assessed gains were as follows:

- 500 tons of plastic are avoided each year
- USD 250,000 cost savings
- 1300 tasks were avoided per member of the retail staff.

As there were obvious benefits for all members of the project and no direct costs (except the time to change packaging specifications and inform all suppliers), it was implemented without major difficulties.

Creating fellowships inside a company is crucial, but it is also important to be a part of one outside the company. In *The Lord Of The Rings*, Frodo would not have managed to reach the Cracks of Doom if elves and humans outside his group from the Shire had not helped him.

Actually, a CSR manager is often lonely in a company. Her/his team is very limited (a junior project manager at best or a trainee), especially when her/his position has been created recently. The CSR manager is most of the time in the position of trying to sell colleagues on an idea, and so has no room for doubt or low energy. That is why organizations such as the C3D (Collège des Directeurs du Développement Durable) in France, where CSR practitioners can meet and share best practices, are truly precious.

Becoming a member of a professional association specialized in a particular sector permits a gathering of forces and generates global improvement within the industry toward significant sustainability. For example, in France, many garment retail companies—even competitors—are members of the ICS (Initiative for Compliance and Sustainability). Their vital objective is to share social and environmental audits of shared suppliers and to develop common training methods and projects to implement workers' voices in shared factories.

We developed many projects with other companies that we would not have had the means or the budget to fulfill on our own. The benefits were beyond the actions implemented, and they favored new internal action.

The Power of Action

As previously mentioned, a successful CSR response requires two conditions:

- Involving decision makers and experts from different departments on the same project.
- The three dimensions of sustainable development: environmental, social, and economic.

I would suggest to take into account a third yet significant dimension: geography.

Globally, in the retail sector, stores are spread out over many regions and countries, and a CSR manager is working mostly at the headquarters. As opposed to other jobs, such as sales, the CSR manager has fewer opportunities to build relationships with store staff because most of the main sustainability projects are undertaken in central departments such as purchasing, marketing, and merchandising.

How can we involve sales staff, apart from asking them to separate their trash and switch off the window lights at night?

I came to the conclusion that one had to associate the sales staff with a major project they could see in the store where they worked. For instance, we had an extended eco-design project with the design and purchasing departments involving all product categories: shoes, coats, T-shirts, and more.

There are multiple ways to express eco-design through clothing and shoes:

- Choose eco-materials: Organic cotton, recycled polyester, European linen, etc.
- Organize clean production processes, especially at the dyeing and finishing steps.
- Extend the lives of garments with more quality fabrics, wearing options, and repair services.
- Collect and organize a reuse and/or recycling service.

Our project focused on the first three ways, and we created a specific label so that customers could identify eco-designed products within all price ranges. The name was proposed by and voted on by many members of the sales staff and other employees.

This rather simple and easy-to-implement measure triggered many other projects suggested by stores, such as a collection of secondhand clothing and partnerships with local shoemakers to repair shoes.

In conclusion, I attained the difficult objective of involving the employees in the stores as well as affecting real local change through action. This helped to cement my position as CSR manager and gave me the confidence to launch new projects.

The journey to sustainability had begun.

Claire Coletti is a consultant in corporate social responsibility (CSR) strategy, eco-design, and responsible buying. She specializes in fashion, luxury, cosmetics, and tourism and has been working on sustainable development topics for over 10 years. Claire started her sustainability journey as a consultant at Vigeo Eiris, an extrafinancial rating agency. She oversaw CSR auditing and advised numerous clients such as Clarins, Suez, Disneyland Paris, and SNCF on their CSR roadmap. She then joined Vivarte Group, a retail group specializing in fashion and accessories, where she was in charge of elaborating and implementing the sustainable development strategy at the group level and for each retail outlet. She led various projects, such as the creation of a contest on sustainable fashion, the elimination of plastic packaging, and the coordination of extrafinancial reports. Before her career in sustainability, Claire was product development and purchasing director at L'Oreal for 6 years and collaborated with several fashion designers as marketing director. Claire Coletti graduated from the University Paris Dauphine with a Master's Degree in Sustainable Development. She also holds a Master of Science in International Fashion and Luxury Management from the Institut Français de la Mode and a Master's in International Business Development from ICN Business School.

Part II

Exploring Environmental and Social Challenges

15

Earth Restore: A Story of Resilience Among Adversities

Nayan Mitra

Nothing comes as an accomplishment instantly.
Success does not come overnight. Patience is the key!
Grow up and be the tree; but remember it takes dry and wet seasons
to become a fruit bearer, achiever and impact maker!
Israelmore Ayivor (Source: The Great Hand Book of Quotes)

Year 2021. It was the peak of the coronavirus disease second wave. Horror stories were pouring in from all directions. A genuine sense of helplessness engulfed the world. People were hoarding hospitals and medical stores for oxygen cylinders. The coronavirus disease (COVID-19) has crossed over 177,358,938[1] cases worldwide and has claimed over 3,905,161 lives. India, having the second largest population in the world, was reeling from the pressure of patients and a collapse of the medical system with doctors succumbing to the disease or just extremely tired, having fought consistently for over one and half years by then. Most importantly, people were petrified of this

---

[1] https://ourworldindata.org/explorers/coronavirus-data-explorer?zoomToSelection=true&time=2020-03-01..latest&facet=none&country=USA~GBR~CAN~DEU~ITA~IND&pickerSort=asc&pickerMetric=location&Metric=Confirmed+cases&Interval=7-day+rolling+average&Relative+to+Population=true&Color+by+test+positivity=false

N. Mitra (✉)
Sustainable Advancements (OPC) Private Limited, Salt Lake City, Kolkata, India
e-mail: nayan@sustainableadvancements.com

unknown catastrophe. India, by then, had 29,823,546[2] COVID-19 victims and over 385,137 who had already succumbed to the disease. There was not one family that had not lost a near or dear one in this devastation.

It was at this time that I felt that something needed to be done. Maybe more long-term than just the short-term interventions that we were focusing on. Incidentally, at this time, the New Town Development Authority (NKDA) was looking for Adoptive Partners for their Green Verges. New Town is a fast-growing, planned satellite city—a green, smart, modern, eco-friendly city developing into a natural extension of the metropolitan city of Kolkata to the East of India. Under the able leadership of Mr. Debashish Sen, the Chairman of NKDA, several Green Verges were designated as pockets of green zones during urban planning. These Green Verges were situated strategically at regular intervals amidst built-up spaces and reserved in almost every residential block within New Town to improve the overall green cover of the city and break the monotony of an urbanscape.

However, the Government was looking at Adoptive Partners from Foundations, Corporate Bodies, Non-Governmental Organizations, Citizen Organizations, or Individual Citizens to adopt Green Verges of their choice for further development, beautification, and maintenance under certain terms and conditions. It was a tendering process.

Under my leadership, my Company, Sustainable Advancements (OPC) Private Limited, applied to adopt a Green Verge from among the 50 available for adoption. A "Green Verge" typically refers to a strip of land or area, often found alongside roads or pathways, that is landscaped or maintained in an environmentally friendly and sustainable manner. This area may be planted with trees, shrubs, flowers, and other vegetation, and it might incorporate sustainable landscaping practices to enhance biodiversity, reduce water usage, and improve the overall environmental quality. In the face of the challenging times brought about by COVID-19, we recognized the need to take action. The pandemic had not only affected lives but also livelihoods. Business was slowing down. Nevertheless, we firmly believed that adopting a Green Verge was the only right thing to do, our contribution to addressing this global pandemic, our way of advancing sustainability. We were allotted Green Verge 9 of Action Area 1, which we adopted. The task seemed easy—buy saplings and plant them. How challenging can it be? (Fig. 15.1)

---

[2] https://ourworldindata.org/explorers/coronavirus-data-explorer?zoomToSelection=true&time=2020-03-01..latest&facet=none&country=USA~GBR~CAN~DEU~ITA~IND&pickerSort=asc&pickerMetric=location&Metric=Confirmed+cases&Interval=7-day+rolling+average&Relative+to+Population=true&Color+by+test+positivity=false

15 Earth Restore: A Story of Resilience Among Adversities

Fig. 15.1 Earth Restore before plantation (Photograph by: Srijoni Mitra. All rights reserved)

We embarked on this journey in the fateful month of April 2021. We had by then done research on the ecosystem of the area. This land, approximately 1.8 acres, had 142 plots in the vicinity, within which 12 of them were planned as co-operative houses with the provision of 32 flats in each co-operative. The land had 22 housing cooperatives or houses directly surrounding the project area. The ecosystem had a direct potential to cater to approximately 4500 people within its community. The members of the community living in these houses were dependent on the government to take care of the Green Verge quarterly and barely interacted with this open space available to them. They would, on the other hand, dump their garbage into this space. Throwing household wastes from balconies onto the verge was not uncommon.

On April 18, 2021, closer to the Earth Day, we went to our Green Verge with 100 bamboo saplings (Fig. 15.2). We named the project the Earth Restore. Earth Restore, a Sustainable Advancements initiative, called for actioning our responsibilities over rhetoric, of changing behaviors, of taking small but decisive steps, however minuscule that might be, to give back to the planet what we have snatched from her. Earth Restore represented and still represents the power of action over thought!

We had already done thorough research on the plants and found that bamboo releases 35% more oxygen than any other plant. It has high carbon

Fig. 15.2 One hundred bamboo saplings ready for plantation (Photograph by: Srijoni Mitra. All rights reserved)

storage potential, particularly when harvested culms are transformed into durable products; high growth potential and the ability to store large amounts of carbon facilitate sequestration; and provides environmental and socioeconomic services that can help communities in developing countries such as India. Moreover, bamboo is also known as "green gold" and is a versatile crop that can be used in different ways: consumed as food, used as a substitute for wood, can help in the generation of electricity, making various useful products and handicrafts. Its other benefits include more rapid growth than any other tree, the ability to yield within 3–4 years after planting, and resilience against drought.

It seemed to be the right sapling to plant. The soil conditions in New Town were conducive to bamboo plantation. However, we were met with shocks that we were not prepared for (Fig. 15.3).

The first shock came when we discovered the land allotted to us lacked suitable soil for planting. Just imagine! The land is allotted, we are ready with our plants, and we have allocated resources for the planting (time, money, and human resources)—but the soil is not ready. It had turned into semisolid with all types of concrete and cement waste dumped into it from nearby construction work. The worst is that with so much housing around it, no one was

Fig. 15.3 Nayan Mitra on the land (Photograph by: Srijoni Mitra. All rights reserved)

Fig. 15.4 The land allotted had no soil conducive for plantation (Photograph by: Srijoni Mitra. All rights reserved)

willing and able to take responsibility for the situation. It was always some contractor or some laborer who did it without the knowledge of the house owner. Yet, we decided to carry on. We were determined. We dug up the concrete and planted the saplings. What was predicted to take a few hours took us the entire day to plant the saplings (Fig. 15.4).

The second shock emanated when the COVID-19 situation worsened immediately after the plantation and the location became a "quarantine" area.

We could not allot resources to water the plants. No one could travel into the neighborhood. We were concerned. However, the plants, being hardy in nature, survived with approximately 25% losses, but it is then that the next shock happened.

Our third shock occurred when the plants were eaten by cows. The Green Verge was naturally fenced by the backyard wall of the 22 houses that surrounded it, but some parts of it, that still had vacant plots, were unfenced. Cows from nearby villages would often graze in these empty plots thereby getting access to the Green Verge, and the delicious freshly planted young saplings provided a good snack to them. We liaised with NKDA and got the land fenced and replanted 100 new saplings closer to monsoon.

Our fourth shock arose when we realized that a part of the plot did not have human access due to no road. We liaised with NKDA once again on this and extended an existing road to access this part of the plot.

Our fifth shock originated when, in the monsoon season, we realized that there was water logging in the land (being low-lying and not capable of water absorption due to the nature of the land) that was detrimental to the growth of the fledgling saplings. We realized we had to transport soil to this area if we wanted the saplings to survive and thrive. Those who know how challenging it is to access and transport soil for plantation in an urban area will appreciate the ordeal that followed.

And this was our sixth shock. To identify soil sources, we had to wait for several months until a nearby canal was being cleaned, and we could arrange with the local contractors to purchase fourteen truckloads of soil from the canal. The plants needed this soil, which is rich in organic matter. It would contribute to both the purposes of feeding the plants with nutrients as well as raising the land to prevent water logging.

By this time, we had already taken care of our seventh shock of construction debris that lay discarded on the land. We segregated them into larger chunks and smaller ones. For the larger chunks, we brought together and created rock gardens at strategic places; for the smaller chunks, we lined a section of the boundary and sunk potted plants within them to beautify the place. The rest of the land had rich soil sourced from the canal.

However, still, it was not enough. The eighth shock was when we realized that the composting pits that we had dug were not enough. What would we do with specific areas earmarked for the creation of composts? The entire land area needed organic matter. Therefore, when we cleaned and pruned, we put the mulch on the land itself, which was then subjected to the various weather conditions and quietly converted into composts for the plants. It also added to the biodiversity of the area with various species, making them their homes, thus enriching the soil and the growth ecosystem.

The ninth shock came when we became aware that we had a divide among the community, with two types of communities coexisting in this geographical area that have two extreme connections with the land. One belonged to the urban community (mostly the land owners), and the other was the migratory population, mostly from the rural or semiurban areas, who worked as laborers and service providers to this urban populace. While the former wanted a manicured garden, the latter wanted sustenance from this land. The latter were definitely many times more numerous, were new in an urban setup, and had a deep connection with the soil coming from the rich hinterlands of rural India. They wanted to nurture the soil, grow food consumables, and depend on the soil for herbs and medicinal requirements. They were often illiterate or semiliterate and shy to visit a doctor when needed. However, they knew their plants and recognized what worked for them. Hence, there was a

Fig. 15.5 Earth Restore turned into a lush green forest within two years (Photograph by: Srijoni Mitra. All rights reserved)

need to consciously add some medicinal plants and vegetables to this land. But where do we start?

Our research showed that one of the pertinent problems in India is anemia among women and children, with over 50% under this condition. We, therefore, started to consciously plant vegetables such as green banana and fruits such as pomegranate and guava that would add to the nutritional requirements of these people to combat anemia. Lemon was also grown to bring out the connection between iron and its fortification through the vitamin C of the lemon. The migrant community's interest in caring for the land grew. Simultaneously, we deliberately cultivated a variety of flowers for the other urban community, flowers like hibiscus, plumeria, jasmine, peri-winkle, nine o-clock, gulmohar, and more. These flowers blossomed adding beauty to the area and attracting butterflies, bees, and other creatures (Fig. 15.5).

The tenth shock happened when we realized that we had overshot our original budget in our pursuit of creating and sustaining impact. We collaborated with several stakeholders to help us bridge over the financials. We found some good corporate CSR funding, civil societies such as the Rotary Club, family funds, and individuals who came forward to help us partly bridge this challenge.

The media spoke about the impact of our first Earth Restore Project, the Government identified it as an exemplary project, and we were allotted two more lands to replicate the model. This land alone sequesters 150+ tonnes of carbon. This has been presented multiple times as a case study in Academic Institutions of Higher Learning worldwide.

Growing Earth Restore has indeed been a humbling experience, with learning opportunities at every step. It is now a space that has completely transformed the interactions between human to nature, human to human, and nature to nature—with a thriving urban forest where life and relationships thrive. This has catalyzed an ecosystem of change. Neighbors, who never interacted with the space, have now built gates in their backyards to access the forest; patches of green are visible on their terrace and balcony now, where they have grown their own patches of potted plants. Young people come here to play and interact with nature, as do many other insects and birds that have made it their home.

Nayan Mitra is a distinguished figure in the fields of sustainability, corporate social responsibility (CSR), and responsible leadership. She leads Sustainable Advancements (OPC) Private Limited, a woman-owned company dedicated to advancing the Sustainable Development Goals (SDGs) through advocacy and impactful projects.

In addition to her academic career, Dr. Mitra is also a sought-after consultant and advisor for international think tanks. She spearheads the India CSR Leadership Interview Series, facilitating insightful discussions among prominent corporate leaders. Her contributions have earned her the Author Award at the Indian CSR Leadership Summit (2017–2019) and recognition as one of India's 25 most impactful Sustainability Leaders.

Deeply committed to women's issues, Dr. Mitra serves as the National President of the Women's Indian Chamber of Commerce and Industry (WICCI) Sustainable Businesses Council. She contributes pro-bono to advisory boards of renowned Indian NGOs dedicated to women and children's welfare.

Website: www.sustainableadvancements.com

16

What Is a Climate Neutral Company and How Do You Become One?

Bernhard Schwager and Gabriele Renner

Climate change and the emission of greenhouse gases continue to be critical issues facing society. Strategies and actions to reduce carbon footprints remain important, and companies are still responding to this issue in various ways. In some markets, carbon neutrality is seen as an important indicator for consumers wishing to choose greener products and services. Carbon neutral means a condition in which, during a specified period, there has been no net increase in the global emission of greenhouse gases to the atmosphere as a result of the greenhouse gas emissions associated with the organization during the same period.

Pervormance International, the company that developed and patented the revolutionary cooling clothing system we discussed in the former story, has been climate-neutral since 2013. It is a participant in the UN Global Compact and was awarded the 2019/2020 Climate Protection Prize by the European Senate of Economy and the 2023 Sustainable Impact Award by Handelsblatt/Wirtschaftswoche.

The application of waste fibers and appropriate upcycling for clothing, as well as the use of renewable energy and other environmental protection measures, reduces CO_2 emissions to the greatest extent possible. All unavoidable emissions are offset by a certified forest protection project in Para, Brazil. All of these practices make E.COOLINE cooling clothing the world's first

---

B. Schwager • G. Renner (✉)
Pervormance International GmbH, Ulm, Germany
e-mail: b.schwager@pervormance.de; g.renner@pervormance.de

climate-neutral air conditioning system—wearable and suitable for both indoor and outdoor use.

Holistic climate protection follows three key principles. First, avoid unnecessary emissions, then reduce existing emissions, and finally, offset unavoidable emissions. So-called climate balances or carbon footprints provide companies and organizations with a tool for identifying significant avoidance and reduction potentials, defining a suitable climate strategy, and tracking the effectiveness of climate protection measures over time. A company, process, or product is defined as climate-neutral if its unavoidable CO_2 emissions have been calculated and offset by the purchase of emission certificates. The mechanism of CO_2 compensation is based on the fact that greenhouse gases are evenly distributed in the atmosphere, and the concentration of greenhouse gases is therefore approximately the same everywhere in the world.

It is, therefore, irrelevant where on earth emissions are caused or avoided. Emissions that cannot be avoided locally can be offset mathematically by climate protection measures at another location. This can be achieved through climate protection projects. Such climate protection projects must meet internationally recognized criteria and standards and have to be certified accordingly.

The most important criteria are as follows:

1. Additionality

    It must be ensured that a project is only implemented because it receives additional financing through emissions trading. The project must therefore be dependent on revenues from emissions trading to cover its financing needs.
2. Exclusion of Double Counting

    It must be ensured that the saved CO_2 emissions are only credited once to the owner of the certificates. This means in particular that certificates may only be sold once and must then be deactivated.
3. Durability

    The emissions savings must be permanent. This means that the binding of CO_2 in forests must be long term. Afforestation cannot generate emission reduction certificates as a climate protection project if, after a few years, the land is transformed back into pasture for livestock by slash-and-burn clearing.
4. Regular Inspection by Independent Third Parties

Climate protection projects must be reviewed in all of the above criteria at regular intervals by independent third parties (e.g., environmental auditors and auditing organizations). During this review, the actual amount of CO_2 saved is determined retrospectively.

However, that is not all. The principles of creating a corporate carbon footprint in accordance with the guidelines of the Greenhouse Gas Protocol Corporate Accounting and Reporting Standard (GHG Protocol) have been set. The GHG Protocol is an internationally recognized standard for the accounting of climate-damaging corporate emissions. It was developed by the World Resources Institute (WRI) and the World Business Council for Sustainable Development (WBCSD).

Five basic principles must be observed when preparing a climate balance sheet or corporate carbon footprint and the corresponding reporting system. They are:

1. Relevance

    The principle of relevance requires that all significant sources of emissions be considered when establishing a carbon footprint for a company and that the report should be useful for decision-making within and outside the company.
2. Completeness

    The principle of completeness means that all relevant emissions sources must be considered within the system boundaries. All emissions that are to be regarded as insignificant can be omitted. This is the case if less than 1% of the total emissions occur in an emissions category.
3. Consistency

    Of course, to enable a comparison of the results over time, the accounting methods and system boundaries should be defined and maintained for the following years. Any changes in the methodology and system boundaries must be identified and justified.
4. Accuracy

    Distortions and uncertainties should be reduced as much as possible so that the results provide a solid basis for decisions.
5. Transparency

The results should be presented in a transparent and clearly comprehensible manner. Pervormance International's corporate carbon footprint was drawn up to identify the largest sources of emissions within the company, as well as up and down its value chain. It forms the basis for the development of a climate-protection strategy in which targets, measures, and responsibilities for reducing greenhouse gas emissions are defined. In the coming years, it will check target achievements, identify progress areas, and pinpoint where further CO_2 reduction actions are required.

A CO_2 balance also requires a clear definition of the system boundaries to which the carbon footprint refers. The system boundaries describe the organizational unit, the time period to which the carbon footprint refers, and the operating system with all the emission sources that are considered. To distinguish between different emission sources, the GHG Protocol distinguishes between three categories, also known as "Scopes":

- Scope 1 includes all CO_2 emissions that can be directly controlled by the company preparing the balance sheet (direct CO_2 emissions). This includes the combustion of fossil fuels (mobile and stationary), CO_2 emissions from chemical and physical processes, and refrigerant leaks from air conditioning systems.
- Scope 2 shows indirect CO_2 emissions caused by the combustion of fossil fuels during the production of electricity, heat, cold, and steam by external energy suppliers. By reporting in a separate category, double-counting when comparing CO_2 emissions from different companies is avoided.
- All other CO_2 emissions that are not under direct corporate control are reported in Scope 3 (other indirect CO_2 emissions). This includes, for example, CO_2 emissions associated with products and services used or processed by the company preparing the balance sheet. In addition, there are CO_2 emissions associated with the use of products and services sold if these cause direct CO_2 emissions.

In accordance with the requirements of the GHG Protocol, the reporting of CO_2 emissions in the Scope 1 and Scope 2 categories is mandatory. Pervormance International also reports on all emissions in Scope 3.

The data acquisition and calculation of CO_2 emissions are based on consumption data and emission factors for conversion into CO_2 equivalents. A distinction is made between primary and secondary data when collecting and evaluating data in terms of quality. Primary data are collected with direct reference to an object of investigation. Secondary data are obtained by processing and modeling primary data. Both primary and secondary data from scientific databases are used to convert consumption data into CO_2 equivalents.

Of course, all greenhouse gases are considered, but climate balances or corporate carbon footprints show all emissions as CO_2 equivalents. This means that the calculations take into account not only CO_2 but also the five other greenhouse gases regulated by the Kyoto Protocol: methane (CH_4), nitrous oxide (N_2O), sulfur hexafluoride (SF6), and fluorocarbons (HFC and HFC). These are converted into the greenhouse potential of CO_2 and thus form CO_2 equivalents (CO2e).

16 What Is a Climate Neutral Company and How Do You Become One?

In the example of Pervormance International, Scopes 1 and 2 accounted for 10% of the company's combined carbon footprint, commanding 5% each. Scope 3 accounted for 90%. Upstream indirect emissions contributed 58% to this and downstream indirect emissions contributed 32% (see Fig. 16.1). Figure 16.2 shows the shares of the balance sheet items in the total emissions.

For the calculation of the Product Carbon Footprint (PCF), the entire life cycle of all cooling textiles was considered. The system boundaries correspond to the "cradle to grave" approach recommended by the GHG Protocol. For the calculation of the phases after leaving the factory gate (distribution, use, disposal), conservative scenarios were developed.

The PCFs of Pervormance International include the emissions of all life cycle phases. Nonproduct-specific emissions (e.g., overhead emissions) are included in the calculation under "Production" via a unit-related allocation. Compared to the previous year, the emissions per product are slightly lower—this is due in particular to the lower production emissions per unit produced.

Of course, CO_2 reduction can only go so far. Pervormance International's cooling clothing has the potential to deliver huge energy and CO_2 savings by reducing the need for air conditioning in response to global warming. As the first climate-neutral textile company in the world, Pervormance reports its emissions by product and updates these figures regularly every year. However, savings alone will not deliver climate neutrality.

The company voluntarily offsets all accrued emissions by means of climate protection certificates. Pervormance International offers its entire product range of cooling textiles in a climate-neutral manner. The CO_2 savings initially came from a forest-protection project in Sofala, Mozambique, which was certified by the Rainforest Alliance. Since 2016, this has been a

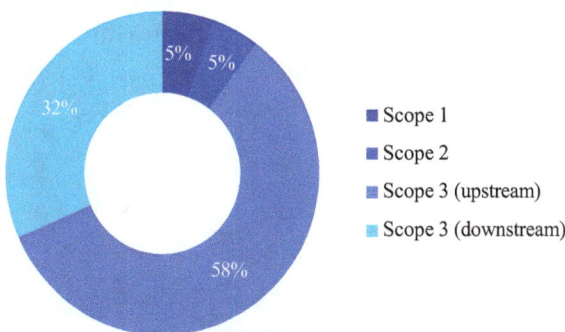

Fig. 16.1 Scopes' shares of total emissions (Image by: Pervormance. All rights reserved)

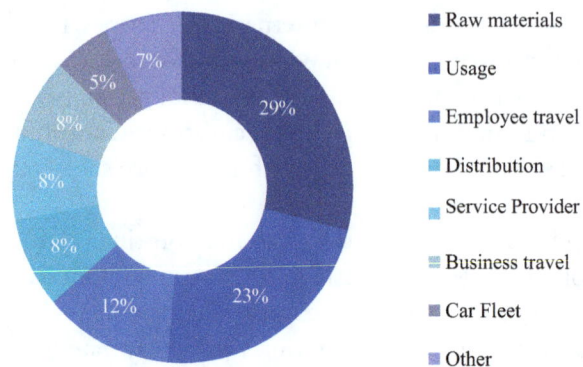

Fig. 16.2 Share of balance sheet items in total emissions (Image by: Pervormance. All rights reserved)

forest-protection project in Papua New Guinea, and now it is a forest-protection project with social impact in Pará, Brazil.

The aim is the reforestation of heavily degraded habitats, the protection of rainforests, the preservation of sustainable habitats, and the promotion of biodiversity. The livelihoods of the population are thereby protected. A regular update allows Pervormance to track changes and to communicate its commitment to climate protection to employees, suppliers, and customers.

The GHG Protocol also identified avoided emissions as emission reductions that occur outside of a product's lifecycle or value chain but as a result of the use of the product. Increasingly, this brings another category of emissions into the field of sustainability, which is referred to as "Scope 4." This refers to avoided emissions, which are important because they save emissions. This is also relevant in the case of Pervormance. Compared to air conditioning systems, efficient cooling products save over 90% CO_2 and 100% energy, as well as chemical and environmentally harmful refrigerants. Thus, Pervormance's products have enormous leverage in terms of sustainability. Especially due to the increasing number of air conditioning systems with enormous emissions, it is important to realize climate-neutral cooling that nevertheless improves climate adaptation and reduces health-related heat problems.

How cool is that?

Bernhard Schwager holds a master's degree in environmental science. He worked as an internal consultant for Siemens AG for 20 years, specializing in environmental protection and technical safety. He joined Robert Bosch GmbH in 2005 as Head of the Sustainability Office. Since July 2020, Bernhard has been a board member of OmniCert Consulting GmbH, advocating for sustainability and representing the company in various national organizations. Since January 2023, Bernhard has been active as an independent environmental assessor. He has held prestigious leadership roles, including President of the German Association of Environmental Professionals (VBU) and Chair of the German Environmental Management Systems and Audits Committee, which is part of the German Standards Institute (DIN). Bernhard is an author and coauthor of numerous books and articles.

Gabriele Renner , a pharmacy graduate from the University of Regensburg, has a rich career in the pharmaceutical industry. She worked as a clinical consultant before joining Merckle, where she managed prescription and OTC brands. In 1999, she founded Marvecs, a prominent service company in the pharmaceutical sector. Following maternity leave, Gabriele established Pervormance, a consulting firm specializing in business concepts for healthcare companies and government organizations. Since 2010, she has been the managing partner of Pervormance International, a German company that develops and sells patented cooling textiles and medical products globally. Gabriele is actively involved in sustainability efforts, serving as a board member of Südwesttextil and chairwoman of the Commission for Sustainability and Climate Protection in the German Senate of Economy. Her expertise contributes to discussions on corporate social responsibility, compliance, and sustainability.

17

Mass Reforestation: Combining Tech and Nature to Fight Climate Change

Fernanda Tsujiguchi and Diego M. Coraiola

The year 2023 is poised to be the warmest year on record, and that might be just the beginning of a series of record-breaking temperatures. From deadly heatwaves to waterfloods, countries in different parts of the planet are witnessing the impacts of climate change, and it is likely these events will become more of a regular occurrence (The Guardian, 2023). Against the catastrophic scenarios projected for the planet, scientists, activists, and international agencies have been pressuring governments to reduce carbon emissions. In 2019 alone, human activities released 43 billion tons of carbon into the atmosphere (Hausfather, 2019), including 1.76 billion tons of CO_2 produced by wildfires, which is equivalent to more than double the annual CO_2 emissions of Germany (World Economic Forum, 2021).

The negative impacts of climate change also contribute to increasing the frequency and intensity of wildfires worldwide. The World Resources Institute (2022) affirms that since 2001, forest fires have caused the loss of 9.3 million hectares of trees, an area roughly the size of Belgium. This means that if we

---

F. Tsujiguchi (✉)
London South Bank University (LSBU) Business School, London, UK
e-mail: tsujiguf@lsbu.ac.uk

D. M. Coraiola
Peter B. Gustavson School of Business, University of Victoria, Victoria, BC, Canada

IAE Business School, Universidad Austral, Pilar, Argentina
e-mail: dcoraiola@uvic.ca

© The Author(s), under exclusive license to Springer Nature Switzerland AG 2024
B. Bernard-Rau (ed.), *Sustainability Stories*, https://doi.org/10.1007/978-3-031-52300-7_17

want to combat the current climate crisis, we all need to work together to restore ecosystems and mitigate the global crisis.

The revised goal of the Paris Agreement to limit global temperature to 1.5 degrees Celsius by 2030 calls for rapid solutions worldwide (UNEP, 2022). Achieving that target requires a global effort to mobilize our expertise and inventiveness to come up with creative, sustainable, and inexpensive solutions that provide efficient ways for us to tackle rising temperatures.

Luckily, one of the best technologies for carbon capture already exists: trees! As powerful natural devices to absorb CO_2, trees are key elements to mitigate the effects of climate change. For instance, a single Silver Maple can capture approximately 25,000 pounds of CO_2 in a fifth-year period (Kilgore, 2023). In addition, the Earth is 31% covered by forests that shelter 80% of the terrestrial biodiversity and stock more carbon than the entire atmosphere (UN, 2023). Tree reforestation thus offers a path for trapping carbon from the atmosphere and fostering the regeneration of the environment.

However, there is a downside to reforestation, as it involves a time-consuming and extenuating process. Planting trees requires covering vast terrains, which can be physically taxing and strain the body. Once the trees start to grow, monitoring their progress and assessing the effectiveness of the results becomes challenging. Moreover, trees take time to grow, "and immature trees sequester far less CO_2 than older ones" (Montaigne, 2019), which is not very good news when we need to act quickly to deter the climate inflection point.

Although there is a growing demand for reforestation (UK Parliament, 2022) and a heating market for tree planting (New York Times, 2022), the challenge is how to quickly increase the number of trees and monitor the effectiveness of our efforts to fight against natural and artificial deforestation and mitigate the effects of climate change.

The current challenge is not so much on how we can deaccelerate and revert to past ways of doing things but how to mitigate the harm we have caused and regenerate the natural ecosystems we rely on. The major difficulty is how we can ensure that we change our mindset and focus on doing things in a sustainable way. To do so, we need to be entrepreneurial and rethink the divide between nature and technology to ask how they can work together to help us more efficiently address pressing global challenges such as the current environmental crisis. How can we use the scientific and technological advancements we have developed for the good? How can we mobilize technology to foster environmental regeneration? The case of Flash Forest provides a case in point.

Flash Forest is a fast-growing startup founded in Toronto, Canada, in 2019. It is one of several startups that began to use cutting-edge drones and data analysis to spread seeds in deforested areas (New York Magazine, 2022). Flash Forest has made "rapid post-wildfire reforestation" their core mission (Flash Forest, 2023). Natural reforestation takes time, and there are many difficulties in accessing blazed areas to perform the manual reforestation of trees. Flash Forest has thus created a solution to mitigate the alarming consequences of forest fires, using technology to reforest post-wildfire areas considered hazardous for human planters. For the Flash Forest team, the goal of using drones to plant trees is to supplement human efforts to help regenerate nature (CNN, 2021). Working with distinct stakeholders such as corporations, nongovernmental organizations, forestry companies, universities, and government, Flash Forest widens efforts to reach more areas and speed up reforestation (Forbes, 2020).

Combining drone technology, artificial intelligence, geographic information systems (GIS),[1] and ecological science, the aerial company employs a data-driven approach centered on biodiversity at scale, aiming to regrow ravaged and resilient forests. AI has the capability to rapidly learn from large datasets and recognize patterns and signals in real-time during emergent situations. With "accuracy, precision, and speed" to work at scale, the company proposes a sustainable and reimagined solution that combines human inventiveness with the benefit of natural systems. In contrast to the labor-intensive and time-consuming process of traditional tree planting, doing so from the air enables the company to make reforestation more efficient and reach areas of difficult access and risky environments such as post-burn sites.

The company has its own approach to reforestation. First, the company sends out a drone to map a replenishing area to obtain a terrain configuration and create a flight path, deviating areas unproper for seeds to grow, such as roads and bodies of water (Canada's National Observer, 2021). The mapping technology permits the company to evaluate the site to identify areas to avoid flights and areas where to plant (New York Magazine, 2022). Once the drone lands, the acquired information is shared with the drone fleet. In a clean area, the drones "can fly as low as three meters above the ground in a cleared area and up to 20 meters above if going atop the canopy, and either drop pods or fire them into the ground at about 180 feet per second" (Canada's National Observer, 2021). Through sensors and AI, the location is mapped out, and they use machine learning to indicate the best places to plant trees. Its precision ensures that the planting process works effectively. Drones are used to fire

---

[1] Geographic Information System (GIS) is a technological tool that analyses the terrestrial space through overlapped information and displays information geographically referenced separately or together (USGS, 2023).

seedpods with precision and speed (World Economic Forum, 2023) at the right density of 1000–2000 trees per hectare (Forbes, 2020). Attached to the drone, the hardware embeds them beneath the surface soil, and the software performs the after-seeding monitoring (Bloomberg, 2021). Visits to the seeded areas are also taking place to verify the seedlings and their condition and check the status of the planting (Forbes, 2020).

Essential to their efforts has been the development of new proprietary technologies that can speed up and increase the rates of successful seeding, such as seedpods.[2] Instead of using drones to plant seeds directly in the soil, they use seedpods to guarantee that the seedlings "a jump start for the critical first few years of life" (Flash Forest, 2023). Contrary to the energy-intensive nursery phase found in traditional tree planting, their production of compact seed pods reduces waste and energy in transportation. The company's capacity of production is over 200,000 seedpods per day. They contain a mixture of tree seeds, fertilizer, additives to retain water, good bacteria and fungi, minerals, and nutrients, and a conditioner that promotes germination, healthy growth, and resilience of trees (New York Magazine, 2022). Seedpods are customized to the forest environment to include a variety of native species in each area, which widens biodiversity and guarantees that diverse forests prevail over managed forests and monocultures (Forbes, 2020; New York Magazine, 2022). Their customized drones are equipped to insert the pods under the soil surface without the need to prepare the site (Flash Forest, 2023).

In 2016, an enormous wildfire took over Fort McMurray in Northern Alberta, Canada. Emissions Reduction Alberta (ERA), an organization in charge of implementing the climate change strategy of the Canadian province of Alberta, allowed Flash Forest to test the technology in the post-wildfire area, which shelters a particular and difficult biome with harsh winters and shorter growing seasons (CNN, 2021). Their solution has also been tested in other biomes in the country, including the wet rainforest on Vancouver Island, northern and southern British Columbia, Ontario, and northern Alberta (Canada's National Observer, 2021). While a traditional method with greenhouses full of seedlings and workers with shovel plants from 1500 to 2000 trees in a day, it is estimated that Flash Forest can plant approximately 100,000 trees by drone at the cost of 50 cents per tree (New York Post, 2021; Canada's National Observer, 2021), which is equivalent to a quarter of the cost of most tree restoration processes (Forbes, 2020). After Canada, the company wants to expand to Brazil and the Netherlands. "We want to scale the rate of

---

[2] Pods protect the developing seeds encapsulating them to keep away pests and pathogens (Bennett et al., 2011).

reforestation and to pull as much as carbon out the atmosphere as possible" (CNN, 2021). The company is an example of how technology and nature can hold hands to secure a better future for the planet and the survival of the human species.

There is a disparity between the rate at which forests burn and the speed at which they regenerate (The Index Project, 2021). Since the pre-industrial era, emissions have been increasing dramatically, exceeding the absorptive capacity of the environment (Newsweek, 2020). Uniting tecno-scientific knowledge with natural elements "is a material way of tilting the scales for the climate" (Canada's National Observer, 2021) and giving a hand to regeneration. Drones and seedpods show that combining nature and technology may lead to quick and inexpensive solutions that help ensure a future for new generations (The Index Project, 2021). This also opens up an opportunity for entrepreneurs and activists to come together and connect nature and technology to promote major solutions for grand challenges such as climate change (Daily Mail, 2020).

Anybody interested in entering the business needs to know some of the inherent challenges involved. Running a business of this magnitude requires a good amount of technical knowledge and well-developed managerial skills. The battery of a drone, for example, lasts 20 minutes on average. This requires planning and coordination to cover all areas in an efficient way. In addition, better ways of measuring performance are required. There has been excessive emphasis on the number of seeds dropped at the expense of how effectively roots are developed (New York Magazine, 2022). Operators have also been quite secretive about their technology and the efficiency of their results. More transparency is thus needed about the rates of seed survival and the use of open-source workflows to promote the participation of the community (Mohan et al., 2021). Moreover, not every seed will become a tree, and not every investment will produce a successful technology. New dead trees can worsen climate change by releasing the carbon they absorb over their lifetime back into the atmosphere (Washington Post, 2021). It is therefore important that investments in reforestation account for their own emissions to ensure that they provide a solution instead of adding to the problem of climate change.

As the climate crisis accelerates, nature-based climate solution (NbCS) technologies such as those developed by Flash Forest are becoming more decisive in our fight for survival (WWF, 2021). Flash Forest drone technology integrated with seedpods shows how we can use the best human ingenuity in tandem with the inherent capabilities of the natural world to enhance the way we monitor, manage, and actively conserve nature and preserve life on the planet (WWF, 2021). The goal is not to disrupt the tree-planting status quo (Canadian Business, 2021) but to bring regeneration up to speed to even the fight against environmental degradation. The restoration of forests with the combined power of technology and nature provides a small glimpse of what we can achieve if we change our mindsets and work together to save the planet. It is thus time we follow the example of Flash Forest to build more humanity with machines and seed hope with every single tree.

British Columbia is one of the most beautiful and biodiverse places in North America. For all the people and species living there, protecting the environment is imperative to ensure a sustainable future for future generations. Teaching Responsible Business and Entrepreneurship in the context of grand environmental challenges is a defiant mission. Climate change and wildfires are some of these tasks for humanity. Wildfires are not a local problem; they are a global issue. Living in Canada, we have witnessed firsthand how forest fires negatively impact the economy, society, and environment. The solution? Educating people through examples of responsible business, innovative technologies, and commitment to the well-being of people and sustainable nature. Through this story about mass reforestation, we hope to help raise awareness and better understand how our forests are paramount living pillars for Earth and a good life for communities. Flash Forest provides an exemplary case that proves that it is possible to change the direction and consequences of climate change by combining the prowess of human invention with the regenerative power of nature.

References

Bennett, E. J., Roberts, J. A., & Wagstaff, C. (2011). The role of the pod in seed development: Strategies for manipulating yield. *New Phytologist, 190*, 838–853. https://doi.org/10.1111/j.1469-8137.2011.03714.x

BNN Bloomberg. (2021, October 22). *Flash Forest uses drone to plant trees for carbon sequestration potential: COO.* https://www.bnnbloomberg.ca/video/flash-forest-uses-drone-to-plant-trees-for-carbon-sequestration-potential-coo~2306532

Canada's National Observer. (2021, Jul 2). *Toronto start-up Flash Forest aims to regrow world's forests with drones.* https://www.nationalobserver.com/2021/07/02/news/toronto-startup-flash-forest-regrow-forests-drones

Canadian Business. (2021, Oct 7). *Flash Forest is in a race to scale up its business and save the planet.* https://www.canadianbusiness.com/ideas/flash-forest-environmental-tech-start-up/?fbclid=IwAR0EyLz4x5L2YHPLDFAIRnIVxkBwi7PlyArWyrhuZ-iJmpGN4l9b2LiqJwc

CNN. (2021, Aug 11). *Arbor Day: These drones can plant trees faster than we can.* https://edition.cnn.com/videos/tv/2021/08/11/exp-flash-forest-drone-reforestation-hnk-spc-intl.cnn.

Daily Mail. (2020, Jan 3). *Canadian company wants to plant a billion new trees by 2028 using a network of drones that shoot out seed pods that grow 'flash forests'.* https://www.dailymail.co.uk/sciencetech/article-7840823/Canadian-scientists-develop-plan-plant-billion-trees-using-drone-swarms.html

Flash Forest. (2023). *Flash Forest.* https://flashforest.ca

Forbes (2020, September 30). *Drones can reforest the planet faster than humans can.* https://www.forbes.com/sites/jamesconca/2020/09/30/drones-can-reforest-the-planet-faster-than-humans-can/?sh=4ac3f041341f

Hausfather, Z. (2019, Dec 4). *Analysis: Global fossil-fuel emissions up 0.6% in 2019 due to China. Carbon Brief - China Policy.* https://www.carbonbrief.org/analysis-global-fossil-fuel-emissions-up-zero-point-six-per-cent-in-2019-due-to-china/

Kilgore, G. (2023, Apr 20). *How much CO2 does a tree absorb? 29 Trees & plants ranked by most CO2.* https://8billiontrees.com/trees/how-much-co2-does-a-tree-absorb/

Mohan, M., Richardson, G., Gopan, G., Aghai, M. M., Bajaj, S., Galgamuwa, G. A. P., Vastaranta, M., Arachchige, P. S. P., Amorós, L., Corte, A. P. D., et al. (2021). UAV-supported forest regeneration: Current trends, challenges, and implications. *Remote Sens, 13,* 2596. https://doi.org/10.3390/rs13132596

Montaigne, F. (2019, Oct 15). *Why keeping mature forests intact is key to the climate fight.* https://e360.yale.edu/features/why-keeping-mature-forests-intact-is-key-to-the-climate-fight

New York Magazine. (2022, Jan 28). *The future of reforestation could be in the sky.* https://nymag.com/intelligencer/2022/01/the-future-of-reforestation-could-be-in-the-sky.html

New York Post. (2021, Oct 30). *7 climate science innovations that might actually help save the planet.* https://nypost.com/2021/10/30/7-climate-change-innovations-that-might-help-save-the-planet/

New York Times (2022, Mar 14). *Tree planting is booming. Here's how that could help, or harm, the planet.* https://www.nytimes.com/2022/03/14/climate/tree-planting-reforestation-climate.html#:~:text=Reforestation%20can%20fight%20climate%20change,and%20make%20nature%20less%20resilient.&text=A%20tree%20planted%20for%20every%20T%2Dshirt%20purchased

Newsweek (2020, Jan 2). *Scientists say they'll plant 1 billion trees by 2028 using drones which plant pods filled with 'secret' ingredients.* https://www.newsweek.com/scientists-plant-1-billion-trees-2028-drones-plant-pods-secret-ingredients-1480019

The Guardian (2023, Jul 28). *Blistering US heatwave spreads from south and scorches 190m Americans.* https://www.theguardian.com/us-news/2023/jul/28/heatwave-temperatures-new-york-city#:~:text=July%202023%20has%20been%20 declared,due%20to%20the%20climate%20crisis

The Index Project. (2021). *Index award 2021 winners.* https://theindexproject.org/award/winnersandfinalists/flash-forest-home

The World Resources Institute. (2022, Aug 17). *New data confirms: Forest fires are getting worse.* https://www.wri.org/insights/global-trends-forest-fires#:~:text=In%20fact%2C%202021%20was%20one,loss%20that%20occurred%20that%20year

U.S. Geological Survey. (2023, Jul 25). *What is a geographic information system (GIS)?* https://www.usgs.gov/faqs/what-geographic-information-system-gis#:~:text=A%20Geographic%20Information%20System%20(GIS)%20is%20a%20computer%20system%20that,Where%20are%20USGS%20streamgages%20located%3F

UK Parliament. (2022). *Tree planting. Third report of session 2021–22.* House of Commons Environment, Food and Rural Affairs Committee. https://committees.parliament.uk/publications/9364/documents/160849/default/

United Nations. (2023). *Issue brief. Forests, energy, and livelihoods. Prepared by FAO, IUFRO, UNDP and UNFF Secretariat in Support of the Initiative of the UNFF18 Bureau.* https://www.un.org/esa/forests/wp-content/uploads/2023/03/ISSUE-BRIEF-Forests-Energy-Livelihoods-March2023-FINAL.pdf

United Nations Environment Programme (UNEP). (2022). *Emissions Gap Report 2022.* https://www.unep.org/resources/emissions-gap-report-2022

Washington Post. (2021, Oct 21). *A few idealistic Canadians are trying to replant the world's forests with flying machines.* https://www.washingtonpost.com/technology/2021/10/21/innovations-trees-drones-climate-change/

World Economic Forum. (2021, Dec 10). *This is how much carbon wildfires have emitted this year.* https://www.weforum.org/agenda/2021/12/siberia-america-wildfires-emissions-records-2021/

World Economic Forum. (2023, Feb 13). *This start-up uses drones to reforest after wildfires.* https://www.weforum.org/videos/28460-naturetech-cohort-flash-forest-uplink-yt

World Wide Fund for Nature. (2021, Jul 6). *Can 'nature tech' rise to WWF-Canada's Nature X Carbon Tech Challenge? (That's Up to You).* https://wwf.ca/stories/nature-x-carbon-tech-challenge-2/ReferenceList

Fernanda Tsujiguchi 's research looks at how multiple actors, such as entrepreneurs, corporations, and the state, can build a sustainable environment of pro-innovation through institutions that incentivize creative and entrepreneurial thinking, opportunities, and new venture creation. She is particularly interested in the symbolic, cultural, and historical aspects related to the actors and organizational practices that can enable and disable new ventures, innovation, and different business models. She teaches Responsible Business at London South Bank University (LSBU) and works on the Croydon campus to bridge academia and the local community in initiatives in the field of business and sustainability.

Diego M. Coraiola 's research focuses on collective action and social change. He applies cultural and historical approaches to analyze how managers and entrepreneurs use symbolic resources to create, perpetuate, and transform organizations, markets, and institutions. His current research projects focus on collective memory and the strategic uses of the past, Indigenous organizing, and historical injustices. His work has been published in journals such as *Strategic Management Journal, Journal of Management Studies, Organization Studies,* and the *Academy of Management Annals*. He is currently Associate Editor at the *Academy of Management Learning and Education.*

18

As Simple as a Lady's Slipper

Bonnie Lewtas

They call me Island Girl.

When I was a kid, I had a secret place. I'll give you directions. Behind the blackberry bushes, run down the path past Elephant Hill. Gain momentum to jump over the bubbling brook. Elephant Hill has four giant pines. They look like the legs of an elephant. Grab the roots to climb up the sand dunes. If they're thick enough, you can swing like Tarzan. You've reached my secret spot when you see the sole lady's slipper, a magenta-colored flower from the orchid family. Can't find it? I'll tell you a story …

Summer, 1994: On a day before exact dates were necessary. I am at my secret spot with my grandmother. Actually, our secret spot!

Stuffed full of blackberries with purple hands and mouths, we decide to head home. My mom wants to make a pie. It is my job to fill it. That could be a challenge. My purple hands are quite incriminating.

I eye the pink lady's slipper. So proud it stands alone in the forest, surrounded by rabbits' bed, a type of mossy ground covering that offers the perfect mattress, either for me or a rabbit. I bend down to pick the flower and bring it home to my mom. I might not have blueberries but, surely, she would love a beautiful flower.

"Bonnie dear. You shouldn't pick that." said my grandmother.

"Why?"

"If you pick it, it will die. If you leave it, you can enjoy it again and again."

B. Lewtas (✉)
TurtlCo, Amsterdam, The Netherlands
e-mail: bonnie@turtlco.com

I might be 5, but her logic makes sense.

"See you here next time, Miss Lady Slipper"

We slide down the Tarzan roots and make our way home (Fig. 18.1).

Fast forward at least 10 years: April 20, 2007: The snow is melting. It smells like spring. That smell means you're free. It means you've made it. I skip down the path. Everything starts to spin. I fall to my knees. Where am I? Where is Elephant Hill? Where is the rabbit's bed? I don't recognize this place. Clear-cut and bulldozed, all the trees lie flat. A big orange "X" spray painted on the owl's house.

What does Joni Mitchell say? They paved paradise and put up a parking lot.

You won't find my secret spot. You can't go somewhere that doesn't exist. I was so angry. Why can't they understand? Do they have no common sense? Sustainability is as simple as not picking a lady's slipper!

Another 10 years: September 18, 2017: I hang my feet in the water. Is something going to bite off my toes?

"No, no. There's nothing like that here," he says.

I skeptically leave my feet in the water, dangling off the wooden boat paddling through the dense rainforest jungle. It's hard to believe nothing will bite off my toes. Seems like the perfect home for an alligator or the arapaima I saw on Jeremy Wade's River Monsters.

"This is it," he says. "This is where they shot that scene from Pirates of the Caribbean. This little wooden hut. Actually, the medical students love this

Fig. 18.1 Bonnie in her secret place many years ago (Photograph by Bonnie Lewtas. All rights reserved)

place. They come here to study. It's their secret spot. Deep in the forest and only accessible by rowboat. Quite a good place to focus."

"That does make sense. I would come here to focus."

Later that day, we stopped at some lodges on the beach. The owner takes me on the "unofficial tour." I live for unofficial tours. With my notepad still slightly moist from the river, I write down the monthly kWh consumption.

"Can I see the garbage? Where do these bottles go?" He gives me Cory's cell.

"You should talk to him. He's building a small compressor. Making all kinds of things from them."

"And the sewage?" "Come with me," he said.

I'll spare you the details. After the tour, we're down by the water. He cuts a coconut for me and my dad. Delicious.

"It looks like it's heading this way. Are you worried?" I asked.

He didn't seem concerned. "No, no. They're not that bad. The last big one was David in 1979. That was awful. Destroyed the whole island."

My dad looks around awkwardly; that is his name, after all.

"I might board up my windows. But maybe I'll have a rum instead. It's only going to be a 2. If a 2 blows your roof off, it was never fixed to begin with." he answered.

We drive back to our hotel.

Our pre-hurricane meal is grilled local breadfruit I got at the market. I top it with some.

Gardein sweet-and-sour vegan pork and a bunch of veggies.

"How awesome they have Gardein here, best meat replacement ever! But nothing beats breadfruit. I could live off breadfruit."

We wash it down with a Kabuki lager and buckle in for a night of intense wind. Around 5:00 p.m. the news cuts off, and the lights go dark. Her name is Maria! She is on her way. Hurricane Maria has increased to a Category 3 hurricane, which signifies a moderate level of danger.

"A 3 is not that bad. Is it?"

There seems to be a waterfall coming through my bedroom door. I can't get through. We've used the lamp cables and the strings of my bikini to tie the mattresses to the chairs, which hold down the doors. Pieces of the ceiling are falling. The wind is howling and banging at the door. Despite what Paul McCartney says, I don't think I should let 'em in.

Everything goes silent. The eye is here. I can hear the neighbor's rottweiler barking. "Who would leave their dog out in a hurricane?!" I yelled.

"Grab your to-go bag, we need to get out of here." Answered my dad.

We make way to the staircase. Bad idea. The waterfall is here too. After the eye, the wind will change direction. That means it will smash the kitchen. We retreat to the far-back storage room.

A few hours later. There is less wind. Around 6:30 a.m., I fall asleep. I wake up at 8:00. We untie the bikini and move the chairs and mattresses away from the bedroom doors (Fig. 18.2).

"Holy s***! Where is my room?"

I look over the edge. It seems to be on the street four floors down. But where is the street? I think that's my couch. Or at least part of it? From the ledge of my newly formed infinity pool (what I used to call a bedroom) I can see the town of Canefield. The dog is still barking. They didn't leave him outside, but there were no roofs.

"It looks like in the computer game, The Sims," I say.

I can see people searching through brightly painted rooms. I can see some wall divisions.

I look at the formerly dense jungle hillside. Looks like a desert.

Everything starts spinning. All the trees lie flat. I don't recognize this place. "That was not a Category 3," says my dad.

Nothing makes sense (Fig. 18.3).

Maybe sustainability is not as simple as a lady's slipper.

At its core, island tourism sells beautiful scenery and pristine nature. So why does it end up destroying the local environment? From an early age, this self-destructive paradox has both frustrated and fascinated me. So much so that people even started calling me Island Girl. After years of research on this topic, I am confident that, if done correctly, tourism can fuel the growth of

Fig. 18.2 Outside of Canefield, Dominica the day after Hurricane Maria, September 2017 (Photograph by Bonnie Lewtas. All rights reserved)

Fig. 18.3 The newly renovated suite above us the day after Maria, Canefield, Dominica, September 2017 (Photograph by Bonnie Lewtas. All rights reserved)

environmental resources instead of degrading them. This is not an easy task and requires many different stakeholders to cooperate across industries.

My passion for island sustainability has made me very aware of how vulnerable coastal areas are to climate change. However, it was in September 2017, while working on a project on the island of Dominica, that the true urgency hit me. I experienced Hurricane Maria, a Category 5 hurricane that turned the entire country to rubble in only a few hours. This was a wake-up call for me. Despite the importance of the research I was doing, this experience showed me that the window for action that actually makes a difference was closing.

To help island nations become more resilient against catastrophes such as the one I experienced, I look at the big picture, break it down, and identify steps that can be taken to achieve the long-term desired results. There is no one-size-fits-all solution. That is why I work on creative projects with businesses, governments, and local stakeholders, helping them on a strategic and implementation level.

My challenge is helping islands protect their environments in a way that makes both common and financial sense, specifically protecting animals and their habitats. I believe that this goes hand-in-hand with creating long-term economic and social prosperity—even when it is not as simple as a lady slipper.

Bonnie Lewtas is the founder of TurtlCo, an organization whose activities focus on sustainable hospitality on islands. TurtlCo designs and implements holistic sustainability strategies helping islands around the world become self-sufficient and resilient against climate change. Bonnie specializes in innovative energy, waste, water, food, and conservation solutions for hospitality. Her work has taken her to many different islands, such as the British Virgin Islands, Grenada, Dominica, Barbados, Antigua, Azores, Madeira, Sicily, the Swedish Islands, the Dutch Islands, and many others. TurtlCo recently partnered with Island Growers to bring the first-ever hurricane-resistant hydroponic greenhouses to Caribbean resorts. Bonnie is currently working with the government of Friesland on the EU Interreg Islands of Innovation project and several other organizations that support island sustainability.

19

The Tourism Paradox: Can Tourists Improve an Area They Visit?

Khalid El Housni

This story explores the paradoxical relationship between tourism and local development, focusing on the region of Tahanaout, a village located amidst the High Atlas Mountains in Morocco. Through a narrative lens, the author reflects on personal experiences growing up in Tahanaout and later engaging in the sustainable tourism sector. The narrative is mingled with insights from academic studies, highlighting the transformative potential of tourism in enhancing economic opportunities and fostering environmental awareness. The author's involvement in the Terres d'AMANAR project serves as a case study, illustrating the complex dynamics of integrating tourism with environmental conservation and community development. By engaging with this inspirational story, readers are exposed to innovative strategies and diverse perspectives for utilizing tourism as a driving force for positive societal and environmental changes within local communities.

Tahanaout is surrounded by beautiful landscapes, and it was here that my sensitivity to nature was forged. I spent the years of primary school between the agricultural fields of Tahanaout and the soccer field. It was only in college that I discovered the world. Every path I have taken led to this college, which was the center of the universe for me. I remember the bicycle that I used to ride during the fall and spring months. In the rainy or snowy seasons, I would race back home, although going through the fruit gardens was, for me, of course, mandatory. In autumn, I would climb fig trees and, in summer, fruit

---

K. El Housni (✉)
Cadi Ayyad University, Marrakech, Morocco
e-mail: khalid.elhousni@uca.ma

© The Author(s), under exclusive license to Springer Nature Switzerland AG 2024
B. Bernard-Rau (ed.), *Sustainability Stories*, https://doi.org/10.1007/978-3-031-52300-7_19

trees. Unfortunately, this area has changed substantially, partly due to urban planning and the extension of the administrative district.

Tourism as a Field of Study

I chose to study tourism and sustainable development because of my passion for the industry and my belief in its potential to drive positive change in communities and the environment. From a young age, growing up in the village of Tahanaout, surrounded by the majestic High Atlas Mountains, I witnessed the transformative power of tourism. The arrival of visitors to our region not only brought economic opportunities but also raised awareness about the importance of preserving our natural and cultural heritage.

Studying tourism and sustainable development allowed me to delve deeper into the industry's complexities and understand how to maximize its positive impacts while mitigating potential adverse effects. I wanted to acquire the knowledge and skills necessary to develop and implement sustainable tourism practices that benefit communities and the environment.

Through my academic journey, I have discovered the immense potential for research and practical initiatives to contribute to the advancement of sustainable tourism. By conducting research, I can explore innovative approaches, identify best practices, and address the challenges faced by the industry. I am driven by a desire to bridge the gap between theory and practice, translating academic knowledge into actionable strategies that tourism organizations and destinations can implement.

Looking ahead, my goal is to continue contributing to the field of sustainable tourism and environmental conservation. I am driven to conduct further research, explore innovative approaches, and collaborate with stakeholders to create more sustainable and inclusive tourism practices. Terres d'AMANAR has provided me with a strong foundation and a sense of purpose. I am eager to continue my journey as a responsible tourism practitioner and researcher, making a lasting impact on both local communities and the environment.

My postgraduate studies in tourism and sustainable development needed professional experience as a way to shape my new career. Therefore, the adventure in sustainable tourism began when I met Jean Martin Herbecq, the founder of Terres d'AMANAR in Tahanaout. He was an incredibly inspiring person who was determined to make his venture a success. Terres d'AMANAR was an ambitious tourism project offering many creative activities, lodging, and catering. Jean Martin offered me a chance to join the Terres d'AMANAR team. My contribution as an employee/collaborator was in the commercial/

Fig. 19.1 Outghal, one of the surrounding villages of the project (Photograph by: Khalid El Housni. All rights reserved)

operational aspect and the development of the environmental and societal needs of the region.

I was also involved in the AMANAR Lands, "made by, for, and with the local population"—a phrase Jean Martin adopted to launch his dream project. The great challenge was integrating this tourism project with the conservation of the environment to positively impact the local economy and protect the natural resources of this semi-arid zone (Fig. 19.1).

Creative Activities, Lodging, and Catering

Terres d'AMANAR offers an array of captivating activities that immerse visitors in the wonders of nature and the richness of local culture. These experiences include guided hiking and trekking tours, scenic walking trails, and exhilarating Zipline tours through the breathtaking High Atlas Mountains. Cultural performances showcase the region's vibrant heritage, while eco-friendly accommodation options, including eco-lodges and sustainable camping experiences, connect harmoniously with the environment.

Additionally, Terres d'AMANAR prides itself on its catering services, which emphasize using locally sourced ingredients and traditional recipes, giving visitors an authentic taste of the region's culinary delights. Furthermore, the eco-activities available at Terres d'AMANAR encompass various categories, each promising a unique and memorable experience such as:

- Trekking
- Introduction to climbing
- Mountain biking
- Roller board
- Kayak rafting and tubing (when appropriate)
- Sightseeing
- Orienteering
- Bounty hunting
- Sports challenges

Cultural experiences include:

- Botanical runway
- Horse carriage
- Craft workshops
- Runs in Moroccan slippers (babouches) and djellabahs
- Berber bowling
- Shooting at rings
- Slingshooting
- Ring throw
- The Berber rickshaw
- Donkey polo

Team-building challenges include:

- Multi-activity week
- Olympics

By engaging in these diverse eco-activities, visitors can forge a deeper connection with nature and the local culture, leaving cherished memories and a heightened appreciation for the region's beauty and traditions (Fig. 19.2).

Fig. 19.2 A part of the accommodation "Ecolodge" (Photograph by: Khalid El Housni. All rights reserved)

The Positive Impact on the Local Community

One of the most remarkable achievements of Terres d'AMANAR has been the creation of over 150 local jobs in the region. These employment opportunities have not only provided a sustainable source of livelihood for many families but have also significantly contributed to poverty reduction, enhancing the overall well-being of the community. The project is deeply committed to prioritizing the hiring of residents, ensuring that the economic benefits generated by tourism stay within the community.

Moreover, collaboration with local associations and tour operators has played a crucial role in preserving and promoting local traditions while generating income for the community. Terres d'AMANAR actively engages with these organizations to offer cultural activities and experiences for visitors. This collaboration not only showcases the region's rich cultural heritage but also provides valuable income-generating opportunities for local artisans, craftsmen, and performers.

To further empower employees and enable them to take on leadership positions, the project has initiated language classes for the staff. These classes enable employees to improve their communication skills in languages commonly spoken by tourists visiting the region. Additionally, Terres d'AMANAR offers various professional development programs and workshops aimed at building essential skills for employees. These programs may include training in customer service, hospitality management, cultural awareness, sustainability practices, and other relevant topics. The ultimate goal is to equip employees with the necessary knowledge and abilities to excel in their respective roles within the project.

The positive impact of Terres d'AMANAR is evident in the lives of individuals and families within the community. For instance, heartwarming stories abound of individuals who have found stable employment through the project, allowing them to provide for their families and significantly improve their standard of living.

The transformative power of Terres d'AMANAR is truly remarkable, and the project continues to make a lasting difference in the lives of local residents. By fostering economic growth, preserving cultural heritage, and investing in the professional development of employees, Terres d'AMANAR sets a shining example of sustainable and community-centric tourism.

The Positive Impact on Local Women

Furthermore, Terres d'AMANAR has empowered women economically and promoted gender equality. In a region where traditional gender roles often limit women's participation in the workforce, the project has offered employment opportunities that empower women to contribute to the local economy and take control of their financial independence. Women have been employed as hospitality staff in guest services, reception, and customer relations. Their welcoming and nurturing approach has added a unique touch to the visitor experience, creating a warm and inclusive atmosphere. Terres d'AMANAR has been an agent of change by breaking down barriers and providing equal opportunities, promoting gender equality and women's empowerment in the community.

Consider Amina,[1] a widowed woman living in the village of Tahanaout, as an example. Amina had always relied on her husband, who was the sole provider for their family. However, tragedy struck when her husband passed away, leaving her with the daunting task of supporting herself and her children. With limited resources and opportunities available, Amina's future seemed uncertain. However, Terres d'AMANAR stepped in and became a beacon of hope for her and many other women in similar situations. The project recognized the potential of empowering women such as Amina, providing them with the means to overcome adversity and secure a better future for themselves and their families.

In fact, economic empowerment was crucial for women like Amina, who faced financial challenges due to the absence of a male provider. The project

---

[1] Please note that the name "Amina" used in this story is purely fictional and has been altered to protect the privacy and identity of the original person.

created employment opportunities tailored to their skills and abilities, ensuring that they could earn a sustainable income. Through this opportunity, Amina not only gained financial independence but also regained her self-confidence and a sense of purpose. Her income allowed her to provide for her children's needs, guaranteeing that they had access to education, healthcare, and a brighter future.

Through its commitment to gender equality and community development, Terres d'AMANAR played a pivotal role in reshaping Amina's life and the lives of many women in the region. The project empowered women like Amina to become self-reliant, resilient, and active contributors to the local economy by providing employment opportunities, skill development, and mentorship. Amina's journey exemplifies the transformative power of Terres d'AMANAR in breaking the cycle of dependency, fostering independence, and instilling a sense of hope for a brighter future.

Therefore, the employment opportunities created by Terres d'AMANAR have had a transformative effect on women in the region, enabling them to contribute to the tourism industry, support their families, and gain a sense of empowerment. By breaking traditional gender roles and promoting equal opportunities, the project has set an example for other initiatives in the industry and demonstrated the positive impact that inclusive employment practices can have on individuals and communities.

My Journey from CSR Practitioner to Researcher

Corporate social responsibility (CSR), or social and environmental responsibility, has become essential for companies as a significant strategic tool for product differentiation and positioning. While it is sometimes used as a sales tactic, the Terres d'AMANAR project goes beyond this "utilitarian" approach, recognizing CSR as a vital aspect of social and environmental responsibility.

This innovative tourist concept aims to serve as a "natural energy reserve" for visitors, putting human beings and nature back at the heart of the action. Its ultimate goal is to encourage a return on investment that extends beyond financial gains, positively impacting the environment and local communities. By prioritizing respectful and sustainable tourist development in this rural region, Terres d'AMANAR becomes an active advocate for responsible tourism practices.

As the person in charge of development and the environment, my mission was to train employees, evaluate areas for improvement in their daily practices, and make tourists and the region's inhabitants aware of ecological issues. In this sense, it is crucial to mention our different achievements in sustainable development on three levels: environmental, social, and economic (cf. Table 19.1). Overall, the project provides a living for more than 200 families in the region. Suppose the balance is sometimes tenuous between respect for traditions and tourism development (and the openness it represents, especially for women). In that case, Terres d'AMANAR has made great strides

Table 19.1 Terres d'AMANAR's achievements in sustainable development

Environmental level	• Reduction of impact through regional construction materials—adobe walls, earthenware bricks—using the latest ecologically friendly methods.
	• Watering of plantations by capillary action; several systems are being tested to be generalized to the entire site and region. Use of drip irrigation systems and traditional watering jars.
	• Implementation of a composting, recycling, and selective sorting system.
	• Regular re-evaluation of water and energy consumption to determine what changes may need to be made.
	• Keeping staff, clients, and the local community informed of achievements and highlighting exemplary individual performance.
	• Use of renewable energy sources, such as solar.
	• Selection of local drought-resistant plants for landscaping.
	• Linkage of the drainage system to a sewage treatment plant for wastewater management and reuse for the entire site.
	• Use biodegradable detergents and cleaning agents compatible with wastewater treatment technologies.
Social level	• Policy of communication with all the actors involved: public, NGOs, heads of local families, and project staff.
	• Setting up specific training courses with outside contributors and the transmission of internal know-how.
	• Empowerment of employees by encouraging their independence in taking control of tasks.
	• Applying a management philosophy that values contributions and stimulates creativity and encourages awareness of the importance of personal initiative.
Economic level	• Continuous training for the benefit of local employees, especially language classes.
	• Development of "solidarity tourism" by putting local associations in contact with tour operators who organize cultural activities for their customers, encouraging tourists to buy locally produced goods and supporting local service providers.
	• Creation of more than 150 local jobs.
	• Continuous training for the benefit of local employees, especially language classes.
	• Development of "solidarity tourism" by putting local associations in contact with tour operators.

toward convincing the community of the value of the project through the opportunities it provides.

Terres d'AMANAR has received the Green Key environmental certification, an eco-label awarded for excellence in environmental responsibility and sustainable operation. In that same vein, the project also received the Responsible Tourism award, a trophy validated by our peers within the tourism industry.

All these achievements have improved my position as a "practitioner" in the field, which later became the position of "researcher" through doctoral studies in CSR and tourism that I conducted at *Cadi Ayyad University* in Marrakech. It has been a journey that created a new identity by integrating these two worlds: a practitioner who seeks and a researcher who practices.

Imagination has no limits! It is an expression that Jean Martin constantly repeated and that the entire team at "Les Terres d'AMANAR" appropriated during the evolution and development of the project. Imagination was a tool that allowed the collaborators to develop ideas from a consciousness imbued with the cultural, natural, and human richness of the region—ideas that quickly led to action in line with a responsible and sustainable vision. This dynamic was also made possible by the "participative" management method introduced at the start of operations.

Challenges That I Faced and Managed to Overcome

Throughout my journey with Terres d'AMANAR, I have faced some challenges, but each one has been an opportunity for growth and learning. One of the major challenges was finding a balance between respecting local traditions and promoting tourism development. It required delicate navigation and close collaboration with the local community to ensure that the project's activities aligned with their values and aspirations. Through open communication, active listening, and building trust, we were able to bridge the gap and create a project that was mutually beneficial for both the community and the tourism venture.

Another challenge was changing mindsets and raising awareness about ecological issues among both staff and tourists. This required continuous education, training, and communication efforts to highlight the importance of sustainable practices and encourage behavioral changes. Overcoming this challenge involved:

- Developing engaging and informative programs.
- Leveraging the region's natural beauty to inspire visitors.
- Leading by example in implementing sustainable practices within the project itself.

Personal and Professional Growth

My involvement in the Terres d'AMANAR project has been a transformative experience that has significantly influenced my personal and professional growth. First, being part of a project prioritizing sustainable practices and environmental conservation has deepened my understanding of the interconnectedness between human activities and the natural world. Witnessing the beauty and richness of the nature surrounding Tahanaout and recognizing the need to protect and preserve it for future generations has instilled in me a deep sense of responsibility and stewardship for the environment. Moreover, working in sustainable tourism has highlighted the importance of responsible and ethical practices in the industry. I have come to realize that tourism can significantly impact local communities and their environments, and it is our duty to ensure that this impact is positive and sustainable. This realization has shaped my perspectives on tourism, emphasizing the need for a holistic approach considering environmental, social, and economic factors.

Unity, Solidarity, and Resilience: Morocco's Response to the 2023 Earthquake and Its Impact on Sustainable Tourism

On the night of September 8th, 2023, the peaceful surroundings of Morocco were shattered by a sudden and violent event. The clock had just struck 11 PM, and the quiet region of Al Haouz located within the Moroccan High Atlas Mountain range was shocked by a formidable force from beneath the earth. Buildings trembled, walls fractured, and the once-tranquil scenery turned into a panorama of chaos and devastation.

Tourism, a cornerstone of Morocco's economy, took a hit from this natural disaster. The vibrant city of Marrakech and its region, known for its historic monuments, beautiful landscapes, bustling Souks, and lavish resorts, are major attractions for tourists from across the globe. The earthquake somehow disrupted the flourishing tourism industry, resulting in some cancellations and closures that lasted for approximately 1 week. Certain tourists found themselves stranded, grappling with fear and uncertainty about the safety of continuing their travels.

Indeed, the earthquake vividly demonstrated the unyielding solidarity of the Moroccan people as they stood united, offering support, shelter, and resources to those in need. The spirit of togetherness and resilience emerged as a formidable force, reaffirming the strength and unity of the nation during challenging times. Drawing from personal connections, I witnessed this solidarity firsthand. With numerous childhood friends from the affected villages, I endeavored to contribute and show solidarity, inspired by fellow Moroccans from all corners of the country. One such effort led me to reach out to a friend known by the nickname "Krimou," an active community member in Ouirgane,[2] a village greatly affected by the earthquake. His response was humble and generous: "There are other villages in the inaccessible mountains that are in greater need than us." This genuine reaction speaks to the remarkable solidarity and mutual assistance among all the villages.

In the wake of the earthquake, the importance of sustainable tourism was strongly emphasized. It triggered a full reevaluation of construction practices, infrastructure resilience, and emergency preparedness to ensure that Morocco's allure could be sustained without compromising the safety of its visitors and inhabitants. This seismic event sparked a trend toward sustainable development by putting a focus on eco-friendly initiatives and community engagement in tourism-related projects. The aim was to ensure that the industry would not only flourish but also contribute to the welfare of the community and the preservation of Morocco's natural and cultural heritage.

Local communities and stakeholders rallied together and were determined to rebuild and restore the affected areas. The earthquake became an educational experience, nurturing resilience, and fostering stronger community bonds. Collaborations were forged between the government, local communities, and tourism experts to devise strategies that would help mitigate the impact of future disasters on the tourism sector. The earthquake served as a somber reminder of the delicate balance between nature and development, urging everyone to prioritize sustainability and safety in the quest for a prosperous future. Despite the devastation wreaked upon walls, narratives, and personal recollections, the essence of memory remains intact. This enduring memory will serve as a cornerstone for the reconstruction efforts in the present era, driving the renewal and modernization of traditional local trades.

---

[2] A rural commune in the province of Al Haouz, located on the High Atlas, 65 km south of Marrakech.

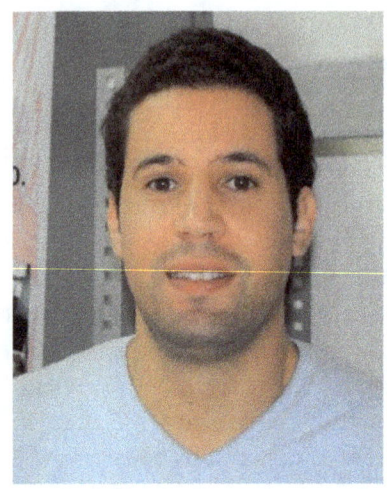

Dr. Khalid El Housni is a professor and researcher at Cadi Ayyad University, with a faculty position at the Essaouira Higher School of Technology (ESTE). Specializing in tourism and territorial management, he is recognized for his work in social and environmental responsibility within travel and tourism companies, particularly focusing on sustainability indicators in tourism projects. His expertise encompasses ecotourism, tourism economics, sustainable development, and corporate social responsibility (CSR) among tourism managers. Dr. El Housni has also made significant contributions to the study of tourism and digital transformation.

Outside academia, he has practical experience in responsible tourism, collaborating with establishments such as Terres d'AMANAR in Morocco. He has a global reach, serving as a visiting professor in Paris and Sofia and leading ESTE's "Management, Tourism, and Communication" department. Dr. El Housni's commitment extends to organizing international tourism symposiums, representing his university at COP22 Marrakech, and contributing to projects similar to the H2020-funded GEOPARK initiative. He also holds the prestigious position of vice-president at the Centre "Résilience", further emphasizing his dedication to advancing tourism research and expertise.

20

Plugging Zimbabwe's Brain Drain

Fungai Mettler

Zimbabwe is one of the most beautiful countries in the world. On its northern border with Zambia, the Zambezi River thunders over Victoria Falls, the world's widest continuous waterfall. The noise of Victoria Falls can be heard from a distance of 40 km, while the spray and mist from the falling water rise to a height of over 400 m, visible from a distance of 50 km. It is no wonder that the local tribes used to call the waterfall Mosi-o-Tunya "The smoke that thunders."[1] Aside from the majestic Victoria Falls, Zimbabwe is home to many national parks, such as Hwange National Park. It contains some of the densest remaining wildlife concentrations on the African continent, has an area of more than 12,000 km^2, and stretches from the Bulawayo–Victoria Falls railway line westward to the Botswana border.

The country is also one of the world's richest in terms of natural resources. Gold, nickel, copper, coal, diamonds, and platinum are all locked beneath Zimbabwe's fertile soils, which were once some of Africa's most productive. Despite these great resources, and although Zimbabwe was once seen as the breadbasket of Africa, it is now one of Africa's poorest countries. A staggering 5.5 million people are currently facing food insecurity in rural areas, as poor rains and erratic weather patterns are impacting harvests and livelihoods. In

---

[1] A child-headed household is a family in which a minor child or adolescent—under the age of 18 years—has become the head of the household taking parental responsibilities for the younger siblings, and providing childcare, breadwinning and household supervision (Phillips, 2011; Van Breda, 2010).

F. Mettler (✉)
SwiZim Trust, Kilchberg, Switzerland

urban areas, an estimated 2.2 million people are food insecure and lack access to minimum public services, including health and safe water.

The nearly 14 million people who call Zimbabwe home are the country's most precious resource. With an adult literacy rate of 88%, the country is one of the most literate in sub-Saharan Africa, where only 65% of the population can read and write. Zimbabwe's high literacy rates can be credited to large investments in education since attaining independence in 1980. One would imagine that a high literacy rate automatically equates to opportunities, but that is not the case in Zimbabwe and many other countries with economic instability. The World Bank's modeled estimates, based on International Labor Organization data, put the unemployment rate as low as 5% in 2016, while Zimbabwe's largest trade union claimed that the jobless rate was as high as 90% in 2017. This high unemployment rate is evident when one walks through the streets of Harare, the capital, where many young people are scattered and restless due to a lack of jobs.

The relative riches and stability of neighboring South Africa, Botswana, and Namibia have created a brain drain through which the country's brightest people disappear in search of jobs and opportunities. For those left behind, the struggles continue. Research on the causes and effects of Zimbabwe's brain drain concluded that there were 479,348 Zimbabweans in the Diaspora. However, the study team is aware that there is a large number of Diasporans it could not contact. The Diaspora destinations of a majority of Zimbabweans are the United Kingdom, Botswana, and South Africa.

Plugging Zimbabwe's brain drain, or at least reducing the flow of young talent through it, will be crucial to building a brighter, more sustainable future for the country's young people. Without educated, talented people, the country's natural wonders are in peril, its natural resources are at risk of being squandered, and future generations could face further decades of hardship. Building a sustainable future is also dependent on the ability to innovate and break through existing barriers, which are numerous in Zimbabwe.

A feasibility study we conducted in 2019 shed light on the immediate need for spaces for people to dream, grow, and create. That's why we, as SwiZimAid Trust, have opened the country's first "Nook," in partnership with Indian NGO Project Defy. The Nook is one of nine centers across Africa and Asia to help foster innovation among local people in an open, free environment. With technological support such as free internet access, computers, tools, and stationery, users can share and jointly develop ideas for solving common problems.

We identified a location to establish the Nook in Nkulumane, a high-density suburb in Bulawayo. We began working with the local community, aided by 30 volunteers from the area, to completely renovate the building, and we installed solar panels to meet the center's energy requirements. The Nook was a year in development and is completely free of charge for users. It is funded entirely by donations, which help pay the salaries of the staff who manage the center and run the activities within it. Aside from computers, the Internet, and solar panels, we also set up a workshop consisting of hand tools and machines that our learners can access free of charge to create prototypes of their innovations. We also offer computer literacy training sessions to those who need it and have partnered with a local school and availed our computers and laptops to enable computer literacy to be integrated into their school curriculums.

The Nook, which we call the Nkulumane Innovation Hub, has great potential to reach the populations that need it most and help to open up new opportunities and brighter futures in their host countries. Opportunities for young people are scarce in Bulawayo, Zimbabwe. HIV and drug abuse are rife. Teenage pregnancies and child abuse are common, and many do not finish school. For school dropouts, the range of opportunities is even narrower. Many resort to crime or prostitution or follow the path taken by more educated Zimbabweans and leave the country altogether.

Of course, change requires thinking outside the box, but new ideas cannot be imposed on a community. You have to work closely with people on the ground to identify their needs and how these can best be met. We strongly believe that sustainable social impact needs to be holistic, which is why we are implementing projects in poverty alleviation, mental and physical health, and education. Under poverty alleviation, we support child-headed homes by providing assistance to food-insecure child-headed households, and this will alleviate their situation and meet their immediate nutrition requirements. With the help of our donors, the SwiZimAid Trust has supported more than 1000 children in child-headed households to date, and we intend to continue raising funds and supporting as many as possible for as long as they need support.

Our biggest lesson as an organization is that ambition alone, without opportunity or resources, does not equate to success. We all have dreams, whether we were born in Harare or Hamburg. So often, the only things preventing dreams from becoming a reality are resources and opportunity. It is often overwhelming to think of tackling all the problems at once, and that is why it is important to take a step back and start where you can. We are a small organization that is making a difference one life at a time, and through our work, more people have a better chance of realizing their dreams.

References

Breda, D. A. (2010). The phenomenon and concerns of child-headed households in Africa. *Sozialarbeit des Südens, 3*, 259–279.

Phillips, C. (2011). *Child-headed households: A feasible way forward, or an infringement of children's right to alternative care?* Leiden University Universiteit.

Fungai Mettler is a multi-passionate social impact-driven professional on a mission to help people and organizations positively impact their communities. She has spent the last decade driving social impact in Europe, the Middle East, and Africa through various roles in academia, nonprofit organizations and the private sector. She currently serves as the Social Business Innovation Director for Eastern Europe, the Middle East, and Africa (EEMEA) at MSD Merck Sharp & Dohme. She is on the verge of completing a doctoral degree at Geneva Business School, that is, exploring the relationship between business decision-making and ESG and assessing its influence in creating shared value. Fungai is a co-founder and director at SwiZim Trust, which is an organization supporting marginalized communities through strategic partnerships that foster innovation. She is a board member at Conscious Influence Hub and Friends for Matibi—which are organizations driving equity and social impact. In 2022, Fungai was named Woman Investor of the Year by Inyova, a company aimed at creating a more sustainable world through investing as a recognition of her commitment to impact investing.

Website: swizimtrust.com(Photograph by Amaru Kueng. All rights reserved).

21

Gender Equality Is Essential for Establishing a Climate Just World

Annika Degen

I love stories. I could listen to the stories people tell me for hours and paint according pictures in my head. It is an honor for me when people open up to share their experiences, their emotions, share the beautiful and the dark sides of their lives. Over the centuries, humanity has built up a wealth of knowledge by telling stories that are not only beautiful, vast, and essential to our survival but also regionally and locally specific. While our ancestors could largely rely on traditional knowledge and were therefore conscious of when the rainy season would start, when it was time to move on, or when the water holes would be filled, this, unfortunately, is no longer the case today. Anthropogenic climate change is throwing a spanner in the works—and an existential one at that. An increase in the number of natural disasters and extreme weather events, together with the loss of biodiversity, are now realities that people worldwide have to deal with, whether they want to or not. For a number of decades now, it has been clear that it is not only our planet with its flora and fauna that is suffering from rising temperatures but also humanity. However, the fact that women tend to suffer more than men from the effects

A. Degen (✉)
Podcast "Gender & Climate", Hamburg, Germany
e-mail: info@annikadegen.com

of human-made climate change is something that only a few people are aware of. I have made it my mission to change that.[1]

Before going into my story, mission, and how I go about my work, I would like to both explain the link between climate change and gender injustice in a schematic and simplistic way, and why we need to think about them together. I draw the information from the results of scientific studies, from my own research, and from the many, many stories that I have collected over the past few years.

The consequences of climate change are clearly evident. Human-induced climate change increases the frequency of extreme weather events such as droughts and heat waves, heavy rainfall, and floods. My aim in this sustainability story is not to talk about tipping points and planetary boundaries but rather about the humanitarian side of climate change impacts. The countries most affected by climate change tend to be in the global south. In these countries, men have traditionally been more inclined to work outside the home, while women have typically assumed the roles of home caretakers, looking after children, the elderly, and the sick. This means they tend to stay home more often and do the bulk of the care work, even in the twenty-first century, up to seven times as much as men in some countries. In addition, they are often responsible for collecting clean water and providing firewood for the household. With the increase in extreme weather events such as droughts, women and girls have to walk many more kilometers (often up to 25 km) to fulfill their water collection responsibilities. Walking many more kilometers than before because of dry wells means they spend more time doing this—time they cannot invest in education, political engagement, or economic participation. This lack of time is often compounded by legal or social constraints that prevent women and girls from active economic or political participation. As a result, it is still predominantly men in elite circles making decisions that affect the entire population of the village/city/region/country. Voices from populations not represented in these circles are therefore not heard, or only insofar as the dominant groups bring them into the discussion. It is easy to imagine, however, that the focus is not on the people who are not at the negotiating table. If we look at the gender binary, there are about as many women as men in the world. This means that when decision-making bodies have only men or a disproportionate number of men, the voice of the other half of the world—women—goes largely unheard. However, numerous scientific

---

[1] Due to the complexity of the issue, I only highlight the impact of climate change on binary genders in this Sustainability Story. The impact on people who identify themselves as members of the queer community differs greatly between regions. To discuss this here would go beyond the scope of this Sustainability Story.

studies have shown that the more diverse decision-making bodies are, the more comprehensive and, therefore, better decisions they make. This is evident in countries and companies being led by diverse teams. They are more innovative, environmentally friendly, and socially responsible than those led by homogeneous groups, and their actions contribute more to mitigating climate catastrophe. There is much more to be said and reported about the gender-climate-nexus—but long story short: Women bear the heavier burden of climatic changes (Fig. 21.1).

So, how do we get out of the predicament we are in?

While studying for my Masters in Sustainable Business Management at the University of Ulm, Germany, I became involved in the gender and climate nexus through one of my reading assignments.

As soon as I read about the link between these two issues for the first time, it was clear to me: This is the scientifically based connection that I have been longing for such a long time; this is exactly what I am so passionate about and what I want to immerse myself in! This short part of the reading had a transformative effect on both my worldview and life.

Thanks to my family, I developed a great love for nature in the early years of my life. Through various people, I have been taught which plants or mushrooms are edible, which animals live in the forest and what they eat, and how all these species reproduce themselves. This is knowledge that has been developed and passed on from generation to generation. From a young age, I came to understand and appreciate the interdependence of ecosystems. When we actually observe the processes on our planet, we quickly realize that everything is perfectly coordinated. Let's take the water cycle, for example: Water evaporates from bodies of water and rises into the atmosphere, clouds form, and the water returns to the Earth in the form of rain, hail, or snow. The sun is the engine of this cycle, causing the water to return to the atmosphere repeatedly.

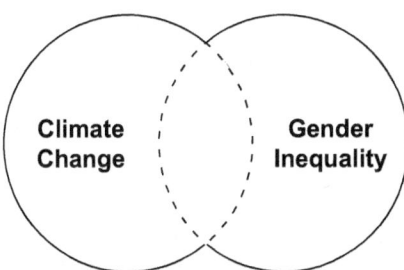

Fig. 21.1 Schematic illustration of climate change-related gender inequalities. (Image by: Annika Degen. All rights reserved)

Without these functioning cycles on our planet, it will be difficult, if not impossible, for us to continue to live here in the long term. In a nutshell, human existence depends on a healthy earth, functioning ecosystems, and ecological cycles. Climate change poses a massive threat to these and, thus, to our own existence. In other words, what we ourselves cause with climate change ultimately harms us all.

While climate change is mostly seen as a primarily ecological phenomenon and solutions are sought for its cause, i.e., the excessive emission of greenhouse gases, we must not forget the social component of it. It should be clear that we will not be able to mitigate climate change in all its breadth and depth without taking into account its social components and that we therefore need to consider a social science approach. To take the necessary measures to mitigate climate change, we need to look at the socioenvironmental interdependencies and implement solutions to them. As outlined earlier, the problem of gender inequality is inextricably linked to the effects of climate change, so these two components must be seen as interlinked. Seeing, highlighting, and presenting these connections is what I believe needs to be done (more). It is not for nothing that diverse teams are more successful, more innovative, and more creative because they do not look at challenges from just one point of view but approach them in different ways and from different angles.

But what to do about it? And this is where my own story comes into the picture:

For a long time, I shared my passion for reading, listening, and telling stories only with my family, friends, and acquaintances. One day, however, someone asked me if I had ever thought about making more of this "secret passion" of mine, considering that she loved listening to my stories, found my voice pleasant, and admired my enthusiasm. Well, what did I do? I took the compliment gratefully but did not pursue it further, thinking, "What stories should I tell?" Surely, no one wanted to hear about my walks, my sporting activities, my favorite recipes—so I put the compliment aside and, like many women before me, did not act on it.

Approximately six months later, I received an almost identical message from my boss at that time. "Maybe," I thought, "there's more to my stories than I had thought." So, I went on to think a lot and tried to figure out how to communicate something that I was really passionate about: climate change-related gender inequalities.

It was a gray, rainy November day, and I was sitting in my small apartment in Hamburg, Germany. The rain was whipping against the windows, the colorful leaves were swirling through the air, and I created an account. An account that has changed a lot since then. On November fifth, 2021, I published the very first episode of my podcast "Gender & Climate"—a podcast that invites guests from all over the world, from Mexico to the Philippines, from Kenya to the UK, and from New Zealand to India. In this podcast, I interview experts about the nexus of gender and climate change and discuss how people around the world are affected by it. My aim is to raise awareness of the deeply interconnected topics of gender equality and climate justice, to give people a stage, to help speakers raise their voices and to represent underrepresented groups in the public sphere. Believe me, I would never have thought that I would be a podcaster, never in my life. However, life has this beautiful way of just happening, and here I am now, being a podcaster.

Every single person in this world has an individual story to tell. With the Gender & Climate podcast, I have made it my mission to share the stories of people who are not being heard. I have made it my mission to share the stories of people who do not have a voice and to amplify the voices of all the people who will not attend the World Climate Conference (even though I will not be there either). It is about giving marginalized people a platform. It is about putting them at the center of the discussion, about putting them in the spotlight so that the whole world can listen to their experiences, to what they have to say, and thereby learn about their situations and struggles. In each episode, we discuss how these very people are affected by climate change and climatic disasters, how gender injustices are being shown, and what survival strategies exist. It is about the whole complexity of the topic and shedding light on it from very different angles. Water management, migration, agriculture, economic empowerment, climate finance—the range of issues is endless. We address North–South disparities, the gap between the rich and the poor, notions of privilege and global justice.

However, the most important aspect is that, unlike in other podcasts, I talk to those people, not about them. It is them raising their voices; it is them being in the spotlight.

In my podcast, the term "expert" is not defined by academic training, entrepreneurial or business success. It is the experiences, actions, and backgrounds of my guests that make them experts. I talk to people who are experiencing the effects of the climate catastrophe firsthand, people who are discriminated against on a daily basis because of their gender, and people who are fighting against these realities. In my eyes, all of these people are s:heroes. They are fighting for a better world, fighting to curb climate change, and fighting to save what can still be saved. They are fighting for women and men to have equal rights, both legally and socially—because in the majority of countries around the world, neither is a given.

My podcast is meant to educate about these grievances and how we can solve them.

My podcast is a place to share first-hand stories.

My podcast is a stage for the everyday s:heroes of our time.

That said, there is one more piece of information about s:heroes that I would like to share with you: It was a woman named Eunice Newton Foote who connected the dots in 1856 between carbon dioxide and planetary warming. In 1859, a man named John Tyndall published a more detailed work on heat-trapping gas, which is typically credited as the foundation of climate science. They had different starting points, and yet both made significant contributions to science, so both deserve their credit. Please… let us not repeat history.

That is why I have five specific takeaways that you can implement yourself:

Takeaway #1: All Hands on Deck!
Humanity is colorful. We shall always be aware of that. It is the multitude of stories and experiences that give rise to innovations and thus bring about the sustainable change we urgently need. Therefore, I love to encourage this slogan in my podcast: "We need all hands on deck in order to overcome the crisis of our time—because only together can we change our world for the better."

Takeaway #2: It Is About Equity!
Women and girls make up half of the world's population. However, they are too often left out or even excluded from (public) discussions, politics, engineering, finance, and especially decision-making. Our world is constructed by men for men. When planning a panel, make sure there is a balanced representation of women and men (plus voices from the queer community), different ethnicities, etc.

Takeaway #3: We Need More S:heroes!
We need to stand up for justice and for each other. Feminism means standing up for equal rights regardless of gender. If there is a woman around you who is better qualified, let her go first. If you are invited to sit at the table, then bring other women with you and people who are marginalized in a variety of ways. We need each other's support because fighting each other will not get us to the goal of climate justice.

Takeaway #4: LeaderSHEp
Money makes the world go round—we all know the saying. If we take an honest look at what got us into this crisis, we quickly realize that it is about

money, power, and prestige. For too long, we have focused on those things. We need economic, effective solutions to tackle the climate crisis. We need leadership that recognizes current and future challenges and leadership that guides and leads society. We need transformative and feminist leadership that embraces the diversity of humanity.

Takeaway #5: You Have It All!
When I released the first episodes of the podcast in November 2021, I did not know where the journey would take me or what to expect. I still do not, but I do know that it is worth getting started, that the first steps will be bumpy and not perfect, but that something wonderful can emerge in the end. Therefore, if you have a project or a passion that keeps your mind busy and driven: start it and go about it! Doors will open—doors you would never have expected to open. You may not be able to plan the path to the end, but you will be guided, and you will have support. You have it all!

Annika Degen, Founder and Host of the Podcast "Gender & Climate". Annika Degen is an entrepreneur at heart, advocate for Climate Justice and an equitable world for all. She grew up in an entrepreneurial family in rural Germany. Over the past decade, she has lived in South America, North America, Asia, and Europe, experiencing first-hand impacts of global inequalities on the ground while working with one-person start-ups and global market leaders across industries. She has extensive experience in sustainability, fostering diversity and collaboration, with strategic and analytical clarity. Her focus on gender and climate change links holistic sustainability, diversity, new work, peace, and security at micro and macro, personal, business and policy levels. She brings this experience not only to every podcast episode and guest selection, but also to every consulting and speaking engagement. She believes that the most important solutions are the establishment of diverse decision-making bodies at both the political and economic levels and a sustainable economic system that works for a socially and environmentally sustainable future for all.

Website: www.annikadegen.com
E-mail: info@annikadegen.com
LinkedIn: https://www.linkedin.com/in/annika-degen

22

Our People Make Our Firm

Raquel Flórez Escobar

Lawyers, particularly those working at a leading corporate law firm, have traditionally been white males from exclusive schools. While these demographics might have been a reflection of the business world, they are not a reflection of society as a whole. Lawfirms are now working hard to attract and retain diverse talent. This article looks at initiatives taken at Freshfields and the lessons we have learned so far.

Law firms have recognized this as a problem for some time, and there is no doubt that their people are becoming more diverse. However, these demographic changes are trickling upward only very slowly, and firms continue to struggle with the promotion and retention of people from different backgrounds.

Law firm Freshfields Bruckhaus Deringer (later Freshfields) is no exception. Perceived by some as an "elite" (and therefore perhaps "elitist") organization, the firm has had to work hard to attract–and retain–diverse talent. This means showing a strong commitment to diversity and rewarding great performers, recognizing difference and the value this brings.

The drive for diversity is also becoming more urgent because clients are demanding it. We are seeing more requests for proposals/quotations containing questions around diversity and procurement decisions being based at least in part on the ability of external advisers to field a diverse group of people.

R. F. Escobar (✉)
Freshfields Bruckhaus Deringer, Madrid, Spain
e-mail: raquel.florez@freshfields.com

Furthermore, of course, beneath this all is the abundance of data showing that diverse entities are better and more profitable than those that are not.

If there is one lesson that we have learned from the pandemic, it is that change can happen quicker than we think—see how many businesses, including law firms, switched to mass remote working within days and continue to provide their services in difficult circumstances to a high standard.

Hopefully, the events of the last few years will accelerate the drive for diversity, too—and we want to do our bit. Becoming one of the first elite global law firms to appoint a female leader was a step in the right direction. However, we also need to continue our efforts to attract and retain the best talent, serve our clients in an innovative, collaborative way, and offer the sort of dynamic, diverse, and inclusive culture where people are motivated to bring the best of themselves to work.

The drive to become more diverse is made more challenging as the situation is not the same for different groups. For example, while firms still have a long way to go to achieve gender parity, more women serve as partners and law firm leaders than in the past. However, women of color hold fewer senior positions than their white counterparts.

This means that we need to have initiatives that not only target underrepresentation based on particular characteristics such as disability, race, and social mobility, but also look at diversity holistically.

"Holistic" Initiatives

Diverse Perspectives, Freshfields' reverse-mentoring program, is an opportunity for professionals from across the firm's various global networks (our Black Affinity Network; HALO, our LGBTQ+ network; our women's networks; our Mental Health Affinity Network; and our Enabled Network for people with disabilities, etc.), as well as anyone who identifies as being a part of an underrepresented group, to connect with a senior colleague, learn from each other, and share perspectives.

The program is open to all colleagues in every office across the firm. For junior mentors, it allows their voices to be heard and builds relationships with the firm's leadership. For the senior mentee, it is a chance to seek guidance and input from more junior colleagues, see the workplace through different eyes, and gain a wider perspective on Freshfields' culture. The program also helps build diversity of thought, which in turn helps to promote new ways of thinking and novel approaches to solving complex problems.

In addition to addressing issues of diversity and inclusion, the program offers participants a chance to focus on professional development and learn more about topics such as client relationships, innovation, and technology.

Targeted Initiatives #1: Gender

We want to ensure that Freshfields is gender diverse at all levels, particularly within the partnership, where the gender imbalance is greater than in other parts of the firm.

To achieve this aim, we use a range of measures, including setting targets for partner promotions.

We also have a range of initiatives, such as our Global Sponsorship Program for Women (GSP). This is a 12-month program that aims to retain our high-potential female talent and support their progress to senior roles at the firm/partnership. It has three main components: each lawyer has a sponsoring partner, attends external coaching sessions, and attends a bespoke learning and development curriculum. Of our 2020 promotions to partner and counsel, 55% are GSP graduates (50% counsel and 75% partner).

We know we need to create a working environment that is equally welcoming to all, regardless of gender identity. We also understand the benefits of bringing together people with shared interests and common goals, and our women's networks are an integral part of this. Outside our firm, we take an active role globally in the 30% Club, a group of business leaders committed to achieving better gender balance at all levels of commerce.

Launched in November 2018, the EDGE (Every Day Gender Equality) commitment was developed by our Women's Network in London in collaboration with colleagues across the firm. It aims to promote gender equality across the firm by empowering our people to take very practical, everyday actions in their working lives that will cause incremental, tangible changes. More than 2000 people across the Freshfields global network have signed up to EDGE since launch, which involves them committing to 10 everyday actions that will help foster true equality across the organization.

We are also passionate about promoting gender equality in the wider legal industry. In recognition of the underrepresentation of women in international tribunals, in 2015, members of the arbitration community (including Sylvia Noury, a dispute resolution partner) drew up a pledge to take action. The Equal Representation in Arbitration Pledge seeks to increase, on an equal opportunity basis, the number of women appointed as arbitrators to achieve a fair representation as soon as practically possible, with the ultimate goal of full parity.

Targeted Initiatives #2: Race and Ethnicity

As a global organization, we want to broaden the firm's representation among different races and ethnicities, particularly at senior levels.

Our efforts in this area include our global Black Affinity Network (BAN), which brings together lawyers of Black African and Black African Caribbean heritage from across the firm. In 2020, BAN created a network of non-BAN Freshfields colleagues who are committed to taking practical action to support ethnic diversity and inclusion within the workplace. These representatives would be senior ambassadors for the BAN community (informally known as BANbassadors), helping to foster an inclusive environment that values ethnic diversity and galvanizes support throughout the firm.

We celebrate Black History Month in both the USA and the UK, hosting talks and other events with a number of our clients.

In the USA, the firm's Legal Outreach program, which was launched in 2007, equips New York high-school students from nontraditional backgrounds with writing and reasoning skills to empower them to achieve academic success and admission to elite US colleges. BAN members mentor these students as they become exposed to the culture and types of work at a corporate law firm.

In the UK, the Freshfields Stephen Lawrence Scholarship Scheme aims to address the disproportionate underrepresentation in large commercial law firms and other city institutions of black men from less socially mobile backgrounds.

We also partner with the Black British Business Awards and organizations such as SEO (Sponsors for Educational Opportunity). Furthermore, we are a founding signatory of The Charter for Black Talent in Finance and the Professions and have recently signed up to the Rare Race Fairness Commitment in the UK.

Building a More Inclusive Workplace: Four Lessons Learned

1 *Involve your leaders*

Having senior leadership commitment is key. Working bottom up is important (see our reverse mentoring program), but without the commitment of management, it will be difficult to make real progress.

2 Take a holistic approach to diversity

Having networks for different groups has clear benefits. However, just as important is having initiatives that have a positive impact on multiple groups at the same time, such as inclusive leadership and behaviors and bias training (both of which Freshfields offers to leaders and colleagues globally).

3 Understand the challenges that each underrepresented group is facing

It is important to understand the unique lived experiences and specific barriers different groups experience and set up tailor-made initiatives depending on the relevant issue. For example, in the case of women in law, generally speaking, the problem is not recruiting gender-diverse talent, but retaining and providing a platform for women to develop their careers—hence, our global sponsorship program.

In other instances (e.g., access to the legal profession for black talent), it is important to tackle the barriers as early as possible, hence our Legal Outreach program in New York and the Freshfields Stephen Lawrence Scholarship Scheme in the UK.

4 Combine global with local

Organizations with global reach still need to bear in mind local specificities and complexities, which means allowing more decisions to be made at the office/regional level. For example, social mobility may be a key priority in the UK, while in countries such as Spain or Italy, the current focus may be more on gender and LGBTQ+ inclusion.

Raquel Flórez Escobar, Partner, Freshfields Bruckhaus Deringer, Spain, At the law firm Freshfields Bruckhaus Deringer, Raquel leads the People and Reward practice in Spain and co-heads the Global Markets group. She oversees and provides guidance to responsible business initiatives in Spain. With expertise in employment-related and pension issues, Raquel serves a diverse clientele, handling both advisory and contentious work. Her clients are mainly listed and non-listed US and EU companies, as well as financial institutions. Raquel speaks Spanish, English, French, and Italian.

LinkedIn: https://www.linkedin.com/in/raquelflorez/

23

Women at the Margins: Organizations, Social Structures, and Gender Norms in Rural India

Hemalatha Venkataraman

Governments across the world acknowledge that poverty and gender inequality are two of the major and serious Sustainable Development Goals that need to be addressed by 2030. According to the World Bank, global extreme poverty rates fell from 10.1% in 2015 to 8.6% in 2018, living on less than US$2 a day. However, while nearly a quarter of the world in 2017 still lived on less than US$3.20 a day, the recent pandemic has substantially increased these figures. According to the World Bank, the global poverty rate increased sharply from 8.3% in 2019 to 9.2% in 2020, the first rise in extreme poverty since 1998 and the largest since 1990. This means that an additional 93 million people worldwide were pushed into extreme poverty because of the pandemic. The World Bank estimates that the situation of people living in poverty is bound to worsen because of rising food prices, the impact of the Ukraine war, and climate change. The Bank estimates that another 95 to 100 million more people will be living in extreme poverty for the reasons mentioned above.

H. Venkataraman (✉)
An Independent Researcher, Coimbatore, Tamil Nadu, India
e-mail: v_hemalatha@cb.amrtia.edu

Neither these figures nor the impact of the war, food prices, or climate change bode well for people living in the global south, especially for women residing in rural parts of India. This sustainability story is precisely about women at the margins. Poverty and gender inequality affect women disproportionately and far more negatively than men because of women's relatively lower education levels, lack of access to financial capital, perceived lower status, and being deprived of basic freedoms because of restrictive social institutions, such as gender norms. Gender norms are embedded in values, beliefs, and specific social and cultural settings and tend to place structured disadvantages on women's access to diverse opportunities, including economic, health, and justice. Women in India face economic and structural barriers to participating not only outside the household but also within the household. Structural barriers include social expectations, i.e., having to obey and follow traditional gender norms, adhering to gender social roles, and skewed power relations within the household that prioritize men and their needs over women and their needs. Economic barriers could include aspects such as the inability to participate in economic activities because of lack of education, poverty, investment capital, knowledge, or the inability to open a bank account. The complexity and way in which poverty and gender inequality intersect have had serious consequences for women and their family's overall well-being.

Taking an interdisciplinary lens is best suited to address issues of poverty and gender inequality within a developing country context such as India because women in rural India face several significant barriers. The questions I ask here, in this sustainability story, have to do with what it takes for women living in rural India to develop their entrepreneurial capacity to escape poverty. What is the role of social structures such as microcredit groups and intermediary or social service organizations [nongovernmental organizations] in facilitating this? What is the effect of women's participation in the social structure of the microcredit groups and the development of their entrepreneurial capacity on traditional gender norms of women and men in rural India?

A Little Context: Rural India

Rural India is home to over 833 million people. According to the census of India of 2001, India has well over 122 major languages spoken and over 1600 dialects spoken in distinct communities, thus making it one of the most diverse countries on earth. The government of India has identified several elements of social and economic infrastructure that are critical to the quality of life in rural areas. These include water supply, housing, telecommunication and information technology, roads, electrification, and irrigation. India's rural economy employs 350 million people, which is 68% of the total workforce and contributed to nearly half of the nation's overall GDP in 2019–2020. India's economy has grown at approximately 6% (conservative estimate) per annum.

Given that the rural economy plays a crucial role in India's growth, it is speculated that women entrepreneurs in rural India can become an important part of this growth story by fostering rural prosperity by way of creating and sustaining their own businesses and thereby "lifting" families out of poverty. It is estimated that women comprise around 14% of the total entrepreneurs in India, which works out to approximately eight million individuals. Around 10% of all formal enterprises are owned by women. The reason for this abysmal number of women entrepreneurs is that women face multiple barriers to creating and sustaining their own businesses. Most of these barriers are institutional in nature and include limited mobility, low education levels, lack of economic opportunities, knowledge, and business skills, restrictive gender norms within the community, and limited opportunity to own land and access to credit to invest in the business.

Skewed gender norms within the community that favor men's needs over women's needs stem from the patriarchal belief system, which is deeply rooted within society and within rural India. Gender inequality exists in the form of predefined gender roles and gender-based discrimination. This can limit women's access to education, healthcare, and productive resources, as well as their opportunities for economic and social advancement. For example, in India's patriarchal system, families prefer to have a son rather than a girl child because as the son gets older, he becomes an asset to the family. Thus, many families do not prefer investing in a daughter's education because once she grows up, she may not provide the returns to investment that a son can provide, as she will be married into the family of the husband.

Caste is another social structural barrier that many families and women face in rural India. Caste is a social hierarchy that has existed in India for over 3000 years. People are born into a caste grouping, and hence, the possibility of changing one's caste is very difficult. Caste has the potential to dictate the profession a person can work in as well as aspects of their social lives, including whom they can marry, speak with, and move around with. Working outside the home is deemed to be of lower status for married women from upper caste backgrounds, while women from lower caste backgrounds are "permitted" to move freely and can actively participate in economic activities outside the home.

Given the myriad difficulties and barriers faced by women living in rural India, evidence shows that men receive more capital investments, are unfairly favored in regard to obtaining, maintaining, and benefitting from credit, and have better access to loans and grants compared to women. Despite these difficulties, over the past four decades, Self-help groups have come to play a significant and crucial role in helping women control and manage how they save, how much they save, and where they save, and more importantly access to credit. Self-help groups (SHGs) in India typically comprise of 10 to 20 individuals, primarily women, who come together voluntarily to form a savings and credit collective that, in many instances, also acts as a support mechanism to discuss pertinent issues related to their own health, financial inclusion, livelihood opportunities, education, family, and community. While there is mixed evidence of the benefits that the SHGs offer women and their families, evidence suggests that it does take women and their families out of poverty (Fig. 23.1).

Often, women are facilitated to form SHGs by nongovernmental organizations, microfinance organizations, and government agencies willing to provide loans to communities of people living at the margins. The primary objective of almost all SHGs is to help their members learn to save regularly and to leverage their savings to access credit and other financial services. SHGs act as a vital link in providing microfinance services to their members. Women pool their savings and avail themselves of small loans from banks or financial

Fig. 23.1 A self-help group in progress in the evening around 6 pm when most women are free from their household chores/duties. Kolar Region, Karnataka, India. (Photograph by Pushpa Gowda. All rights reserved)

institutions, which enables them to start small businesses or meet emergency expenses.

Despite the benefits that SHGs offer for women in rural India, there exists mixed evidence of the impact of SHGs on the lives of women and their families. Some evidence suggests that women are more credit-constrained despite having access to credit and that the credit that they receive is invested in the husband's business. The evidence is also mixed with respect to the empowerment potential of SHGs. While some evidence suggests that SHGs empower women by allowing women greater say within the household, opportunities for mobility, and increased confidence, other studies suggest that SHGs are useful to the extent that they help families mitigate consumption expenses.

Given the mixed evidence of the impact of SHGs on the lives of families and women, SHGs face challenges such as sustainability, effective management, and financial linkages with formal institutions. Thus, there is limited knowledge of how SHGs form, the role that organizations play in this formation, and the SHGs sustenance to get families out of poverty. Furthermore, what is less known is the role that SHGs play in facilitating women's business ownership and the combined effect of the SHG and being a business owner on traditional gender norms within the household and the community. In the following section, I address these concerns from the insights I have gathered through my own research both in northern and southern India.

My research addresses the initial concern of how do SHGs form, what role do organizations play in this process, and what is the sustenance of SHGs to get families out of poverty? My research suggests that, strategically, organizations draw upon two distinct yet interrelated and practical organizing principles: the market and the community. By integrating these broad organizing principles, organizations introduce market-based activities aimed at enhancing the social and economic well-being of rural women and their families, ultimately contributing to poverty alleviation (Fig. 23.2).

My research shows that organizations can strategically leverage and use organizing principles of the market and community to create social structures such as self-help groups to enable the market participation of women in rural India. The organizing principles of the market emphasize transactions, money transfers, and the accumulation of money, whereas the organizing principles of the community are characterized by group membership, community participation, relations of affect, loyalty, common values, and reciprocity. The creation of self-help groups or social structures hinges on the simultaneous building of community values and market principles without challenging the existing norms of the community. First, organizations build trust and solidify already existing interrelations within the community to introduce and

Fig. 23.2 Hemalatha interviewing a woman entrepreneur who runs a sewing shop within her house. Hemalatha is seated with her translator and field research assistant collecting data in Kolar region, Karnataka state, India. (Photograph by Pushpa Gowda. All rights reserved)

legitimate new forms of social organizational structures such as the self-help group. Then, they build the market literacy of women by showing how women can access, avail, and retain money through self-help groups. The organization demonstrates to women that money can be saved, transferred, and accumulated over time and kept safe in the self-help group, where the governing members are the women themselves, and thus, the SHG is entirely owned by them. Alongside building market literacy, the organization can create social obligations by leveraging the community principles of reciprocity and cohesion and market principles, such as paying for services that were rendered to the group members, such as paying a bookkeeper, an equitable share in the interest gained through the savings in the self-help group and taking a loan and repaying on time with interest. The use of such market and community principles for creating and sustaining the self-help group endears it to women. The final phase of the organization is the move to build social loyalty among women such that the organization can build a rural business ecosystem. Social loyalty is built by creating a sense of belonging among women within the self-help group while simultaneously creating a sense of competitiveness between/among self-help groups and creating linkages between the self-help group and local banks. This enables the self-help group members to build their individual rural businesses. The organization can act as a facilitator to help women establish their individual businesses; it can enlighten them of the power of pooling their risks, which provides women with higher negotiating power. The organization builds women's operational skills so that they can manage their respective businesses. This enables women to acknowledge that they are not alone in their business but are a part of a larger entity, a cooperative. Given that individual businesswomen provide produce to the cooperative, each woman understands that her business is linked to the larger entity and to that of other women who, too, provide produce to the cooperative. Thus, in this way, each individual business woman has the potential to influence her peers and has a say in how the cooperative ought to be governed. Thus, the organization builds a rural business ecosystem within the community.

By simultaneously using principles of the community and the market, the social service organization working in rural India can enable the market participation of women, thereby getting women and their respective families out of poverty.

The second of my research concern pertains to the role that SHGs play in facilitating women's business ownership and their effect on changing traditional gender norms within the household and the community. The answer to the first part of the preceding concern is that SHGs play a positive role in facilitating women's business ownership by providing not only credit but also a larger support system and peer group access to a network for women to gain knowledge and skills. The self-help group acts as a platform for women to apply their newly acquired knowledge and skills (Figs. 23.3, 23.4, and 23.5).

While women self-select themselves to form self-help groups, in many instances in rural India, women are facilitated to form into groups by nongovernmental organizations, microfinance institutions, or banks. The basis on which groups are formed or facilitated matters for the sustainability of the group and for reducing traditional gender norms within the household. While forming groups of women, non-government organizations approach women with the suggestion that groups are a useful vehicle through which women can save money, be in control of their cash, and invest the credit received through the group for "productive purposes," such as establishing and running their own business. The market and community principles are used to facilitate groups and skill all the group members in the governance system of the self-help group. Groups formed by banks, microfinance institutions, or other government agencies such as the local municipality or the department of women and child development (i.e., the local government agency) facilitate women to form groups with the explicit purpose of becoming loan recipients.

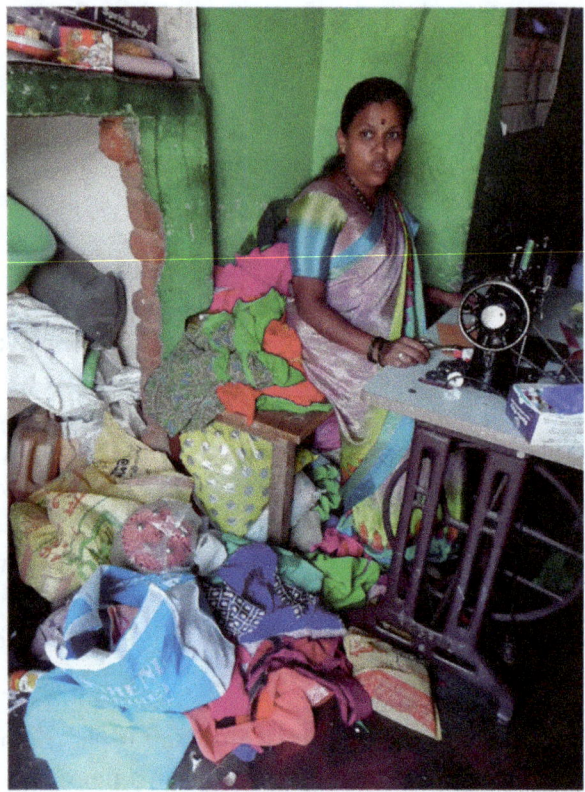

Fig. 23.3 A woman entrepreneur in rural Kolar district Karnataka, who sews bespoke dresses for others in her community. (Photograph by Hemalatha Venkataraman. All rights reserved)

Only a few members of these groups are skilled in taking charge of their group. These members are neither told the importance of the group and the potential benefit it can have for each member nor are women explicitly told that they could use the loan that they will receive for "productive purposes." This contrasts with members of groups formed by nongovernmental organizations, where *all* members learn skills related to administering the group's responsibilities.

What women are communicated and how they are communicated with about the self-help group, its objectives, and its functioning matters for several reasons. First, it matters for the practices and processes of the group's functioning. When the objectives of the group are conveyed and women are suggested that the group belongs to everyone, its responsibility lies with each

Fig. 23.4 A woman entrepreneur sitting at her machine inside her home sewing clothes for others. Kolar region, Karnataka, India. (Photograph by Hemalatha Venkataraman. All rights reserved)

member and that each member must learn the market skills to be able to administer the group effectively. More likely than not, women are bound to become accountable for the way the group functions. Second, the survival and sustenance of the self-help group hinges on the initial communication with respect to the group: this anchors the members of the group and the groups as a whole to the possibilities that the groups can offer each individual member. Once members are suggested that the group is being created for the sole purpose of savings and credit, members of the group seem to be unable to look beyond this. However, when members are informed that the group offers more than just savings and credit—such as opportunities for skills development and support groups—it expands the women's perception of the group's potential. Third, the initial communication about the group matters

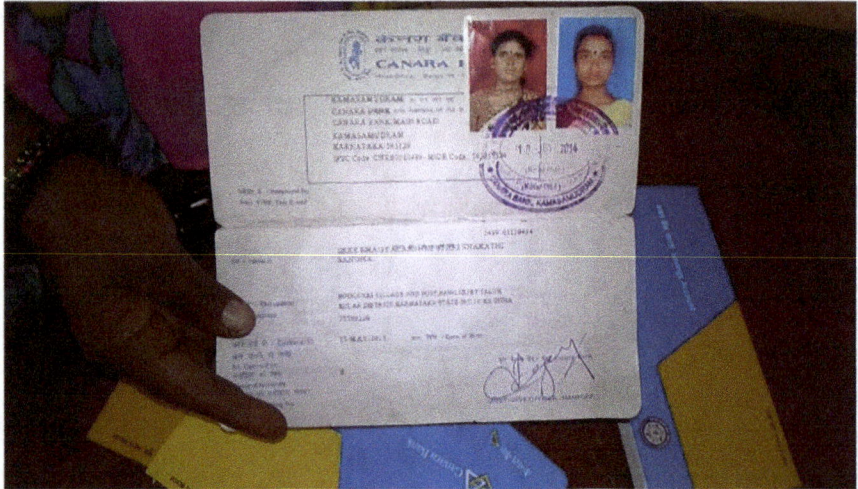

Fig. 23.5 A self-help group passbook where credit and savings are noted down. Each group member is provided a book as a safe keep and can refer to it to understand how much savings they have accumulated over the past months or years; how much credit they have taken, and how much interest they must pay. (Photograph by Hemalatha Venkataraman. All rights reserved)

for women's capacity to establish a business because many women see the group as a path to fulfill their dream to be able to contribute positively toward their family by earning a living without leaving their homes. Fourth, communicating the various possibilities that the group can offer matters for women's belief in their ability to challenge and change traditional gender norms. Thus, the cascading effect of the basis on which groups are formed plays an important role not only in poverty alleviation but also in the empowerment of women.

Only when all the women in the group are skilled in the governance system of the group can they graduate to learn the skills needed for the market so they can participate in establishing their business. Once they have successfully established their business, their level of earnings increases in a (rural) context where opportunities for being gainfully employed for both men and women are rather limited. This new founded monetary gain, along with the practice of the skills gained in the self-help group, especially with respect to interpersonal and negotiation skills, allows women the capacity to modify traditional gender norms within the family.

While governments across the world aim to improve two major sustainable development goals—gender equality and poverty—governments need to take cognizance of the complexity and intertwining of these two issues. Taking an

Fig. 23.6 Hemalatha (extreme right) doing fieldwork with her field assistants and her then-main advisor Prof. (Dr.) Patrick Vermeulen (fourth from right)

interdisciplinary lens to understand the complexity of the issues in rural areas of countries in the global south is important because poverty and gender inequality affect women disproportionately and far more negatively than men. This is because restrictive social institutions, such as gender norms, deprive women of basic freedoms, creating barriers to accessing education, financial capital, and society's perceptions of women as lower in status. Given that gender norms are embedded in values, beliefs, and specific social-cultural settings and tend to place structured disadvantages on women's access to diverse opportunities, working with women and their respective families who live at the margins, especially in rural parts of the global south, becomes imperative. Social service organizations play a critical role in poverty alleviation and creating gender equality.

Social service organizations can mitigate some of the economic and structural barriers that women face in participating both outside of the household and within the household. Organizations can facilitate social structures outside of the home by understanding the context in which women live in and build their capacity, which can enable them to face both economic and structural barriers. Furthermore, this can enable women to question the skewed power relations within the household that prioritizes men and their needs over women, their needs, and their family's well-being (Fig. 23.6).

Dr. Hemalatha Venkataraman currently serves as an Assistant Professor of Management in the Department of Organizational Behavior and Human Resources at the Amrita School of Business, Amrita Vishwa Vidhyapeetham, Amrita Nagar, Ettimadai, Coimbatore. Prior to joining Amrita School of Business, Hemalatha was a full-time international fellow and doctoral candidate at the Nijmegen School of Management, Radboud University, Nijmegen, the Netherlands (2021). Hemalatha has trained in Organization Studies from Tilburg University, the Netherlands (Master of Science, 2011) and Psychology from Delhi University, India (Master of Arts, 2001). Her research interests lie broadly at the intersection of organizational studies and development. Hemalatha has worked in the social/development sector in northern India, especially around mental health, psychosocial care, and disability. She has undertaken a few international research assignments within the South Asian region. She has conducted several focus group discussions around mental health and rehabilitation in the Maldives and in the National Capital Region, Delhi, India.

24

Empowering Communities Through Social Entrepreneurship: The Label Créole Project

Marie-Lou Nazaire

The Label Créole project aims to promote fine handicrafts from two islands, Haiti and Zanzibar, and to support social entrepreneurship there. The project was born out of an enormous love for the creativity and fine art of living in both Haiti (the Caribbean) and Zanzibar (Tanzania, Africa). It is also the result of a long reflection on the crucial role of social entrepreneurship for development that would be truly sustainable and, perhaps most importantly, dignified.

A craftsman who works under good conditions and gets a decent salary supports not only his family but also a whole socioeconomic network on a small scale. This is what clients of Label Créole support when they fall in love with the unique creations of the project's partner workshops.

Social Entrepreneurship Empowers Communities

Sustainability is not just a trend: it is an everyday challenge that requires faith, creativity, patience, a strong will, solidarity with others, and hard work. In that sense, one can find many kinds of help to achieve his/her goal. A country can benefit from international aid on an ad hoc basis via

---

M.-L. Nazaire (✉)
Label Créole, La Hulpe, Belgium
e-mail: marielou@labelcreole.com

nongovernmental organizations (NGOs) or charity campaigns. Artisans sometimes receive local subsidies or foreign funds to build their businesses. Nevertheless, the first and main actors in the sustainable development of a country are its own people. No matter how considerate your international partners are, you cannot afford to depend on them in regard to the long-term development of your country!

Actively and sustainably contributing to their country's development is what social entrepreneurs do, since they not only create economic activity or establish commercial relations locally and internationally. Their work is not only about earning money and growing bigger. Of course, any business is about earning money! However, social entrepreneurship involves a proactive commitment to improving the lives of workers and, through those workers, empowering a whole local community.

Starting Point

Born in the Ivory Coast of a Haitian father and a Belgian mother, I have lived in different countries, and I feel at home a little bit everywhere. During my upbringing, I developed a passion for travel, and my understanding of different cultures, religions, and races continued to grow. In one of my travels, I traveled to the islands of Zanzibar in the Indian Ocean and fell in love with them. It reminded me so much of Haiti, my father's bit of an island in the Caribbean Sea. Inspired by the crafts and arts of the inhabitants of those islands, I decided in 2015 to launch the Label Créole project. In fact, I was also tired of hearing only defeatist comments about Haiti. I knew how much talent and creative wealth there was in that country, and I needed to share it with the rest of the world. I also deeply believe in social entrepreneurship as a driving force to achieve dignified sustainable development.

In both Haiti and Zanzibar, there are ultradynamic entrepreneurs who do business with strong social commitment. I felt the need to talk about their work and show it to the part of the world where I live, to bring some nuance to the recurring dominant discourse.

I also wanted to address some stereotypical ideas lots of people have. In Belgium, where I live and work, both Haiti and Zanzibar are the objects of collective fantasies (clihés) that are diametrically opposed: Haiti is seen as a "cursed island," doomed to poverty and instability, while Zanzibar is idealized as a tourist's paradise. Of course, the reality is much more nuanced! Both islands have gifted people, as well as their share of problems.

How We Work

The artisans who are partners in the Label Créole project employ between 6 and 125 workers each. Particular importance is given to working conditions (wages, hours, meals, equipment), insurance coverage, training, eco-responsible methods, and gender equality.

Handmade objects from the Caribbean or the African continent can be seen as expensive by the European market. The cost of transport and import taxes is indeed added to that of the know-how of professional designers who offer either unique or limited-series pieces (Figs. 24.1 and 24.2).

While the European public still regularly associates "made in the Caribbean" or "made in Africa" items with the cheap trinkets sold to tourists on exotic beaches, the customers who take the trouble to read up on the subject do understand our constraints and prices. Would we expect European artisans to slash their prices? Would we find it acceptable for them to set their selling prices without considering their production costs, raw materials, or transportation? In Europe, when faced with local creations, do we bargain in luxury boutiques, fashion stores, or jewelry shops? Of course not, because that would be absurd and disrespectful! So let's question why such behaviors would be more acceptable when it comes to the work of artisans from elsewhere?

This is why raising awareness of international solidarity and of solidarity-based economic issues is crucial. Our best customers are aware that their

Fig. 24.1 Creation Chako, Zanzibar. (Photograph by Marie-Lou Nazaire. All rights reserved)

Fig. 24.2 Creation Caribbean Craft, Haiti. (Photograph by Marie-Lou Nazaire. All rights reserved)

consumption is, somehow, a form of political commitment. Of course, they are buying a foreign object, but why would this be incompatible with "buying locally"? Certainly, the purchase of a Haitian or Tanzanian creation can cost more than a purchase in a supermarket, but they get a refined and unique object just like in a European designer boutique. In addition, yes, some southern countries' governments may have a bad press, but supporting workers does not mean supporting their country's leaders.

What's Next?

As my project is still modest, I take care of most operations myself, from contact with my suppliers, to sales, to communication with our clients. This is exciting, because I have learned a lot, but working alone is also a long-term weakness. I am now fully aware that, to push my project forward, I must think bigger and partner with other people!

My current way of working is suboptimal, especially considering that my goal extends beyond merely being a reseller or an influencer. I am currently thinking about a larger project. I now wish to organize a joint delegation of high-level Haitian and Tanzanian craftsmen for a European fair, such as the *Maison et Objets* in Paris or *Ambiente* in Frankfurt. This would be a wonderful opportunity to establish larger business contacts in Europe and give the social entrepreneurs I partner with a boost toward wealth creation and, as a result, their communities' empowerment and local sustainable development. Slowly but surely, I am working on finding funds and partners to organize such an enormous event.

I am not a businesswoman! (I am just a linguist.) So why did I launch the Label Créole project? Because I met passionate and highly committed people whose enthusiasm and ideals I wholeheartedly share. I work with professional artisans and designers who deal with rather uncomfortable situations, having to compensate for the lack of infrastructure in their countries and, in some cases, the lack of support from local authorities, too.

No matter what, they get up and open their workshops almost every day to create beautiful pieces for their clients locally and abroad and a better living for the community they work in. They spend the money they make on local schools, health centers, shops, and small businesses. This is how a social entrepreneur changes the world, starting with his community. Through the Label Créole project, I take part in the kind of change I believe is fair. My dream is to contribute to opening European minds and markets to the handcrafts of Haiti and Zanzibar. I would like the talents of my two favorite islands to be recognized here at their true value, and for the Label Créole designers and artisans to succeed in showcasing their colors proudly. I am certain that their creations have the potential to captivate audiences worldwide (Europe being the first step), and that very enriching collaborations could be established between here and there! This requires new narratives and an egalitarian approach to partnership.

This journey has already taught me a lot. My partners are role models for me: the constancy of their commitment and their professionalism inspire me. My project, although still small, is all the same useful to raise awareness and connect people.

I have also learned from my own limitations. Just because I was passionate about handicrafts and social entrepreneurship, I thought I could become a saleswoman and manage everything on my own. Today, I know that this is not true! And it's okay: accepting this allows me to rework my project and adjust my working methods. The Label Créole project is not yet a success story, but we're working on it.

Are you hesitating about a project? Just do it! Give it a try, do your best and talk about it to every single person you meet until you achieve your goals! Failing is okay: it means you tried (Fig. 24.3).

Fig. 24.3 Creation Caribbean Craft, Haiti. (Photograph by Marie-Lou Nazaire. All rights reserved)

Marie-Lou Nazaire is a professional interpreter and translator. She studied at the School of International Interpreters, in Mons (Belgium), at the University of Liège (Belgium) and at the University of Salamanca (Spain). Her main work languages are French, Spanish, English, Dutch, and Haitian Creole. Also trained in international project management, Marie-Lou is especially interested in the subjects of social entrepreneurship, international relations, and Caribbean literatures. In 2015, she embarked on a remarkable journey with the Label Créole project, dedicated to empowering social entrepreneurs in Haiti and Zanzibar (Tanzania), while showcasing the most exquisite craftsmanship of these two islands in the European Union. At times, Marie-Lou is also a writer. In 2009, she unveiled her debut book, offering a vivid glimpse into daily life in Haiti during the 1990s, aptly titled "*Chronique naïve d'Haïti*" (Naïve chronicle of Haiti) and published by L'Harmattan.

Website: http://www.labelcreole.com

25

"Entgrenzung": De-Bordering & Breaking Down Barriers

Sigrid Berenberg

Lunch in a downtown business club, Hamburg, Germany, late summer 2012. Three CEOs talking, exuding kind of an air of WASPish heritage in their easygoing manner, me, a guest, mostly listening.

One of them mentions the presence of a quite smart intern within his inner-office team.

How did that intern get the chance to join the team, I inquired, curious about the selection process.

No process took place.

The CEO's decision came about through a casual chat with a trusted golf partner, who brought up a name. As it turns out, the internship opportunity was extended to a college friend of the golf partner's daughter.

As I left the lunch, two powerful thoughts occupied my mind: a well-connected network has a profound impact on one's career and an inherent privilege often comes with a sense of "belonging." Without either of these two elements, navigating the path to leadership, let alone reaching the very top in fields like business, administration, or government, becomes significantly more challenging.

Many children of immigrants are incredibly bright but their parents lack the advantageous network of connections that can open doors to leadership

---

S. Berenberg (✉)
Schotstek, Hamburg, Germany
e-mail: info@schotstek.com

positions. They do not play golf with CEOs. It is not enough for university graduates with a migration background to be ambitious, intelligent, and well-educated. They also need to have access to the right connections. Realizing this was a pivotal moment in my life.

It was not the first time I had been mulling over the issue of fair and equitable opportunities for intelligent immigrant students. Research consistently pointed to the lack of upward mobility within immigrant families in Germany. The blatant waste of talent associated with this disparity became increasingly obvious. This was a call to action.

Schotstek, a scholarship program aimed at encouraging future immigrant leaders, was founded in Hamburg in 2013. It actively encourages applications from outstanding university students, offering them a multifaceted support system. This includes coaching, mentoring, and a wide spectrum of opportunities to broaden their horizons. The program also provides individual and tailored career support, aiding participants in navigating the subtleties of Habitus, unspoken in-group rules through exposure and practice. At its core, Schotstek embodies the concept of de-bordering ("Entgrenzung") and belonging.

Ten years later, Schotstek has evolved to become a large network of students, young professionals and influential figures, movers and shakers, from diverse backgrounds, nationalities, skin colors, cultural heritages, and religious faiths. Its recent expansion to Berlin marks an important milestone. Central to Schotstek's accomplishments is its Advisory Board, comprising renowned and respected individuals in the fields of business, science, culture and politics, many of whom are second or third generation immigrants. Their strong support has been instrumental in advancing our missions since the very beginning.

The key to any program is its effectiveness, and Schotstek's narrow focus delivers a tangible outcome: visible immigrant role models do snowball the message that education is the first step toward self-empowerment. This message is crucial and Germany needs to encourage ambitious high-school students from immigrant backgrounds to join the ranks of an increasingly diverse university student body, and subsequently to move on to become part of multidiverse teams across all fields of work.

Schotstek's financial backing comes from a blend of corporate sponsorship, support from philanthropic foundations, and private donations. Securing funding was not without challenges and this, at times, slowed down the growth of Schotstek. In the initial phase, prospective partners preferred a wait-and-see approach. Fortunately, however, support was granted based on the founders' track record.

25 "Entgrenzung": De-Bordering & Breaking Down Barriers

The focus on encouraging exceptional students pursuing leadership roles does imply an element of elitism. Some prospective partners raised eyebrows and expressed reservations due to a certain stigma attached to the concept of elites within certain segments of the German public. However, we strongly argued that, as Germany's immigrant population continues to grow, the country will benefit from the inspiration provided by elite role models. In a diverse society, it is essential that children of immigrants recognize a clear path to leadership positions and feel welcomed to actively contribute to shaping the future of their adopted homeland.

At its core, Schotstek is a people-focused business, and our job is to communicate effectively. Our modus operandi involves the identification of outstanding, ambitious, and diverse university students across a wide spectrum of academic disciplines. We achieve this through our relationships within immigrant communities and collaborating with professors from various universities. Moreover, Schotstek alumni also spread our message.

Convincing bright students to apply is not always an easy task, particularly because immigrant students from low-income families often prioritize, and for good reason, grades and scholarships offering financial aid. The value of a Schotstek scholarship, which does not provide direct financial support, might not be immediately apparent to all. Nonetheless, our selection process, driven by dedicated juries, identifies and recruits 24 to 28 promising individuals every year. In certain cases, Schotstek has welcomed applicants based on their potential and conviction, rather than their academic scores. Each incoming cohort is meticulously chosen to reflect the diversity of migration into Germany. Our mentors are professionals drawn from a wide array of vocations, lines of work and backgrounds, all intimately familiar with the challenges faced by ethnic minorities in Germany. Ten years later, the Schotstek family has grown, with an increasing number of alumni taking on mentorship roles, giving back to the program.

Schotstek aims to foster a profound sense of belonging and cohesion among its participants. The program is designed to cultivate this sentiment. During the first year, Schotstek organizes three weekend-seminars set in countryside locations. These gatherings serve as a platform for starters to learn and build trust, offer support to one another, and forge their own small network within the broader Schotstek network. Additionally, they have unique opportunities to interact with chief executives, academics, artists, and politicians. They spend time in Berlin, immersing themselves in visits to government institutions, and engaging in meaningful conversations with high-ranking members of the Federal Government.

The mandatory two-year program marks the end of the formal curriculum, but the spirit of Schotstek continues to thrive. Alumni and starters remain interconnected, ensuring a strong support system and enduring connections. The experienced alumni gladly share their experience, advice, and inspiration, whether as regards their international careers in companies based in Hamburg, Munich, Berlin, or Dusseldorf, their entrepreneurial endeavor as they have established their own startup, their pursuit of doctoral degrees, their roles in enhancing a team at state-level to improve vocational trade schools, or their successful balancing of family life with their professional careers.

Over the years, Schotstek has witnessed a surge of interest from ambitious young immigrant professionals who, having heard about our mission, seek our support and aspire to join our thriving network. Historically, Schotstek's focus was primarily on applications from university students, deliberately excluding those who had just entered the workforce. Recognizing the evolving landscape and the growing need to provide guidance and support to a broader audience, we took a significant step forward in 2021. That year, we introduced a specialized program tailored to support and mentor young professionals with immigrant backgrounds. This initiative places a strong emphasis on mentorship, expanding horizons, and providing access to our extensive network. Importantly, our program extends an invitation not only to smart and ambitious young students who have graduated from university but also to young professionals who have forged their own unique paths outside of the traditional realm of university education.

As a testament of its impact, Schotstek, a registered nonprofit company, counts three esteemed alumni among its seven partners. In 2023, another alumna, Evgi Sadegie, ascended to the position of CEO. Talented young individuals who benefited from Schotstek's engagement a decade ago are now assuming increasing responsibilities as they step into leadership roles. This Schotstek narrative would be incomplete without the voices and insights of our scholars. Pars pro toto, Anette and Ebrahim graciously share what Schotstek means to them. Let's engage in a meaningful dialogue with them now.

Anette Plics was born in Hamburg to Ghanaian parents. She was selected for a Schotstek scholarship by one of our juries in 2020. At the time, Anette was a 19-year-old economics student at Hamburg University. Anette and her older sister Patience were raised by their working mother.

Sigrid:

25 "Entgrenzung": De-Bordering & Breaking Down Barriers

You first heard about Schotstek from Patience who joined Schotstek in 2014. Do you recall what she told you back then?

Anette:

She spoke passionately about it because she believed it was an exceptional program. Growing up as the children of an immigrant mother, we were constantly reminded in our household about the importance of attaining as much education as possible. In fact, my sister began encouraging me to apply for a Schotstek scholarship a few years before I finished school. I vividly recall her telling me that within Schotstek, I would meet many individuals who shared similar backgrounds and interests as ours. That meant a lot to me. During my time in high school, I had felt a bit different from everybody else right from the start. It took me some time to grasp where this feeling was coming from. For years, I was the only black person in my entire school, including students and staff. I felt an unspoken expectation to excel; I had to work harder than my classmates; without this constant extra effort, I might be overlooked or ignored. The high school I was attending was a Gymnasium, and in such high schools in Germany, the prevailing assumption was that we would all go on to obtain our Abitur[1] and continue our education at a university. Many of my friends from school did not. Among my friends at church, who were also children of West African immigrants, we all gave our best to perform well in school. Nevertheless, I noticed a difference. Even though the schools my friends from church attended were more diverse, some of them encountered greater challenges in accessing the best possible education. After finishing school, a few of them pursued apprenticeships or other job qualifications. Patience was right; I did find friends within Schotstek who shared stories similar to mine.

Sigrid:

You seem to be talking about a feeling of belonging.

Anette:

The diversity at Schotstek put me at ease; there was no pressure to constantly prove myself to get accepted. People didn't view me as different because everybody was different yet similar in some kind of way. It was a place where people generally strove to help one another as much as possible. I distinctly recall the time I was looking for my first Werkstudentenjob (student job)

---

[1] The Abitur in Germany is a diploma equivalent to the A Level in the UK or the Baccalaureat in France, enabling students to qualify for university admission.

within a company. I was eager to gain a deeper understanding of business, beyond what I learned in my economics classes, and I also needed the money. Hashmat, an alumnus of Schotstek, helped me by facilitating an introduction to the right person in a company. Schotstek opened doors for me and provided opportunities that I couldn't have found elsewhere.

Sigrid:

In 2022, you went to Finland for a semester abroad on the European Erasmus program. I was very happy to hear the news. Even more so, since the percentage of German Erasmus students coming from immigrant families seems rather small to me. What made you apply? Why Finland?

Anette:

I became an Erasmus student with a lot of help from my mentor, a consultant at Boston Consulting Group. Without her, I would hardly have had the confidence to apply. She encouraged me in every way possible. She advised me during the application process. I'm really grateful to her. My semester abroad made me value academics in a wider sense than before. It helped me grow as a person. I had never been to Finland before and knew little about the country, I imagined life there would be quite different than in Hamburg. It was, starting with the amount of snow in winter. I lived in a small university town. Our group of Erasmus students, coming from all over Europe, made it a place as diverse as you can imagine.

Sigrid:

You just finished your bachelor studies, you'll be awarded your degree soon. What comes next?

Anette:

Right now, I am working as an intern at Lufthansa Technik. I'm still thinking about what to do next. It feels like I am standing at a crossroads. The prospect of pursuing a master's degree in logistics or a master's degree in business psychology, both hold a strong appeal for me. I can see myself thriving in various fields of work. Moreover, I would like to have a chance to travel a lot, so I might link my master's studies with a part-time job as a flight attendant. I am planning to inquire about flight attendant training.

Sigrid:

I am happy to hear about the diverse pathways ahead of you.

One of Schotstek's partners is alumnus Ebrahim Momenzada, M. A. Social Work, born in Afghanistan, living in Germany since age 7.

Sigrid:

Why did you to apply to Schotstek?

Ebrahim:

Being a "refugee child," one of the labels stuck on me, as well as acting somewhat shy, school, for me, meant life on the sidelines. My grades were average, teachers hardly seemed to notice. I felt kind of lost at sea. I was determined to attend university, though. Nearing graduation time, I still wondered what best to study. I chose political science for my bachelor. It was quite different than what I had expected. This choice had been a logical one to me then, since I had long had a notion that I could somehow contribute to German society and its economy. You might think this made me apply for the program right after hearing about it. No. In fact, I pondered the question of applying for quite some time, doubtful about Schotstek's impact. Plus, my unimpressive grades did not match the profile.

Sigrid:

You took a chance by applying, despite having some doubts. Meeting you, talking to you, made a significant difference to us, the jury in 2015. While you might have seen it as merely "giving it a try," we recognized your immense potential. You have come a long way since 2015. Please tell us about your first day at Schotstek.

Ebrahim:

I was struck by the diversity. What a great group of people. Everyone seemed to have something to give, there was a lot of energy in that room. Schotstek made me understand that broad diversity is a very powerful resource. Regarding noticeable changes in me, the first thing that comes to my mind is that I learned to trust my own thinking and to share it. After that came: Don't wait for a door to open, grab the handle and step forward. Later, I realized that stepping forward worked best for me on paths I could muster with my own talents. Relying on strength-oriented work, in turn, boosted my self-confidence. Mentoring was very helpful. Schotstek's network was crucial to leaving the sidelines of German society. Just three examples: I interned at an educational community center run by a well-known foundation, where I could help opening up toward a more diverse clientele. I also had the opportunity to intern with a Borough President. Schotstek made me serve as a Master of Ceremonies (M.C.) at its publicly held debate on immigration between Olaf Scholz, then Mayor of Hamburg, and several Schotstek students. Who would have predicted anything like this in 2015?

By the way, I have gladly moved beyond my high school days, but I have not forgotten them. A few years ago, I invited some Schotstek friends to help initiate a mentoring program for eighth graders from immigrant families. We started at my old high school, which is far away from middle-class area schools. Our message to the kids is more impactful because first, we look like them, and second, we attended their same schools. Our message is the following: the way "in" and "up" is education; we are all different and, at the same time, all part of one country and society that we should care about.

Sigrid:

Learning is a two-way street. I also learned a lot from our scholars. The true rewards of diversity emerge by opening up, by listening, and sometimes just by setting aside one's own situation. The widening of horizons is a process, enriching all parties involved.

Ebrahim:

I recall the first time I witnessed a CEO expressing gratitude to us students for our discussion, saying that our perspectives had shed new light on a seemingly well-debated matter. Great moment. We made a difference. For me, Schotstek means empowerment. I guess we pretty much agree since you are talking of "Entgrenzung." The encouragement and constructive feedback I received through the years at Schotstek made me stronger; they boosted my confidence in my own viewpoint. Questions, even, helped me grow. Discussing next steps or the outcome of a previous decision, too. This dynamic has been present since my first year at Schotstek. Today, I am one of the partners of Schotstek gGmbH, and this is very important to me. I know that I make a difference. Not in business or science, like many of my fellow Schotstekers. I have set my goals differently. I earned a masters' degree in social work, and I now collaborate closely with civil institutions and local politicians, discussing strategy, joining forces to move society forward.

These two Schotstek students are testament that the decision I have taken to dedicate my time to make a positive change in our society was a good one. I wish all Schotstek students and alumni a continued success in all their endeavors. May their journey and unwavering dedication be an inspiration to others.

Sigrid Berenberg is the founder of Schotstek, a scholarship program for university students with immigrant backgrounds. She previously worked as a criminal defense attorney, as head of communications at an international publishing company, as the manager of a postgraduate film studies program and as an independent communications consultant. Her pro bono work lasted 20 years as head of a nonprofit focused on reproductive health. She also co-founded a public event space in Hamburg. Sigrid started Schotstek with seven of her friends, four of them first generation immigrants.

Website: www.schotstek.com

26

An Idealistic Approach to Temp Work

Ingrid Verduyn

The author is a 'serial entrepreneur' in the temp agency industry. From the start of her career in this industry she witnessed the societal inequalities firsthand and recognized the potential for positive impact through meaningful employment. This led to the creation of Plus Uitzendkrachten, pioneering in involvement and personalized career guidance for temporary workers. Their approach, emphasizing competence, motivation, and sustainable employment relationships, challenged industry norms and garnered recognition. The later evolution to WaW reflects an idealistic business model with employee cooperative governance, emphasizing fairness and inclusivity. The author's reflections underscore the importance of kindness, personal values, and the role of entrepreneurship in creating meaningful societal impact. They advocate for sustainable entrepreneurship and hope to inspire others to pursue idealistic ventures for the betterment of society.

My Sustainability Journey

In my first job after my archeology studies, without knowing it, I was working illegally. My wages were paid correctly but were not declared to the Belgian National Social Security Office. When I found out, I immediately wanted to

---

I. Verduyn (✉)
WaW Jobs, Meise, Belgium
e-mail: ingrid@waw.jobs; https://www.waw.jobs

get out of there. I took a business policy course and soon there- after became a freelance grocery shopper for private individuals. I borrowed 200,000 Belgian francs (approximately 5000 euros) from my parents to buy a van, make leaflets, and advertise, and then I got a contract with a small supermarket that I was able to interest in the concept. The work was very labor-intensive: it was before the computer age, so every morning, I had to wait by the phone for customers to call, then fill out the order forms and go to the store. I filled one cart per customer and then made my deliveries.

When I noticed that my friends were all going out on Friday night while I was still driving around in my van, I stopped. It was the 1980s. I answered a newspaper ad for an office manager at Gregg Interim in the Antwerp office that places workers. I knew that I liked working with blue-collar workers, the people who fill the supermarket shelves and serve customers from behind the butcher's counter. I'd always enjoyed working with them when I was a professional shopper. Against all odds, as a very young woman, I got the job. I was their youngest office manager ever.

It was life changing. Understand that I come from a rather sheltered environment, where it's the rule that one goes to a good school and then to university. My parents and friends were all very similar people from the same background. However...

At this job, I saw something completely different. When someone did not show up for work, I jumped in my car or on my bike to get that worker out of bed. That is how I got to see these people's homes, how I came to see into the lives of men of all ages, ethnicities, and backgrounds. At that time, I wasn't trying to make the world a better place—that would not have worked in this situation anyway—I just thought these people should go to their jobs. For one thing, I had clients who were counting on them, and, for another, I felt that these workers had made a commitment. Sometimes people just need a push.

But imagine this: you are at a house where a man opens the door and you enter, although you notice that he doesn't really want you to. Inside are just rows of beds. The man has seven children, and they all sleep in one room.

That's an image I will not forget in a hurry. Doing this job, I was confronted with real social deprivation, with deep poverty, homelessness, and children who did not appear to go to school. These were situations that I didn't realize existed.

My most truly life-changing lesson was when I experienced firsthand that **one can really transform people's lives—as long as you give people a chance**. One morning, there was a guy on the sidewalk waiting for the office to open at 8:00 in the morning. When I opened the door, he followed me inside. He was there just in case someone did not show up for a job in the hope that he could take that person's place. He sat there for a couple of hours.

Waiting. After a few hours he left, and the next day he was there again. I talked with the man, and it turned out that he was in prison, allowed out every day just to look for a job. Because he had been at the door repeatedly at 8:00 a.m. on the dot, I figured he would be a punctual worker. I called a client, Sus, and asked if he could help such a person with a job. I knew that Sus would be amenable to this, and my client worked there for two years.

In this way, I was able to help a lot of people, people you might otherwise give some spare change to and not think about again. I realized that, through my work, I could do something that's really good for other people. That's how my "social heart" was born, among those workers. It was the most instructive period of my life. I have seen a lot of misery, I was even physically assaulted once, and had to go to the hospital because one of the temporary workers did not receive an advance on his wages and clearly disagreed with that.

In 1995, Gregg Interim was sold to the Vedex Group and went public. This is how a good company, where people are still important, evolves into a pure money-making machine. The pendulum emphatically swung that way, and the business did not suit me at all anymore. I left because my values were obviously clashing with the new company's values.

I then went through a personal crisis. I had loved doing well and succeeding in business. It is a game, and playing and winning the game is fun. However, what I do must be meaningful to me and must contribute something to society. If it is only about money, or if it is only about fun, then it is not enough.

With that entrepreneurial spirit, I created the agency Plus Uitzendkrachten (Plus Temporary Workers Agency) and asked my former boss to join me. He declared me crazy, but after some discussions, he said, "Why not?" **I knew what we had to do: we had to make our temporary workers feel better**. We made a business plan. It was the first company in our field with an outspoken social vision.

We came up with the concept of a "job coach" at our kitchen table. The idea was for us not only to create added value for the shareholders and the customers but also to create added value, in particular, for the temporary workers—for the people who actually come to work for you, for those who make sure you make sales and increase margins. That is how we started with career guidance for temporary—or temp—workers. This approach would give everyone involved much more than just a day's work for a day's pay.

Competence, Motivation, and Sustainable Employment Relationships

To make temp workers feel valued and engaged, you focus on two areas: competence and motivation. You can work on competence by letting people take special classes. That is quite easy. We did that. To work on people's motivation, you have to make sure that these people are working at the right place. At the end of the 1990s, a temp worker would enroll with an agency, and the consultant would open his book of clients, tell the worker what was available, and ask: "Is this something you would like to do?" Some job was chosen, and the temp would go to that client. Is it really what (s)he wanted? Nobody was asking. In fact, things often went wrong because the choice was not well thought through. At Plus Uitzendkrachten, our solution was to work on competence and motivation by offering temporary workers the possibility to **work with a job coach, who would offer them personalized career guidance**.

In the beginning, the professionals in our industry, the temping agencies "club," did have a good laugh at our expense. They told us, "After two months you'll have lost everything, you'll go broke." After a number of years, however, some of them began copying us. For example, we founded a cooperative alongside Plus Uitzendkrachten that we called Puls. Our temporary workers could join the cooperative and obtain hospitalization insurance. It was revolutionary and has always been unique in our field. Our copycats, however, just thought a cooperative would be a good way to bind people to a company. The temp agency Creyf's (now Start People) copied our cooperative idea and made their company a kind of club that temp workers could join. That membership then provided benefits, such as discounts through group purchasing. But they didn't copy our insurance package, as it was probably too expensive, and they did not really copy our career guidance initiative either.

For us, however, the most valuable content was not the hospitalization insurance. Our difference was, rather, in the real content: what is really good for a person, for his development. For us, it was really about career guidance, which is always human guidance.

Our clients appreciated our different approach, and that's how we were able to create a lot of goodwill with them. The other temp agencies may have laughed at us, but the clients weren't laughing at all. We told them what we were doing and how a temp worker who has received career guidance knows what he wants and makes different, better choices. This is good for both clients and temp workers.

We based our business model not only on competence and motivation but also on sustainable employment relationships. Indeed, our clients also saw another advantage to working with us—our approach resulted in a more sustainable story. The temp sector was then driven by what was called the "peak & sick"; that is, the typical temp contract covered the peak periods and replaced workers who were sick. These days, the focus has shifted from "peak & sick" to a steadier flow of work. Sustainable employment relationships are very important because, when hiring a temp worker, an employer hopes for a good match. A match has to be right on many levels, and one of them is the culture of the company. Matches often fail because someone did not take this into account, and so the match will not be a sustainable story. Unfortunately, many agencies place a temp worker and consider their job done. If the client is satisfied, great, and for the rest—well, have fun!

WaW, an Idealistic and Pioneering Approach for Temp Agencies

I will always be a pioneer, because I am always looking for the possibility to do things differently and better. That's in the genes of a pioneer. That is the reason why I have always been looking for systematic improvements, improvements in the ways of work. Therefore, to ensure that my partner and I can continue improving the temporary work industry and the "ways of work" in this industry and doing it the way we want, we are now pioneering another type of temp agency. We decided to call it WaW. What we are doing now with WaW is really special and I do not see the others copying it yet, not directly anyway. But we hope they will!

At WaW, we have an idealistic business model. **In our employee cooperative, the principle "one share, one vote" applies.** In other words, the corporate governance standard we have in place allows everyone to receive a single vote, regardless of the number of shares that one holds. To become a shareholder, one simply has to have at least a two-year membership in the cooperative. We bring all strategic decisions to our shareholders, because they are our partners, not self-employed but employees with a contract. In addition, my partner and I, WaW founders, limit the number of shares that we can dispose of: we cannot have more than twice the combined shares of the other shareholders. Therefore, we will never have more than twice the dividends of any other employee. The ratio is one to two, never more. This is not courageous, this is idealistic! Some might say this is overly egalitarian, but if the company is doing well and we pay out a dividend, we do not want the proportions to be skewed.

I have one vote out of 20; Paul also has one. We must therefore take a good look at our decision-making processes, because we can be overruled. We have annual general meetings with all WaW shareholders—many of them our employees—and the board of directors, where Paul and I sit as managing directors alongside two elected directors where most strategic decisions are taken. In addition, we organize quarterly meetings with our shareholders in which much time and thorough preparation is invested in order to guarantee a better decision-making process. Sometimes the path is clear, and then all is well. However, what if it's not always clear?

I always seek that critical voice, and I am disappointed when everyone nods yes. In fact, if there are no questions at all, I interpret it as lack of involvement. Criticism helps: there's no moving forward if a problem, which may otherwise have negative consequences, is not discussed. There are always issues, concerns that are hard to express, but they need to be said, and that takes guts. Therefore, when there is even one dissenter, we keep looking for a solution to bring that person on board. **We always strive for consensus.**

Reflections on My Journey

Be kind to others and to myself. It is very important to be kind. It sounds contradictory, but it's not. **On the one hand, you have to be brave and have the guts to raise issues; on the other hand, you need kindness, because everyone makes mistakes.** A person may behave very badly and needs to be addressed. However, you can still like the person and show your positive feelings to this person when you speak to him or her. If you do not make your positive feelings clear, you may be cold and hard and not reach the person. That is exactly what happens when you start lecturing people, and that doesn't work.

This approach takes a lot of energy. If I do not take or make enough time to find my peace, to put my own thoughts on paper, to meditate once in a while, then I risk ending up with a kind of tunnel vision where I only see work, work, work. That is not good for me. I really need to take a step back regularly, just push the pause button. My walking shoes are always ready. Walking brings me to myself. It brings me connection.

My beliefs and values. I am a religious person, even though I do not know what I believe in. However, I do know that I am a believing person and that I really need that connection with God and nature, with my partner and myself. That is pure oxygen, a breath of fresh air to me. Strike that out of my life, and I will not last long. In the end, everything that I do, including our new social employment organization, Make it Work, that coaches and employs young adults with a criminal record, arises from my beliefs and values. I think that every human being is born to contribute something to someone else's life. That is my faith. If you can do something that really improves someone's life, I assure you, there is little more you need.

Emulating others. I think it is good that sustainable entrepreneurship is receiving attention. The fact that others in our industry copy us is a good thing; if everyone could copy us, the world would be a better place. The market leader, Randstad, for example, is now also working on sustainable entrepreneurship, and I am deeply happy about that. It is really not to our disadvantage.

I feel proud of what we do, although pride is not my motivation. I do not have to stand on a stage, but when it is appropriate, I will do it, because it is good for the company. **I hope other young entrepreneurs will look at our work and see that idealism works.** I hope that we encourage people to do something good with their lives, because there is so much to do…

Ingrid Verduyn is an entrepreneur driven by creating added value for all stakeholders in the labor market. With over 30 years of experience in the employment services industry, she began her career at Gregg Interim (later known as Vedior) before leaving to establish Plus Uitzendkrachten ("Plus Temporary Employment Services") a decade later. In 2015, she founded WaW Jobs, a company specializing in search, selection, and temporary labor. In 2017, she further expanded her impact by establishing Make it Work, a social employment organization that provides coaching and employment opportunities for young people with a criminal record. Ingrid possesses a keen eye for emerging trends and new opportunities that can bring about positive changes in the labor market.

Part III

Addressing Governance and Financial Matters

27

What Is Compliance: An Open Conversation

Christian Rau

"Compliance, what's that?" This short, eye-opening conversation between a CEO and his Chief Compliance Officer will explain, in a nutshell, what corporate Compliance means.

Judging by the slightly confused look on the CEO's face, his question seemed sincere. I was no less surprised. Here we were, in one of Europe's major business centers, less than 3 hours away from the city where an army of prosecutors and police officers had raided and searched the global headquarters of another well-known, publicly-listed corporation just over a year ago. The case had made headlines, both domestically and internationally. It had also become a kind of "cause célèbre" in legal and compliance circles.

I took a deep breath. Knowing that my boss, the Chief Executive Officer of our multinational group of companies, was quite the sailor (called "The Captain" by some of his friends) and also an avid golfer in his spare time, I suggested the following:

"Compliance basically means playing by the rules, all the time, and especially when nobody is watching."

I continued after pausing briefly.

The following is a fictitious conversation. Any resemblance to real events, companies or persons, living or dead, is purely coincidental. You shall be the judge as to whether such conversation could actually take place in an executive office or boardroom near you.

C. Rau (✉)
GRC EMEA, Hamburg, Germany

"You, as an accomplished sailor, you would never claim to have rounded that buoy which is hard to see from the pier if you really hadn't, would you?"

"Of course not," came the prompt reply. The CEO looked at me with amused interest. His jet-black hair, neatly slicked back on his head, did not move an inch.

"What about golf?" I inquired, trying to sound as neutral as possible. "Would you ever consider moving your errant tee shot, which has gone out of bounds by half a foot, back onto the fairway?"

"Unthinkable, that would be cheating!" he shot back, eyes glistening and with an undertone of growing contempt for my questions which had apparently touched a nerve.

"Not to be disrespectful, I am just trying to illustrate my point: Our corporation is acting in a narrow market with only a few major competitors. Together, we dominate that market, and it is not easy for 'newcomers' to enter."

A somewhat nervous half-smile appeared on his face before he remarked:

"Rrrright, and we'd better keep it that way. After all, that's what has made this company successful for the last 30 years. Plus, even with only a handful of players in total, it is a tough market, competition is fierce, and everyone's prices have been under pressure for the last four quarters and counting. And because of you guys, I cannot even speak to my fellow CEOs without a chaperone. Hell, even at a routine meeting of our industry association, there is a lawyer taking notes and lecturing us on the topics we can talk about and the ones we apparently can't."

"That's correct, Sir, and that, exactly, is part of compliance. Playing by the rules, this time the rules of competition law. They certainly don't allow us to discuss prices and markets with our competitors, especially given the oligopoly in which we are operating."

I was quite tempted to go on as follows:

"And if it hadn't been for 'the likes of you,' creating an illegal cartel in which Player 1 gets to dominate Market x and Player 2 Market y, with regular and coordinated price increases that all parties agree upon at regular secret meetings, and all this neatly laid down in the so-called Golden Rules; hence, if people in your position hadn't made a mockery of free and fair competition, people like me would not have to look people like you over the shoulder at every step."

Instead, I bit my lip and turned to another topic that I felt was no less delicate:

"And what about our two big joint-ventures with state-run companies in the Far East, and what about all those agents and 'facilitators' who helped bring about those deals?"

"What about them?" came The Captain's curt reply. "These mega-projects have been our cash cows for many years in notoriously difficult and sometimes outright impenetrable markets. Besides, that's the way of doing business in that part of the world. Of course, you as a lawyer probably do have a hard time understanding that."

"Actually, I don't. The trouble is that, in the past, we seem to have been bidding in a tender procedure, which was, to put it mildly, opaque. We also apparently paid large sums to several 'middlemen' who claim 'to open doors, establish contacts and facilitate matters.' Last but not least, we have been dealing with government officials, some of whom double as board members of local state-run entities. Senior civil servants, ministers, and, in at least one case, even a member of the local royal court."

"Soooooo. .?"

"Wellllllll …," I replied, allowing myself to let my one-syllable answer linger just about as long as his deliberately provocative, if not dismissive question. I continued: "Let me just politely inquire whether, when entering into Deal 1, we may have paid an unusually high 'commission' to that consultant with the many letterbox companies and offshore accounts and whether, in order to bring about success in Deal 2, we may have been a bit too close to the local vice-minister who initially set and then changed the terms of the tender which we then won, much to everyone's surprise."

Touché?? If so, he didn't show it. Instead, yet another long silence settled over the room while the sun stretched its final afternoon rays over the foothills opposite our corporate headquarters. Finally, the CEO got up, switched on a floor lamp, and adjusted the dimmer, so the lamp gave off a warm, golden glow.

"I'll tell you what," he finally continued. His usual smile was gone, having given way to a sheepish smirk. "I inherited these deals from my predecessor who, during my transition into the CEO role, told me that it had been his habit to delegate a fair amount of things, 'to always stay above the fray,' not to ask too many 'unproductive questions' and, especially, 'to leave the details to the project managers on the front lines.' He insisted that this had been part of the corporation's and his personal success story, and he recommended that I had best follow that example. As CEO, you simply cannot know everything—and you probably shouldn't either."

A piercing glance right into my eyes accompanied his last statement, as if he wanted to gauge the immediate impact of the words he had spoken with considerable executive might.

I deliberately let his last statement hover in the air for a while before clearing my throat: "Hmmm… So, the captain does not know the cargo of his ship, and he is blissfully unaware of the goings-on below deck."

The nautical metaphor worked, again, and I had his undivided attention. It was time to press on:

"Do you know how certain authorities call this 'head in the sand approach' where the leader says he didn't know or didn't want to know? They call it 'willful blindness', and the bad news is that it is not a valid legal defense. In fact, quite the opposite may be true: Just like the captain of a ship will be held accountable for everything that happened 'on his watch,' the CEO has a duty to inquire how such deals came about. And in a more general way, he must install and follow a Compliance Management System in his corporation to prevent, detect and respond to possible improprieties and wrongdoings."

"A Com-pli-ance Man-age-ment Sys-tem," he sighed, slowly repeating every syllable of this bureaucratic monster of a word and rolling his eyes in theatrical exaggeration. "But how do we do this? Do we really need this? Playing by the rules, that's not new so what's all the fuss about anyway? And what about our legal department? Can't they take care of this?"

I decided to wait for another moment, making sure that this most recent flare-up of a smart but notoriously short-tempered industry leader had run its course. Then, I proceeded to address his concerns, careful not to start my next salvo with the dreaded words 'No, but…':

"It's true, compliance is not new. It's just that the amount and complexity of laws and rules have grown enormously over the last years. Add to that the fact that some of these laws, while being made by national parliaments, are being applied—and enforced—worldwide. The number of investigations has increased, and sanctions have become stiffer and more varied.

By now, everyone is aware of fines up to hundreds of millions of dollars, but how about being excluded from government contracts or having your name or the name of your company publicly 'named and shamed,' not to speak of the pressure by investors, shareholders and social media."

Silence.

"And yes, we have a fine legal department. Its strong suit is, no doubt, drafting and negotiating our highly complex, long-term project contracts, documents that can easily stretch over 100 pages. We also have strong IT and patent lawyers. However, as you probably know, a fair amount of our legal work is being outsourced to one of our three preferred law firms."

We made eye contact, the first in quite some time. The CEO returned a quick nod, so I carried on:

"My point is that our fine law department is simply not equipped to provide specific compliance content, much less deliver large-scale online training, monitor business processes and payment flows, or conduct investigations. In order to satisfy today's requirements, we need to do quite a bit more—and yes, it has to be a structure and program which lives up to the standards of a Compliance Management System commensurate with our industry…

Besides, how could we otherwise claim, as we routinely do, that our corporation excels at everything it does?"

Reminding him of our proud company's 'Culture of Excellence' and linking it to the level of compliance I was aiming for seemed to strike a chord. It prompted another nod and a seemingly knowing smile from 'The Captain.' Then, as if shifting up one gear, his look zoomed in on me as he placed the bait:

"So, can you organize and oversee this or will we need the usual army of outside consultants? … Because if you can't, … well I am sure my sailing partner from one of the Big Four is already smiling in anticipation of a juicy project."

Sensing that we had reached a crucial moment in our conversation, I decided to strike while the iron was hot:

"Our company already has a basic risk framework as well as a finance, an HR and—you mentioned it—a legal department. An internal audit function also exists. Furthermore, we have a well-worded and attractively designed Code of Conduct, although it does seem to be somewhat of a 'sleeping beauty' at the moment. We even have a telephone and email hotline through which employees and third parties can raise complaints, even anonymously, if they so choose. What we need now, however, is a specific risk assessment, region by region, which checks our business model, our competitive landscape, our sourcing, procurement, and distribution flows, and several other parameters against competition laws, anti-corruption norms, data protection rules as well as export-control and sanction legislation. Add to that tailor-made training, education, and advice, especially for those of our employees who are most at risk, plus process monitoring, spot checks, and investigations when necessary."

And on I went, confronting one of the tricky parts—money and resources—head-on:

"We'll draw on our corporation's IT systems, and we will closely work with the departments which I just mentioned. We will also liaise with our external auditors, leveraging resources and tools as much as we can. But let me be clear: We will need a certain number of professional, fully-dedicated compliance and data protection specialists. We should be able to reassign some from positions elsewhere in our company and develop them into compliance managers. Others we'll have to hire from the outside."

Nothing in his face gave away his thoughts. So, I concluded:

"There will be regular reports to you, to the entire Executive Board, and to the Audit Committee. You'll have my concept in writing the week after next, complete with a timeline and a full cost estimate. Once you've had the time to study my proposal and clarify any remaining questions, I'll ask for your and the Board's formal approval."

A prolonged silence followed. I tried to read his face again, prepared to go into greater detail or argue any of the points I had just rattled off at a brisk pace. Finally, his easy smile was back, laced with a trace of relief.

"Hmmm …," he said and paused. "Let's go for it!"

Another pause came as I started to slowly close my laptop and pack up.

"Doing the right thing?" he mused, almost as if talking to himself.

"Exactly."

Christian Rau has over 25 years of experience as an attorney, manager, and advisor. He started his legal career with a major international law firm in Berlin before joining a large, publicly-listed US healthcare company in Brussels/Belgium and at its Global Headquarters in New Jersey. While working as a corporate attorney in the USA he also served on the management board of one of his employer's multinational subsidiaries and co-taught a course on International M&A at New York University. Upon returning to his native Germany he took up the position of Global Chief Legal Officer and Global Chief Compliance Officer at a major global corporation listed on the DAX. He currently works as Chief Compliance Officer and Head of Governance, Risk and Compliance (GRC) EMEA at a global medical device manufacturer.

Dr. Rau received his legal education at the Universities of Freiburg/Germany, Geneva/Switzerland, and Georgetown/USA. He holds German and US law degrees and a Ph.D. in comparative constitutional law. He has been a member of several Advisory Boards and of the Executive Faculty at Bucerius Law School's CLP in Hamburg/Germany. His working languages are German, English, and French, and he is proficient in Spanish.

LinkedIn: https://www.linkedin.com/in/rauchristian

28

Navigating Artificial Intelligence Governance Challenges in Organizations

Blanca Escribano Cañas

New Playing Field, New Challenges

Boards need to be well-equipped to ensure that their organizations have a governance structure in place that can be adapted to the new digital playing field. They need to adapt the organizations' internal controls to the new environment. The digital economy has created a paradigm shift that is triggering a change in how organizations govern. As the physical and virtual worlds converge into the metaverse, the value of information and intangible assets is on the rise. As I write this story, it is becoming increasingly apparent that there is an immediate urgency for organizations to think about how they can navigate the challenges posed by artificial intelligence (AI).

The year 2023 will be remembered as the most pivotal year for generative AI.[1] Although AI is not a new technology, the proliferation of foundational models and, in particular, the launch of Chat GPT and its competitors (i.e., Bing AI, Bard AI, Claude AI, xAI) have shaken up the tech market and made more obvious how significant AI is and how it stands out compared to the rest

---

[1] The European Parliament defines Generative AI as *"foundation models used in AI systems specifically intended to generate, with varying levels of autonomy, content such as complex text, images, audio, or video."* European Parliament text adopted on 14 June 2023. (P9_TA(2023)0236 Artificial Intelligence Act).

B. E. Cañas (✉)
Carlos III Madrid University, Madrid, Spain

© The Author(s), under exclusive license to Springer Nature Switzerland AG 2024
B. Bernard-Rau (ed.), *Sustainability Stories*, https://doi.org/10.1007/978-3-031-52300-7_28

of the exponential technologies (e.g., 3D printing, augmented reality, sensorization/IoT).

The potential of AI is enormous, but there is also enormous concern[2] regarding the risks and downsides of using this technology. The characteristic that makes AI most promising is likely its capacity for autonomy and unpredictability. When AI systems use machine-learning[3] techniques, they can achieve a certain (or full) level of autonomy from the coding or the instructions provided by their creators (e.g., designers, developers, data analysts), which can inevitably lead to consequences that go beyond creating a computer program.

To counterbalance these risks, initiatives around the world have emerged to monitor and regulate AI. It seems that previous debates on whether to regulate AI have already been surpassed. In the meantime, plans have been put in place across different regions to set up a specific legal framework for authorities to oversee the use of this technology and mitigate potential damage. The European Union is ahead of the game in this regard, and a specific regulation, the Artificial Intelligence Act [4] (directly applicable in all the member states), is expected to be passed by mid-2024, thus becoming the first general AI regulation enacted in the world.[5] Most likely, the UK, United States, Japan, and China, among others, will soon follow suit.

Governing AI in Organizations Internally within an ESG Context

The impact of using AI in "corporate and organization governance"[6] (COG) can be analyzed from three different perspectives.

---

[2] Elon Musk, CEO of Tesla, X, SpaceX and xAI, and Sam Altman, Open AI CEO, are among the voices that are loudly demanding AI oversight.

[3] For a definition of machine-learning, see https://www.expert.ai/blog/machine-learning-definition/

[4] Proposal for a Regulation of the European Parliament and of the Council laying down harmonized rules on artificial intelligence (Artificial Intelligence Act) and amending certain union legislative acts. COM/2021/206 final.

[5] The European Commission has proposed 3 interrelated legal initiatives that intend to contribute to building trustworthy AI: (i) The AI Act (a European legal framework for AI to address fundamental rights and safety risks specific to the AI systems); (ii) The Liability Directive (a civil liability framework—adapting liability rules to the digital age and AI); and (iii) a revision of sectoral safety legislation (e.g. Machinery Regulation, General Product Safety Directive)

[6] Governance of the digital assets in general and artificial intelligence and algorithms in particular is relevant not only for corporations or companies but also for governmental and nongovernmental organizations. For this reason, this paper will use the term "corporate and organization governance" as a wider term beyond private/public corporations.

The first perspective is related to how AI and other digital technologies can serve as instrumental tools for collecting information when reporting and monitoring sustainability indicators.[7] By using and sharing this information, AI helps us to understand how organizations assess their risks and opportunities, enabling internal and external actors to make better financial and nonfinancial decisions. Today, AI is a key technology for achieving sustainability goals.

Another perspective is the support provided, the replacement of those involved in the decision-making process, and even the substitution of physical board members by AI systems. Currently, there is an ongoing debate about whether the legal frameworks in place should allow directors to be replaced by AI systems.

Both of the abovementioned perspectives are currently very topical and relevant, but this story focuses on a third perspective: how boards and governance bodies address the questions raised by AI and its related technologies and how these advancements impact strategic planning, risk management, and overall control within their organizations. Boards must be adequately prepared to establish a governance structure tailored to the changing dynamics of the Fourth Industrial Revolution (as coined by K. Schwab[8]).

During the last few years, organizations have developed personal data and cybersecurity policies and governance frameworks. Now, the next milestone is to focus on AI systems. These systems are substituting some of the tools and processes for decision-making that were previously performed by humans. In 2017, anticipating the civil liability framework that Europe is putting in place now, EU Commissioner Margaret Vestager stated: *"Businesses also need to know that when they decide to use an automated system, they will be held responsible for what it does. So, they had better know how that system works."*[9]

---

[7] The revised G20/OECD Principles of Corporate Governance 2023 states: *"Digital technologies may also be leveraged to make regulatory compliance less onerous for companies, with a view to maintaining the rigor and scope of corporate governance regulation and corporate disclosure through improvements in the functioning of the existing framework. Adopting digital solutions in regulatory and supervisory processes also comes with challenges and risks. Important considerations include ensuring the quality of data; ensuring that staff have proper technical competence; considering interoperability between systems in the development of reporting formats; and managing third-party dependencies and digital security risks. When artificial intelligence and algorithmic decision-making are used in supervisory processes, it is critical to maintain a human element in place to mitigate against risks of incorporating existing biases in algorithmic models and the risks from an overreliance on models and digital technologies."*

[8] Schwab, Klaus. "The Fourth Industrial Revolution," which describes the shift to smart technologies and its effects. World Economic Forum, 2016.

[9] Margaret Vestager is the EU commissioner responsible for competition. Speech delivered on algorithms and competition at the Bundeskartellamt 18th Conference on Competition, Berlin, 16 March, 2017.

Consequently, and in line with the G20/OECD principles of corporate governance,[10] boards and governing bodies have faced the challenge of ensuring that their organizations have a robust, agile, and fit-for-purpose AI governance structure for setting objectives and monitoring performance.

Since 2018, international organizations, governmental and nongovernmental bodies, and private companies have released responsible AI frameworks. For instance, the UN, UNESCO, the OECD, the World Economic Forum, the European Council, the European Commission, the European Parliament, and more than a hundred public and private initiatives have produced statements describing high-level principles for appropriate governance concerning the development and use of AI, robotics, and related technologies to "*increase citizens' safety and trust in those technologies.*"[11] All these institutions concur on the necessity of providing guidelines, toolkits, or lists of principles for organizations to self-assess the risks that AI entails as well as the means to deploy and implement a governance structure.

Boards have the responsibility to know what their AI systems do and how algorithms work to ensure that their organization has a robust governance structure for setting objectives and monitoring performance. Reports to shareholders and filings sent to regulators should include information about the use and risks of AI, and these should also be detailed in nonfinancial reporting and audited.

In addition, within an ESG (environmental, social, and governance) context, AI governance will gain greater significance. ESG is a tool for investors to look beyond the profits and losses of a company and to recognize other factors when making investment decisions.[12] ESG can be divided into three categories, each addressing the environmental, social, and governance policies and practices of a company. In the past, the environmental dimension has enjoyed heightened scrutiny from both investors and regulators, overshadowing the social and governance dimensions, but this is starting to change.

Organizations should consider AI policies within the governance category of ESG, together with data privacy and cybersecurity. Furthermore, as we will

---

[10] The G20/OECD Principles of Corporate Governance are the international standard for corporate governance. The Principles help policy makers evaluate and improve the legal, regulatory, and institutional framework for corporate governance, with a view to supporting economic efficiency, sustainable growth, and financial stability. The principles were first issued in 1999 and the revised Principles were endorsed by G20 Leaders in 2023. The following five principles include: responsibility, accountability, awareness, impartiality, and transparency.

[11] European Parliament Resolution of 20 October 2020 with recommendations to the Commission on a framework of ethical aspects of artificial intelligence, robotics, and related technologies (2020/2012(INL)).

[12] On AI, sustainability and C-suit, see Empowering AI Leadership. AI C-Suit Toolkit. World Economic Forum, January 2022.

discuss later when addressing trusted or responsible AI, the ethical dimension of AI (AI ethics) can also be incorporated into the social category, reflecting its potential impact on human rights. Investors will increasingly demand disclosure information regarding how AI is employed, developed, and implemented within organizations. They will focus not only on compliance with existing regulations but also on the ethical dimensions of AI. Although ESG regulations do not currently require this kind of disclosure, it may soon become a standard practice.

Noncompliance with AI regulations could trigger serious fines, civil liability, and serious reputational damage. If AI regulations and guidelines are infringed upon, this would make the organization lose trust from customers, employees, stakeholders and investors, subsequently having a negative impact on long-term profits. In contrast, organizations pioneering the inclusion of AI policy information in their ESG reporting would help them gain trust, with a positive long-term profit impact.[13]

Trusted AI: The Three Ingredients

In keeping with the above reference to trust, to be trustworthy or responsible, AI systems should be safe, secure, reliable, and robust to avoid causing any harm. They should comply with the laws in place,[14] which apply irrespective of the underpinning technology. And they should be ethical. Indeed, there is a global consensus that AI governance should include technical, legal, and ethical components. Organizations will be liable and accountable not only for developing and using AI in a legal and technically robust way but also for complying with ethics.

In this regard, the independent High-Level Expert Group on AI, which was set up by the EU Commission in its *Ethics Guidelines for a Trustworthy AI* (2019),[15] recommended that top management and the board of directors should discuss and evaluate AI system development, deployment, or procurement when critical concerns are detected. When describing how this should be implemented, the recommendation that has been made to organizations in the Guidelines is that they should *"adapt their charter of corporate responsibility, Key Performance Indicators ('KPIs'), their codes of conduct or internal policy*

---

[13] Jon McGowan. ESG May Help Regulate AI/ChatGPT Use In Business. Forbes, August 2023.
[14] In addition to specific AI norms, the entire legal system also applies to AI.
[15] The AI HLEG is an independent expert group that was set up by the European Commission in June 2018. "Ethics Guidelines for Trustworthy AI" was made public on 8 April 2019.

documents to add to the striving toward Trustworthy AI" or, in other words, toward a more responsible AI.

In the same vein, the World Economic Forum published *Empowering AI Leadership: An Oversight Toolkit for Boards of Directors*[16] to guide board members when monitoring compliance with AI ethics. The toolkit includes principles very similar to those identified by the EU. This toolkit has a three-stage methodology: the first is for selecting activities requiring governance (ethics, risk/reward, technology, and people); the second is for evaluating governance; and the third is for assigning governance responsibilities, splitting obligations between the ethics board and the board of directors.

In light of the above, boards will also need to ensure that they have a sufficient level of expertise in ethical principles as they relate to AI. The ethical dimension also needs to be measured, either through nonfinancial key performance indicators or ethical compliance certificates.

The ethical component introduces a new dimension to governance frameworks. Organizations become accountable for the ethical spectrum of decisions associated with the development, deployment, and use of AI systems. As a result, large organizations are already developing codes of ethics for AI and appointing someone to be in charge of ethical compliance in regard to AI, or creating an internal/external panel on AI, an AI board committee, or a board member who has received ethical training in AI.[17]

From a practical point of view, the only way to comply is by embedding these "ethics," the ethical principles, into the system "by design," akin to constitutional principles driving outputs toward ethical rather than unethical results. In this regard, in the European Union, the referred Guidelines and proposed regulations state that the three earlier mentioned components of trusted AI should be implemented from the very outset, by design: legal

---

[16] http://www3.weforum.org/docs/WEF_Empowering-AI-Leadership_Oversight-Toolkit.pdf. Retrieved on 23 March 2021. See also "Empowering AI leadership: AI Suit Toolkit," January 2022.

[17] For instance, the AETHER Committee was established at Microsoft in 2017. Google created an AI Ethics board (Advanced Technology External Advisory Council, or ATEAC), but cancelled it after public outcry caused by the controversial behavior of some of the board members. Facebook formed a special ethics team to prevent bias in its A.I. software (https://www.cnbc.com/2018/05/03/facebook-ethics-team-prevents-bias-in-ai-software.html). There are also international partnerships for valuating the impact of AI, such as the *Partnership on AI (https://www.partnershiponai.org/)*, which includes Facebook, Amazon, Google, IBM, and Microsoft; or the *AI Now Institute (https://ainowinstitute.org/)*. Public organizations are also moving in this direction, such as the European Data Protection Supervisor (EDPS), which appeared in the early days creating an ethical board back in 2015 (*https://edps.europa.eu/press-publications/press-news/press-releases/2015/edps-set-ethics-board_en*)

by design, ethical by design, technically robust by design, or in other words, they should adhere to AI ethical practices and to the rule of law by design (X-by-design). Similarly, in the United States and in the context of Generative AI, companies such as Anthropic[18] are talking about Constitutional AI (CAI).[19]

In other words, boards should ensure that the ethical component has been embedded within the AI general strategy of the organization, and they should confirm that the governance structure is adequate for monitoring how AI is employed.

Defining the Ethical Component

However, what does it mean an ethical AI system? While the legal ingredient is certain, the ethical ingredient could become something vague, something that lawyers call an "indeterminate legal concept." In legal theory, a vague or indeterminate concept could indeed become controversial when interpreting compliance with obligations. Ethics are not the same in all corners of the world, which is why organizations are drawing up what an ethical AI should look like based on the values that are the most obviously impacted by the use of AI systems. Therefore, trying to consolidate these ethics in the EU, a group of experts identified principles from the European Charter of Fundamental Rights (EU Charter) and the Treaties of the European Union, highlighting

---

[18] Founded in 2021 by former senior members of OpenAI, Anthropic is an AI safety and research company based in San Francisco (USA).

[19] Anthropic's constitutional AI gives a system a set of principles to make judgments about the text it generates. These principles guide the model to take on the behavior they describe (e.g., "nontoxic" and "helpful"). The principles are used in two places while training a text-generating model. First, one model is trained to critique and revise its own responses by using the principles. Then, another model—the final model—is trained using the AI-generated feedback based on the first model plus the set of principles. Anthropic argues that this approach is superior to the method used to train systems such as ChatGPT, which relies on human contractors comparing two responses from a model and selecting the one they feel is better according to a certain principle. The company believes that constitutional AI is more transparent and requires fewer resources than the methodology used thus far, RLHF (Reinforcement Learning via Human Feedback). Anthropic's constitution is, in theory, taken from several sources, including the U.N. Declaration of Human Rights and Apple's terms of service. The principles include discouraging harmful content, avoiding stereotypes, and refraining from giving specific legal advice. The company claims to include values that are not strictly from Western, rich, or industrialized cultures. It can be understood that embedding principles within the technology is opposite to the Reinforcement Learning via Human Feedback (RLHF).

four principles: respect for human autonomy, prevention of harm, fairness, and explicability.[20]

To implement these four ethical principles, the European Commission suggested seven requirements that AI systems must meet: human oversight, technical robustness, data governance, transparency, avoidance of bias and discrimination, social and environmental sustainability, and accountability. Moreover, in its Resolution from October 20, 2020, with recommendations to the Commission on a framework of ethical aspects of AI,[21] the EU Parliament proposed an AI certification of ethical compliance, mandatory for AI systems developed, deployed, or used within the territory of the EU. The close link between AI and data, the latter being necessary for the former, makes privacy considerations and data ethics also crucial.[22]

There are other organizations and institutions across the world that are trying to define the ethical component; however, making a comparison between all of them would exceed the scope of this story.

Despite ongoing efforts to define the ethical ingredient within AI, it appears that there is still a long way ahead in shaping a comprehensive ethical framework. The necessary ethical component for a trustworthy AI system should be much more precise and, ideally, internationally harmonized.

Finally, and to use an ironic tone, organizations should be transparent and consistent with their own ethics in the development and use of AI themselves and in their relationships with all their stakeholders. Otherwise, the ethical ingredient could serve the opposite purpose and be used as, what is called, ethics-washing, a justification for poor conduct or to mask anti-ethical conduct.

---

[20] Respect for human autonomy is strongly associated with the right to human dignity and liberty (reflected in Articles 1 and 6 of the EU Charter). The prevention of harm is strongly linked to the protection of physical or mental integrity (reflected in Article 3 of the EU Charter). Fairness is closely linked to the rights adhering to Nondiscrimination, Solidarity and Justice (reflected in Articles 21 and following of the EU Charter). Explicability and Responsibility are closely linked to the rights relating to Justice (as reflected in Article 47 of the EU Charter). Explicability refers to the ability for the parties involved to furnish an explanation of why an AI system behaved in such a way. For further reading on this subject, see, for instance, L. Floridi, Soft Ethics and the Governance of the Digital, *Philosophy & Technology*, March 2018, Volume 31, Issue 1, pp. 1–8. Retrieved from the EU Ethics Guidelines for Trustworthy AI https://ec.europa.eu/futurium/en/node/6945#_ftn23 on 18 March 2021.

[21] Framework of ethical aspects of artificial intelligence, robotics and related technologies. P9_TA(2020)0275. https://www.europarl.europa.eu/doceo/document/TA-9-2020-0275_EN.html Retrieved on 23 March, 2021.

[22] Without data, there is no AI. Data are essential for feeding AI; the fairness, legality, and ethics of the data used will condition AI. Machine-learning systems require enormous datasets. Proper data governance requires quality checks of the external sources of data used by AI and puts oversight mechanisms in place regarding their collection, storage, processing, and use, in order to avoid the creation or reinforcement of bias that can lead to discrimination. Choices about how to evaluate the data will affect how the data is used, which, again, means more choices about any final algorithms. Data should be transparent, traceable, interoperable, compliant with privacy and security regulations, and auditable.

Blanca Escribano Cañas has practiced law in international firms for more than 25 years, advising clients at the intersection of law and technology. Blanca is a member of the Advisory Board of the Communications Law Committee of the International Bar Association and a member of the academic board of EU Law LL.M. at the Carlos III Madrid University (Spain).

LinkedIn: https://www.linkedin.com/in/blancaescribano/

29

International Climate Negotiations: "Blabla" or Key Forum to Solve the Climate Crisis?

Axel Michaelowa

How can one, as an individual, influence the global policy process addressing climate change? Isn't one powerless given the enormous resources controlled by fossil fuel interests? Will policymakers not always address short-term issues while shirking the long-term ones? Does a consensus-based process at all make sense when there are so many open and hidden conflicts regarding how to address the global public good of climate change mitigation?

As a student in the late 1980s and early 1990s, I was passionate about the climate change issue and really delved into it, yet I was uncertain about what to do best to contribute to solving this immense problem effectively. But then fate gave me the opportunity to become professionally engaged in designing climate policy instruments. In early 1994, despite being just a PhD student at an economic research institute that had no references on climate change, I was awarded a project to study international carbon markets by the Federal Ministry of the Economy. So, I had a nice budget at my disposal and two years of freedom to pursue the project.

In 1994, the UN Framework Convention on Climate Change (UNFCCC) had just entered into force, and the 1st Conference of the Parties (COP1) was scheduled for 1995 in Berlin. I contacted the UNFCCC Secretariat and asked how one could become engaged in the process. They told me that my institute could get accredited as an observer if it could show its nonprofit status. Thus,

---

A. Michaelowa (✉)
University of Zurich, Zurich, Switzerland
e-mail: michaelowa@perspectives.cc

I sent a one-page accreditation request with a proof of the institute's tax exemption, and one week later I received the formal accreditation (currently the accreditation process takes two years, and one needs to provide a large array of documents).

Thus, in late 1994, I was one of very few researchers accredited with the UNFCCC. Proudly, I took the train to Berlin to participate in saving the world and registered for COP1. But then the awakening was rude. Huge crowds of people thronged the corridors of the "spaceship"-style congress halls. Weird acronyms were used by the initiated. Empty declarations were uttered in high level sessions by heads of state. Large piles of paper cluttered the negotiation rooms. Understanding the schedule and where to engage was challenging. I wondered how to play a relevant role in this giant machinery. So, I tried to find my friends working on carbon markets—a small group in these days—and to attend the most interesting side events to get a grasp of the relevant topics. I participated in a tour to a lighthouse climate change mitigation project offered, free of charge, by the German government—the massive, just refurbished Jänschwalde lignite power plant [1]. Thirty years later, no one in Germany would dare to showcase a coal power plant as climate change mitigation!

Reflecting on the COP1 experience, I was not put off but thought of options to meaningfully contribute. I harnessed several of such options over time. Some are simple and can be taken up by anyone, while others are more complex and require deep immersion in the negotiation process. I start with the former and subsequently address the latter.

Anyone accredited to the UNFCCC process can provide input through the so-called side events on topics that are freely chosen. Official side events are mini-seminars of 90 minutes in rooms provided free of charge by the UNFCCC. Unofficial side events are hosted in pavilions of countries and large institutions or even outside the venue. I have routinely run official side events, way over 100 in total and am very proud of never having a side event proposal refused, even as competition has become very fierce (Fig. 29.1). A good side event makes negotiators and relevant stakeholders aware of a new topic. You can develop your network through inviting reputed speakers and asking relevant questions in side events organized by others. Therefore, over time, you become a respected member of the "epistemic community" of the climate negotiations. And if a suggestion you have proposed at a side event pops up in a country submission or in an official negotiation text, then you have made a difference.

---

[1] The Jänschwalde power plant is located in Brandenburg on the German-Polish border. It is the third-largest brown coal power plant in operation in Germany.

29 International Climate Negotiations: "Blabla" or Key Forum...

Fig. 29.1 Axel Michaelowa speaking at a side event at COP19 in Warsaw 2013. (Photograph by Matthias Honegger. All rights reserved)

Supporting a country delegation as a consultant is the second level of sophistication. This requires that you have acquired yourself a reputation as an expert on the issues under negotiation and that the government trusts you. Of course, funding also needs to be available. I have supported many different delegations over the years and do not want to miss the experience. Cultural and work style differences are significant. Sometimes you exasperate if your input is brushed away due to high level political considerations. Sometimes you feel completely exhausted after successive long night negotiation sessions. But if you manage to use your network built over the years to enable a proposal of "your" country to be supported by others and to find the way into the final outcome, you have made a difference. And there are moments you will never forget like observing huddles fighting for the decisive words in final plenaries where "the wind of history blows"… (Fig. 29.2).

The most elaborate level of input into climate negotiations is supporting the host country of a Conference of the Parties, the so-called COP Presidency. I did this in 2012 in Qatar. The country had submitted its candidacy believing that this would be an event such as a sports championship or large fair where Qatar could show it is a modern country. No one understood the political risks that a failed COP could bring. For a year preceding the COP, I had tried to market my services to Qatari government actors, seemingly in vain. But ten days before the starting date of the COP, I got a call from Doha—"We

Fig. 29.2 Supporting the Moroccan delegation in Article 6 negotiations at COP25 in Madrid 2019 (Photograph by Axel Michaelowa. All rights reserved)

need you!". And the almost comical aspect of that call was that my small company Perspectives was asked to subcontract famous professors from Harvard University who had also been on marketing trips to Doha and then had flatly refused collaboration with me. So, I assembled a team, brought Harvard on board and we descended on Doha two days before the COP. During my reconnaissance, I found out that there were two strands of command in the Qatari COP presidency that fought each other. This is a frequent phenomenon and needs to be taken very seriously as it can doom a COP, as happened in Copenhagen 2009 when the Danish Ministry of Foreign Affairs and of the Environment were openly fighting each other and committed massive blunders such as leaking key documents.

We spent the first week of the COP in getting to understand the exact problems in the two competing strands and to identify serious people with enough power with whom we could work on content. Our machinery then worked well oiled throughout the second week. While we did not directly engage in high-level negotiations, our inputs became highly relevant in the final three-day period, where we worked in shifts around the clock. Fortunately, there were bunk beds in the Qatari office ☺.

Presidency support requires a full grasp of the key negotiation issues on the table and the ability to identify cross-cutting solutions. You need to have a large network that provides you with intelligence around the clock. In addition, you need to understand the dynamics of the key forces—the UNFCCC Secretariat, the "friends of the chair," potential spoilsports, the NGOs, and the media. You need quick wits and the ability to concentrate even if you are

29 International Climate Negotiations: "Blabla" or Key Forum...

Fig. 29.3 The gavel used at UNFCCC negotiations (Photograph by Axel Michaelowa. All rights reserved)

dead tired. However, when the gavel comes down on the final documents of the COP, you feel vindicated (Fig. 29.3).

Last, but not least, you can amplify your impact on the UNFCCC process by building bridges between different actor types. I have done this by straddling the fields of consulting governments, providing input as a researcher, and engaging with media. As a researcher with a large network I became engaged when in 2002 there was a movement to set up a new group of observer organizations in the climate negotiations. Previously, only environmental NGOs and business associations had been recognized as formal "constituencies." Together with my researcher friends, I lobbied with the UNFCCC Secretariat to set up the constituency of "Research and Independent NGOs" (RINGOs). The USA threatened to block this because they feared the emergence of a new group advocating for strong climate change action. Therefore, we painstakingly had to convince the Secretariat that we would not advocate specific causes, and in 2003, the RINGOs were formally recognized. I have been serving on the RINGO Steering Committee ever since. Serving a constituency is very helpful in many aspects. You have direct access to the UNFCCC Secretariat and are respected by its staff. You get access to meetings otherwise inaccessible. You routinely interact with the chairs of the different negotiation streams and the Presidency. You liaise with the other constituencies on matters of general interest. You have access to infrastructure like an office. Sometimes, you provide services that are crucial for sustaining a good spirit. For example, in Copenhagen 2009, the RINGO Steering Committee ran a process to equitably distribute the negotiation access cards allocated by the Secretariat because the host had overestimated the capacity of the venue. Without that, many observers would have left the negotiations and publicly shared their exasperation.

These strategies show that there are many ways to meaningfully engage in the international climate negotiation process. Combining these allow you to "swim like a fish in the water" during a COP. That can be an exhilarating experience.

Over almost 30 years, I have learned how to provide meaningful input into a process that is seen by many as unable to lead us toward a solution to the climate crisis. In my view, however, the UN climate negotiations offer a wide array of opportunities to push good climate solutions.

Side events allow us to bring in new topics and to engage with critical stakeholders. Anyone interested in international climate policy should start with organizing side events and actively attending those of other actors. Young, aspiring people can thus rapidly get involved. The wide range of country and institutional pavilions now available at COPs expands the range of opportunities.

Supporting country delegations allow to directly feed in proposals. This becomes particularly effective if you work with multiple countries from different regions and negotiation groups at the same COP. Of course, you need to guarantee confidentiality regarding country positions, but you can use your information to orchestrate inputs. If you are trusted by negotiators from other countries that you are not supporting directly, your suggestions can gather momentum. Obviously, your input gets more relevant, the longer you have been involved in the negotiation strand and the more people you know.

Supporting a COP presidency enables you to influence the web of decisions of a COP. Of course, you cannot control the high-level influences on the presidency, but you can feed the right people with the right ideas. Especially when pressure is high and time is short, a creative input can make a substantial difference. In the context of presidency support, the depth and strength of an international network are decisive.

Serving a constituency allows you to build bridges between many different actors. Moreover, you will benefit from infrastructural elements such as access to relevant officials and infrastructure that facilitate input into the negotiations.

If all this is combined with a deft media strategy, where one "feeds" good journalists with timely information and then gets the possibility to be quoted or interviewed, even as an individual you can leave your mark.

Obviously, such an approach requires patience and stamina. The results will not "fall from the sky." You need to constantly monitor whether your proposals actually advance the cause, and that you do not damage your reputation. You need to continuously learn. Finally, you need to keep your optimism even if confronted with a failure that seems devastating. I still remember the final plenary in Copenhagen, where the president wanted to call a vote while even a novice participant of a COP knows that the consensus principle reigns paramount. Following that blunder, the plenary broke down in disarray. However, this bad memory is outshone by the memory of French Minister Laurent Fabius gavelling through the Paris Agreement and the plenary erupting in standing ovations. So far, the UNFCCC process has overcome all crises, and I hope I will be able to constructively engage in it until my retirement.

Axel Michaelowa has a PhD in Economics and has worked on international climate policy instruments and the UN Framework Convention on Climate Change (UNFCCC) process since 1994. He is senior founding partner of Perspectives and part-time researcher at the Institute of Political Science of the University of Zurich. Axel was the lead author for the chapter on mitigation policies in the 4th and 5th Assessment Report of the IPCC. He consults private, governmental, and public institutions and has written more than 400 research articles and studies on the design of domestic climate policy instruments and international market mechanisms for mitigation. Axel is a member of the Executive Committee of the Adaptation Benefits Mechanism (ABM). Between 2006 and 2013, he served on the CDM Registration and Issuance Team of the CDM Executive Board; he was a member of the board of the Climate Cent Foundation between 2005 and 2009.

Axel has conducted capacity building initiatives on carbon markets and carbon pricing in over 40 developing countries, ranging from Algeria to Yemen. He has supported various UNFCCC COP presidencies and only missed two out of 28 Conferences of the Parties to the UNFCCC.

Website: www.perspectives.cc

LinkedIn: https://www.linkedin.com/in/axel-michaelowa-863739a/

30

More Than A Seat: Building Sustainable Ecosystems for Youth in Government

Ashley Priore

The 2016 Presidential Election was my first real introduction to American politics. While I studied American political parties in school, most notably Democrats' value of social responsibility and Republicans' belief in individual rights and freedom, I realized I was hardly taught about campaigns. 2016 taught me the power of voter engagement and that political parties weren't so rigid as textbooks made them out to be. As I volunteered for Presidential nomination Democrat Hillary Clinton in Pittsburgh, Pennsylvania, I learned that voters have beliefs on both sides of the aisle. At the end of the day, voters worry less about political labels and just want to be heard and feel like someone in government will listen. Despite the outcome of the Presidential election, I learned the importance of the phrase "every voice counts!" On the campaign trail, Secretary Clinton spoke to the voices who were shut out of positions of power in politics for too long. To me, she practiced public engagement in the truest sense of the word: listen to the voters. They are true stakeholders. This should be common knowledge, right? Every single person who can vote is a political stakeholder. If you pay taxes, you should be able to vote. If you vote, you are the boss of your elected official. Unfortunately, this idea is not practiced in current politics. In fact, it scares politicians. This is one of the reasons current government structures are not sustainable.

A. Priore (✉)
Queenside Ventures & Queens Gambit, Pittsburgh, PA, USA

Flash forward to the 2020 Presidential Election, I was so ready to fight for progressive policies. I had been writing proposals and policy ideas to share with senior staff of the Biden campaign team. I wrote emails every day to the campaign manager and other campaign staffers. I was expecting the stakeholder engagement I had experienced before with Secretary Clinton. I should have known better: when I ran for Pittsburgh Board of Education in 2018, people told me I was too young to be leaping into a political career (their exact words were "It isn't your time."). Still, I was hopeful…until someone on the Biden team told me that the 2020 election was about "voting, not policy."

My first reaction: How do you expect people to vote when you don't have a detailed policy plan? Young people need to know what the President is going to do to make lives better. What are his policies on climate change, student debt, and opportunities to engage in the White House after the election? We shouldn't just be used for our vote. What about being a stakeholder?

> *The truth is, young people aren't supposed to have a "stake" in the gam at least that is what we are taught. Young engagement in government right now is about having a seat at the table, not having a voice. Most governmental bodies have roundtables and listening sessions for young people to share their feelings and reactions to current politics. That type of engagement is not sustainable. It is one-sided.*

The bottle line: young people are stakeholders in government, and in order for the planet to thrive for future generations, we must be a part of the structures implementing policies. I didn't say we "should be" or "need to be" involved in politics. We truly must be. We are stewards of this planet and aim to address issues such as climate change, student debt, and social justice. While existing elected officials might see young people as wanting power, I view the youth in government movement as taking responsibility for our world and wanting to actually have a planet to live on.

After months of networking with former Obama Administration staffers and leading political strategists, I learned that there really never were sustainable, working structures for youth to get involved in government. Every initiative that had been spearheaded in the past had failed because the stakeholders (in this case, young people) never had access to the decision makers (the President, Vice President, or Senior Staff). For example, the individual leading the work related to young people in the White House currently is level 3 staff which means they do not have direct access to the President and are paid under $70,000 annually.

During my fight for youth in the White House, I needed to find a balance between creating a solution that young people deserved and understanding that the existing ecosystems for public engagement in government are broken. Current public engagement in government is what we might call public relations. Instead of "how can we create pipelines for engagement with the American people," it is "how can we share information about what the administration is already doing?" The second question is important in administration communications but is really secondary. Public relations is the job of the communications department. In other words, public engagement is stakeholder based, while public relations is media based.

After months of brainstorming, rewriting, and researching, I found that a White House Youth Policy Council would be the best solution. This idea came about from an existing structure: The White House Gender Policy Council. In January 2021, President Biden signed an executive order to establish the White House Gender Policy Council, formerly the White House Council on Women and Girls. Co-chaired by former Chief Strategy and Policy Officer at TIME's UP, Jennifer Klein, and United States Ambassador to Spain, Julissa Reynoso Pantaleón, the council aims to advance gender equity and equality in domestic and foreign policy implementation. According to the White House, the council works to "instill a strategic, whole-of-government approach to gender equality and gender equity." Upon its creation, Vice President Harris stated that the Council is "restoring America as a champion for women and girls." This got me thinking—why not restore America as a champion for all young people? The formation of a White House Youth Policy Council would ensure a streamlined approach to youth policy. By having advocates within the White House, President Biden and his team can ensure that needs are met and that policies are reflective of what young people care about. The vision for this council is a freestanding policy council focused on youth equity and equality within the Executive Office of the President. For example, the Youth Policy Council could lead a campaign to get young people vaccinated, advise the President on in-person vs. online instruction measures, and support each Council with outreach to young Americans. It would work in coordination with the other White House policy councils—including the Domestic Policy Council, National Security Council, and National Economic Council—and across all federal agencies to instill a strategic, whole-of-government approach to youth equality and equity.

The downside to any Executive Order is that the next President can reverse it. For example, President Biden reversed 15 Executive Orders written by the Trump Administration. However, Executive Orders set some precedent and allow statues, treaties, and provisions of the constitution to run smoothly and effectively in a time of crisis. President Franklin D. Roosevelt signed 3721 Executive Orders during his time in office. A lack of youth engagement is a crisis. Young people are ready to use their vote in 2024. Remember that.

There are three other important elements of the White House Youth Policy Council that speak to building sustainable ecosystems for youth in government. The first is the inclusion of the word "policy." The council's purpose is not to determine ways for the White House to better engage youth with internships and volunteer opportunities. That should be the job of the Office of Presidential Personnel. The council's job is to consider how to create legislation that benefits youth and speaks to their concerns. The council can work with the Office of Legislative Affairs and other senior advisors to create a pathway for youth equity and equality in the White House.

Second, the council allows for numerous youth voices to be heard rather than just one. In order to create sustainable, effective, and robust infrastructures for youth engagement (at any government level), more than one person needs to be doing the work. Many youth engagement techniques fail because there is not one person dedicated to the work or the person who handles youth engagement has other responsibilities. Another way to look at this problem is from a nonprofit sector point of view. Would you have your Program Manager also serve as the Development Manager or Marketing Manager? These three roles are truly three different jobs. As such, the person doing youth work in the White House needs to only focus on youth engagement. As it stands currently, the person leading youth work in the White House is an Associate Director who also leads White House engagement with the LGBTQ+ community and gun violence prevention community. These three important areas of focus deserve three different full-time directors for maximum impact.

Finally, the White House Youth Policy Council would require a Chair or Co-Chairs to work directly with the President. This job would be a level 1 or 2 meaning they would have access to the President and senior staff. Having access and the ear to high-level officials is a must. Oftentimes, information gets mistranslated when too many people try to share it. Having Co-Chairs who serve as level 1 or level 2 staff ensures that youth have direct access to the President.

The White House Youth Policy Council serves as a national model for sustainable engagement by youth and for youth. Elected officials can follow a similar structure that best suits their needs and governing structure. For immediate ideas or suggestions for youth engagement, the best recommendation I can give is to connect with young leaders in your network. One-off conversations do not work. Instead, have 10–15 young leaders serve as advisors in your administration. The best public engagement techniques happen when the stakeholders (aka youth) are the ones who lead the initiative. Young people know young people best! Don't assume what young people want. Ask questions, learn what you can, and listen. Listen more, talk less.

Another suggestion is considering what you want out of your youth engagement initiatives. Young people know when groups only want their engagement for checkbox purposes. If you want policy ideas and suggestions, reach out to leading youth policy groups such as the Greater Good Initiative or Student Voice. There are resources out there, and young people want to help.

If you were to ask me why youth engagement is important in two words, I'd say "the future." Young people are the ones who must live with the decisions made today by their elected officials. It's scary when you feel powerless. Young people have felt powerless for too long. It is the role of the elected official to create policies that are representative of the people and allow communities to feel uplifted and heard.

I will end this story with a brief section of my letter to President Biden. I include this note here because if elected officials are reading this, I guarantee you young people are trying to connect with your office. It's your responsibility to write back. In addition, young people understand that there are other responsibilities that elected officials must handle outside of the youth engagement crisis. However, we view youth engagement as a tool to achieve your administration's goals.

> *"Dear President Biden,*
>
> *In a time of uncertainty about COVID-19 and countless duties and responsibilities to put the United States back on stable footing, I appreciate your administration's commitment to serving young Americans and re-opening schools safely. However, with constant fires to put out, the administration is losing direct outreach to young Americans, leaving many to feel disconnected and disengaged from their government. I understand your vision of a government that works for all, so I'm here to build these relationships back better and support your administration as you further your connections, outreach, and strategy with those under 25."*

Ashley Lynn Priore is an American chess player & coach, entrepreneur, and strategist. She currently serves as the Founder, President, and CEO of Queens Gambit, a national nonprofit using chess as one of the influential tactics in building the next generation of leaders, and as the founder & CEO of Queenside Ventures, a consulting firm leading a tactical revolution where the chessboard becomes a canvas for expansive thinking, unlocking new possibilities in every piece, move, and decision. The author of numerous books, and the youngest person to run for office in the State of Pennsylvania in 2019, she is a nationally recognized leader in youth rights activism and youth policy implementation, writing and submitting an entire playbook for youth engagement in the White House for the Biden-Harris Administration. She is the founder of the White House Youth Movement, advocating for a White House Youth Policy Council via Executive Order.

31

After ESG: Is Impact Investment the New Frontier for Responsible Investing?

Grégoire Cousté

On April 20, 2010, BP's Deepwater Horizon oil platform exploded in the US Gulf of Mexico off the coast of Louisiana, killing 11 people and spewing more than 130 million gallons of oil into the Gulf of Mexico. The impact on surrounding ecosystems and the lives of those affected is still being felt today. It has been described as the worst environmental disaster in US history. Beyond this human and ecological disaster is a financial calamity that changed the lives of ordinary people across the world. BP's stock market valuation fell by 55%, or US$100 billion, in the 2 months after the explosion, jeopardizing the savings of thousands who had bet their pensions on BP, which until then had been seen as a jewel of industry, a safe bet.

However, the warning signs had been there before the disaster. Nonfinancial analysts had warned about the growing risk of accidents at BP since the arrival of then-CEO Tony Hayward, raising concerns over his approach to safety (6 months after the disaster, Hayward resigned). Public equity investors remained oblivious to these warnings. Or if they did, they didn't heed them.

The Deepwater Horizon example crystallizes one of the key challenges the world of finance, and by extension humanity as a whole, still faces today: the separation of environmental and social impact from financial

---

G. Cousté (✉)
Forum pour l'Investissement Responsable (FIR)—Sustainable Investment Forum (French SIF), Paris, France
e-mail: gregoire.couste@frenchsif.org

imperatives in the eyes of investors. For sustainable and responsible investing to gain traction, the concept needs to be clearly defined, measured, and communicated to the general public, retail investors, and pension fund managers.

For the past two decades, we have been advocating for investors to include an analysis of environmental and social impact in their decisions. By scrutinizing environmental, social, and corporate governance policies, one can manage risk far more effectively. After all, this is fundamental to any investor's job. Our argument is as relevant today as it was back in 2010 when the shortcomings of BP's governance had a very real impact on investors.

Another example is the Volkswagen emissions scandal, also known as "Dieselgate." When, in 2015, it was revealed that 11 million VW cars worldwide were emitting 40 times as much nitrogen dioxide as they should because the manufacturer had cheated on emissions tests, its stock market value collapsed. Again, nonfinancial analysts had warned of governance issues that led to this cheating.

A study conducted in France showed that responsible investors had listened to these analysts and, as a result, had found themselves less exposed to the market downturn than their peers. The conclusion is that such analysis is essential for good risk management. It enables arbitrage by integrating varied information that is consistent with companies' business models.

In retrospect, 2015 was a significant year for sustainable development and responsible finance. That September, just 2 months before the United Nations Climate Change Conference took place in Paris, an event shook the international financial community to its core. Mark Carney, then-governor of the Bank of England and chair of the Financial Stability Board (G20 Central Bankers), gave a speech that was to leave a lasting impression.[1]

At Lloyds of London, he spoke of "breaking the tragedy on the horizon," the mismatch between the short- and long-term interests of finance and systemic risk linked to global warming. This historic speech was received with polite applause rather than a standing ovation. Then, at the end of November, at the opening of the UN Climate Change Conference in Paris, Carney began taking the steps he said were needed, launching the Task Force on Climate-Related Financial Disclosure (TCFD), which will become the international standard in a few years. The TCFD urges companies and investors to produce quality data to manage climate risk.

---

[1] https://www.bankofengland.co.uk/-/media/boe/files/speech/2015/breaking-the-tragedy-of-the-horizon-climate-change-and-financial-stability.pdf.

The rationale is clear: to implement corrective policies and prevent "the tragedy on the horizon," first, we must measure the risk. Mark Carney appointed a leader to head the TCFD—billionaire, former mayor of New York City, and one-time US presidential candidate, Michael Bloomberg. This choice illustrates the ambition central bankers now have in addressing the climate issue. This positioning has enabled TCFD to establish itself as the international framework for private players.

But that's not all. In its role as the host of the 2015 UN Climate Change Conference, France is actively demonstrating its commitment to achieving a sustainable future. According to Article 173 of the French law on energy transition for green growth, institutional investors and asset managers are required to disclose their approaches to deal with climate and other sustainability-related issues as well as corporate responsibility within their investment policies.

The approach is somewhat in the spirit of the Anglo-Saxon model: either you comply, or you explain; there is no mandate to act, only an obligation to disclose. Of course, publicly declaring that you are doing nothing to solve the greatest challenges facing humanity would be a PR (public relations) disaster. Consequently, investors who were previously inactive have been spurred to take action.

Today, although not all players have fully implemented relevant policies, there have been substantial shifts in attitude among many French entities, especially the major players who constitute the bulk of the market. Furthermore, this legislation has inspired other regulations, particularly at the European level, steering many financial institutions toward a significantly more sustainable and responsible path.

It was also in 2015 that the UN's Millennium Goals were transformed into Sustainable Development Goals (SDGs). These encompass 17 objectives outlining how, as a species, we will confront the significant challenges of the twenty-first century. These include poverty, inequality, human, education, and environmental preservation. In the context of addressing climate change, a specific and clear objective is to maintain global warming below 1.5 °C.

Companies and investors are progressively adopting the SDGs as a universal framework. However, it is imperative that we adopt a holistic perspective. We cannot only look at one objective in isolation without considering the potential negative impacts this objective may have on others.

For instance, consider a company that has improved the productivity of a crop, claiming a positive impact on eradicating hunger (SDG 2). However, the measures taken to increase crop yield per hectare have contributed to soil degradation and pollution (SDG 15), high water consumption (SDG 6), and have negative effects on workers' health (SDG 3). In this scenario, it would be challenging to conclude that this company has had an overall positive impact. Is it, then, a suitable company to invest in?

Most likely, not! To consider whether a company, on balance, has a positive impact, we must look at all the SDGs affected by a company's products and services, evaluate whether the impact is positive or negative, and make an overall assessment. Only then can it be decided whether we should invest in a company or not.

The European Union is adopting a comprehensive global perspective in the development of its green taxonomy framework. The objective is to qualify and categorize the activities of companies considered green or environmentally sustainable, thus enabling the creation of financial products that align with the environmental goals of investors. Of course, the question is complex. The construction of this taxonomy is, therefore, guided by the principle of "do no significant harm."

Once again, a holistic approach is needed. An activity that excels in pollution control efficiency should not have a significant negative effect on climate or biodiversity, for instance. When it comes to greenhouse gas emissions, we cannot just look at a company's direct emissions (referred to as Scope 1 and 2); we must also consider indirect emissions (referred to as Scope 3), which concerns the upstream supply chain and product usage downstream.

Without taking this holistic approach, the likelihood of success is limited, or even non-existent. Ultimately, the transitions to less ecologically damaging energy sources are undertaken for the sake of humanity—including the people living in the present day.

This transition leads us to the concept of Impact Finance, which is the new frontier of responsible investing. Progressively, the definition of responsible finance is going beyond the influence of environmental, social, and governance criteria in informing investment decisions. Instead, it now involves decisions based on specific positive environmental and social impacts an investment can generate. This approach can be described as "investing for impact."

This shift in mindset holds the potential to contribute to the creation of a better future for us all. The investment community has the real power to hold the corporate world accountable. It can serve as a force for good, compelling companies to act in the interest of us all. By formalizing their environmental and social intentions and giving them equal importance to their financial goals, investors can play a pivotal role in helping humanity avert environmental calamities in the future.

Grégoire Cousté joined French SIF, the founding member of the European Sustainable Investment Forum association Eurosif, in 2009. He is also a member of the French governmental Greenfin Label Committee and a board member of INEC, the National Institute for Circular Economy. Prior to this, Grégoire worked as a journalist at the news radio BFM Business and at the news agency Dioranews, where he managed editorial partnerships. An expert in strategic communication, he led the public affairs and strategic communication activities of Nextep, a consulting firm focused on health economics and the pharmaceutical industry, and was appointed the Communication Director of the International Union Against Tuberculosis and Lung Disease (IUATLD). Grégoire graduated from the French IPAG Business School and CNAM, National Conservatory of Arts and Crafts in Health and Development. He is a part-time teacher at IAE Lyon School of Management (Jean Moulin University Lyon-France), and as an SRI professional, Grégoire is regularly invited to speak in business schools such as ESCP Europe, HEC or Kedge Business School. Grégoire is a coauthor of the book "ISR & Finance Responsable" (SRI & Responsible Finance), coordinated by Professor Nicolas Mottis and published by Ellipses.

32

Why and How We Should Start Measuring Real Impact

Jan Moellmann

The Problem with Today's Sustainability Reports

Sustainability reports do not report on sustainability! The issue at hand arises from insufficient depth in the measurements (pertaining to what is measured and where), shallow reporting requirements (relating to why these measurements are taken), and the inherent challenges of accurately measuring real or tangible sustainability impact (in terms of how it is measured). If we want true accountability, the eradication of greenwashing scandals, and the capacity to make informed sustainability-driven investment and management decisions that maximize impact, we need to change this soon.

Over the last few years, sustainability reporting has finally picked up speed, mainly driven by regulations such as the Sustainable Finance Disclosure Regulation (SFDR) and Corporate Sustainability Reporting Directive (CSRD) in the European Union, or the Act on Corporate Due Diligence Obligations in Supply Chains in Germany. Overall, this is great news! Particularly in the realm of carbon accounting, we see progress with an increasing number of companies reporting Scope 1 and Scope 2 emissions, or even following the Task Force on Climate-Related Financial Disclosures (TCFD) and including Scope 3.

J. Moellmann (✉)
Leonardo, Frankfurt am Main, Germany

Technical University Munich (TUM), Munich, Germany
e-mail: jan@leonardo-impact.com

However, sustainability is often assessed based on a sustainability initiative and not on the outcomes that could, in turn, contribute to a more sustainable future. This is particularly the case regarding the social dimension of sustainability—represented by the letter S in ESG. The problem begins with the regulations that require companies to draft reports in the first place. Too many required indicators are still based on "yes/no" questions such as "Do you have an anti-forced labor policy?" Whether forced labor has actually taken place or not is neither measured nor reported! The policy appears to be sufficient and justifies achieving a high sustainability score. However, the logic is in fact the reverse. Most sustainability reports have traditionally been crafted primarily for the sake of risk mitigation. They tend to focus on a single materiality, addressing just one question in the end: "What is the impact of sustainability issues on the organization's financial and operational performance?" The critical question we should be asking, although, is: "What is the impact of an organization on the planet and the people?"

I do acknowledge that the trend is heading in the right direction. Moreover, I also understand that not every organization has sustainability at its core but of those which do, or which claim to have, we should expect more. Therefore, do the reports that have been drawn up by impact investors and their impact-driven portfolio companies look any different? Rarely so! The general issue here is that reports rely on proxies and secondary data. In the case of proxies, indicators such as sustainability policies or output measures (e.g., the number of delivered products) are used to communicate the sustainability impact of an organization. In the case of secondary data, information is taken from other data sources, regardless of whether it is comparable to the current organization, to assume a distinct impact.

Allow me to give you a concrete example: for an impact-driven organization providing electricity access that is based on solar power in rural areas in West Africa, impact measurement should not be reduced to the amount of paper waste the company has, its electricity consumption, or gender diversity in the management team. Neither should the impact be reported based on proxies or secondary data, such as similar electrification projects in a different geographical setting and a different time zone. To provide a meaningful answer to the fundamental query an impact report should address, primary data directly from the projects on the ground are needed. The real question should thus be: "What is the impact of the organization on the people in rural areas of West Africa and on their environment?"

In summary, the problem is that sustainability is not measured where sustainability effects actually occur. This is ineffective at its best and greenwashing at its worst. Particularly regarding social impact, there is also a philosophical aspect to consider: Can we simply assume the impact a particular organization, product, service, or project has without asking the people who are actually affected?

My Personal Path to Finding a Solution

The solution that I am proposing is quite straightforward: measure sustainability impact where sustainability effects actually occur, that is, outside the organization, in the real world, and ensure that the measurement is based on primary data. And yes, in the case of social impact, this would involve asking those people who have been directly affected.

My conviction comes from having worked for several years in the rural electrification of the Global South (Yes, the example mentioned above has not been made up!). Repeatedly, impact investors were asking for impact reports, and increasingly I was frustrated by the current status of the space, believing that the questions asked and the indicators proposed were not doing justice to the impact the company was generating.

In search of an answer, I started a Ph.D. program at TU Munich to better understand how impact organizations measure and report their sustainability impact. As part of my research, I started interviewing customers of the rural electrification company for whom I was working with the aim of gaining insights into the real impact of the organization's activities on those who are directly experiencing the impact. These interviews were tremendously insightful, shedding light on both potential negative effects and tangible improvements in people's lives. These positive real-life changes had hitherto been concealed behind the overly simplistic metric the company was previously reporting on: "Number of people with access to electricity." I started talking to many other organizations, received similar insights again and again and found the following: (1) organizations would like to understand the real effects (rather than their office paper waste in kilograms); (2) such deep impact reporting would be appreciated by key stakeholders, even if they did not ask for it yet (pointing out a potentially positive ROI (return-on-investment) on deep impact reporting); and (3) obtaining the data for such deep impact reporting is challenging.

To be honest, this challenge is not surprising. Talking to people is both time-consuming and expensive. And so is finding the right indicators for measuring deep impact and collecting, processing, analyzing, and visualizing the data. It does not sound very scalable, does it? And yet, I would still argue that it should be at the heart of what impact-driven organizations are doing and what impact investors request. First, only these data can enable us to transform capital markets and the economy by being able to guide resources into the most impactful projects and organizations. Second, simply because only what gets measured can be managed.

When looking particularly at the letter S in the acronym ESG again, in which the social impact based on primary data is assessed, for example, by asking people who are directly affected by a product or project, we must remember that it also has other important benefit. This should matter to any organization, not only impact-driven organizations; it is the path toward being customer-centric. Understanding one's customers and the effects a product or project has on them is core to the success of any company that has scaled in the past. Therefore, even when this topic is approached from a growth and scaling viewpoint, I would argue that these data are crucial.

So, how do we get this data? How can we unleash its full potential most effectively by making it a crucial part when designing products and projects, managing companies, and guiding resources?

I propose a solution that is based on the following three principles: (1) measure deep impact; (2) follow standardized approaches; and (3) utilize state-of-the-art technology.

Measure Deep Impact

OK, I know I am repeating myself here, but this point still needs to come across. We need to start measuring sustainability impact where sustainability effects actually occur. This requires primary data, the willingness to talk to affected stakeholders, and implementing data inputs outside the boundaries of the organization. Secondary data and proxies suffice for an impact due diligence pre-investment, but they cannot be applicable to impact monitoring or when reporting post-investment. This is because it is just not possible to use this kind of data to take meaningful steps toward optimizing sustainability performance. It is inactionable, impractical, and often irrelevant data that does not answer the questions that should be asked at this stage. Additionally, data on company operations (the paper waste and gender diversity in the board I mentioned earlier) are important to obtain a holistic understanding. Nevertheless, it should not be the main focus in the case of impact investments, as accountability should be bottom-up from the people who are affected and not top-down from a regulatory entity or investment fund.

Follow Standardized Approaches

Yes, standardization is a problem in this jungle of different measurement approaches, manifold metrics, and diverse frameworks. However, it should not be an excuse for inaction, nor should it be necessary to design yet another impact framework or another in-house solution that is not comparable and that could have the risk of not being reliable or valid, that is, the metrics do not measure what they are aimed to measure. Over the past few years, some truly good approaches have been published. The Sustainable Development Goals provide a globally accepted framework and a common language as well as 231 scientific indicators, including clear methodologies on how to use them. Other approaches such as the "IRIS+" catalog of metrics from the Global Impact Investing Network (GIIN) or the Harmonized Indicators for Private Sector Operations (HIPSO) provide helpful frameworks toward consolidation and standardization as well as the Operating Principles for Impact Management or the Five Dimensions of Impact. Moreover, regulatory guidelines and directives can contribute here—even though they often do not go into depth enough, as described earlier. Reporting requirements for Article 9 funds, i.e., financial products with sustainable investment as their primary objective, under the Sustainable Finance Disclosure Regulation (SFDR) are a step in the right direction. I sincerely believe that standardized metrics are possible. At least when we apply them per sector, we should obtain certain indicators that enable impact to be aggregated and compared. This would again provide a major step to guide resources into the most impactful organizations. It would also provide the basis for pricing impact, similar to the development of carbon certificate markets, and thus incentivize organizations to generate more impact by making it directly monetizable.

Utilize State-of-the-Art Technology

Scalability is a challenge here, I admit. However, technology can make the job of impact and sustainability managers much easier. The problem starts with the question "What should be measured?" Then, the answer will hopefully comply with the second principle mentioned above, that is, "Follow standardized approaches." Imagine a recommendation engine that drafts your impact framework in alignment with acknowledged standards all based on a few key inputs, such as your sector, your geographical location, your latest sustainability report, and a few customer interviews. The latest developments from the realm of natural language processing (NLP) appear to be very promising and they could significantly reduce the cost and effort involved in all that needs to take place before even a single measurement has been conducted. After which, impact investment funds and operating companies spend hundreds of hours every quarter collecting, processing, aggregating, and visualizing data for reports. I am not suggesting that technology can solve the entire struggle here. Again, I still believe that data must come from the actual impact touchpoints, involving surveys and data from IoT (Internet of Things) devices and ERP (Enterprise Resource Planning) systems. Nevertheless, integrations, as well as automatically generated, scientifically reliable, and valid surveys, can tremendously reduce the effort. A software solution can automate the entire data pipeline, making the manual processing and aggregation of data points from different data sources and portfolio companies obsolete. Machine learning-powered data validation can spot anomalies and suspicious behavior and thus automatically increase data quality and reporting credibility. This could save hundreds of thousands of Euros that are typically invested in field audits that can currently be afforded only by larger organizations, which sidelines smaller impact organizations from participating in mechanisms such as carbon credits. Credibility is key here, but it can be created through standardized data pipelines that reduce the risk of human error and manipulation while ensuring traceability. This could be the basis for the tokenization of impact performance, which could help to drive more capital into impactful initiatives. Finally, the process of generating insights from vast amounts of data can be simplified through smart visualizations that are automatically displayed on dashboards and in verified impact reports. Imagine analytics features that help to identify patterns and maximize your impact. To the best of my knowledge, this software does not exist. However, the technological progress that has been made, particularly in the realm of NLP and machine learning generally, gets me excited that we are slowly getting there.

These three principles helped me as an impact manager at the rural electrification company to understand more about the socioeconomic impact that the company aims to push forward. The results were not perfect, but they were much better than what was available before, and the stakeholders of the company were impressed. Nonetheless, it also soon became apparent that a single company cannot and should not perform such a technological development project independently—at least not the typical impact-driven organization. Therefore, I embarked on a new journey to build a software solution based on the three abovementioned principles. At *leonardo.*, we are doing just that. We are on a lengthy journey, and we genuinely believe that we can help impact organizations to measure what actually matters. In doing so, we aim to move the entire sector toward reporting real impact (and not just the kilograms of paper waste ☺).

Key Insights and Lessons

I will say it one more time: start by measuring sustainability impact where sustainability effects actually occur. Having said this, I encourage each and every reader to challenge their understanding of sustainability reporting.

If you are involved in impact investing or an impact-driven organization, I challenge you to start measuring real impact. Go deeper. Measure what you truly want to know about your products or investments. Measure whether you are achieving the goals set out in your mission statement, as that is what brought you here in the first place.

If you are involved in a more traditional company trying to juggle the demands of new sustainability regulations: I know it's hard. I also know that much of what I said might feel impossible today when you have multi-tier supply chains and sell millions of products every year globally. Start where you are and ask yourself whether there is a way to move one step further than what you need to measure for regulatory compliance already today. Just one step toward measuring the impact of your organization on people and the planet, and not the other way around. At *leonardo*, we call this "ESG+".

And if you are none of the above, you are still a consumer or perhaps a small-scale investor. Do not underestimate the kind of impact your consumption and investing choices can have. Question the impact of the products you are consuming and the companies you are investing in. Start asking questions. If enough of us do this, then companies and regulators will have to move toward deep-impact reporting.

Jan Moellmann is co-founder and CEO @ *leonardo.impact GmbH*, and a doctoral candidate @ TUM School of Management. After 4 years as the Finance Director of the social startup Africa GreenTec and while conducting research about the topic as a doctoral candidate at TUM, Jan discovered not only the great value that trustworthy impact data have for sustainability-focused enterprises, but also how hard it is to obtain these data—leading him to co-found leonardo. leonardo aims to make deep impact measurement, verification, and reporting easy and credible. Jan holds master's degrees in Engineering Management from Technical University (TU) Braunschweig as well as Industrial Engineering from Georgia Tech, where he focused on sustainability optimization of businesses, processes, and systems through data. He and his wife Lena live in Frankfurt, Germany, and love to hike and bike through mountains whenever they get the chance. E-mail: jan@leonardo-impact.com, LinkedIn: https://www.linkedin.com/in/jan-moellmann-2b8b3611a/.

Part IV

Art as a Driver for Transformation

33

From KALABATOLA to TO BE: A Transformative Journey in the Twenty-First Century

Joël Nankin

Our arrival in this Caribbean space is the result of the deportation of thousands of captured human beings, survivors of the Middle Passage, and resisters who reinvented themselves.

All the violence of these crossings and of the conquests of one world by another are suggested in the *"Gravée dans ma mémoire"* (Engraved in my memory) canvas inscribed in the KALABATOLA series (Fig. 33.1). This series was an imperative to question the humanity in each and every one of us to bring up the submerged truths and open wide doors of memories. Otherwise, how can we build ourselves firmly? KALABATOLA brought together individuals and individualities and gave birth to monologs and dialogs, leaving words historically charged with meaning permanently etched in space. The search for "YO" (them) within ourselves was rewarded by the path of a life rooted in resistance ("NÈGZISTANS"). A little-known history, a repressed history, yet this dark part of our heritage is terribly present. We must reckon with it to be. "To BE" would be the fulfillment of the individual in its depths and within the smallest cell (family) to the largest group (community, city, country) (Fig. 33.2). The decentered character, occupying only the right third of the canvas, seems to want to escape. However, she is very much there, enveloped by two mysterious red forms. She asserts herself through her

---

KALABATOLA is a creole word, which means literally the hold of the ship; there is no memory of a ship except for the one transporting slaves (bateau négrier).

J. Nankin (✉)
Paris, France

© The Author(s), under exclusive license to Springer Nature Switzerland AG 2024
B. Bernard-Rau (ed.), *Sustainability Stories*, https://doi.org/10.1007/978-3-031-52300-7_33

expression. What can be said about the surrounding space? In fact, this individual, before reaching the pinnacle of the pyramid, had to live and confront social tensions in a colonial world. This is also what the Guadeloupean poet Sonny RUPAIRE portrays in *"Cette igname brisée qu'est ma terre natale"* (This broken yam that is my homeland).[1] The canvas titled *"And Red was the City,"* as mentioned in Rupaire's poem *"L'œil,"* is not an illustration of the poem. Rather, it is a reflection on this City, which, despite its weathered appearance of glory in shades of gray and black, radiates the accumulated red of countless lives (Fig. 33.3).

This quickly sketches our almost carceral universe, not because it is island-like but primarily because it is colonial. This bubble makes it difficult to see external things, even the crucial issues and major challenges of this third millennium. Some of these challenges should be calling us, mobilizing us, and doing so massively. The soils of banana-growing regions are permanently contaminated by the chlordecone pesticide (also the waterways by runoff) in a small territory of only 1700 square kilometers. Water, a vital element, is sorely lacking. Renewable and green energy (e.g., hydro, wind, solar, biomass, geothermal), all possible and available sources on the island, would provide us with cleaner air, reduce the production of greenhouse gases, create jobs, increase community revenues, reduce the production costs of nongreen sources, and above all, contribute to our energy independence and more (Fig. 33.1).

But…

The observer's eye could seize the *"Gravée dans ma mémoire"* canvas to embrace the vast concern of migratory waves. These global flows, totaling over 280 million international migrants today, do not concern only the infamous islands of Lampedusa (Italy) and Lesbos (Greece). Guadeloupe also receives nationals from Caribbean countries (Haiti, Santo Domingo, Dominica). These multidirectional migrations are expected to intensify with the projected and anticipated population explosion. This exponential growth of the world population, a revolution even, is a major challenge of this millennium that will exacerbate other social, ecological, and economic challenges. We will inherit a crowded planet where dissatisfaction will reign because our basic needs will not be met due to extreme scarcity. *"And Red was the City"* might be the city of wasted lives, of homeless wanderers, of sick bodies, of dreamless

---

[1] Sonny RUPAIRE, Cette igname brisée qu'est ma terre natale/Soni RIPÈ, Gran parad Ti kou baton, bilingual French/Creole, Edition Jasor, 1971

Fig. 33.1 Joel Nankin's painting titled "Gravée dans ma mémoire" (Engraved in my memory)

minds. The issue of biodiversity is not just the preservation of species and ecosystems. We, Men and Women, Human Species, one species among a million, need protection too (Figs. 33.1 and 33.2).

And if painting, Art, could contribute to strengthening our humanity so that tomorrow, respect for the Other in all their conditions is the guarantor of our survival in this World.

Let us shatter the colonial bubble...

Lasserre, Villa Nusch, 24 September 2023.

Manifesto

Pictorial art has swept over me with a force that surpasses even the primal violence of our entry into this world. This emergence, described poetically as a "poorly shod tooth in the dazzling dentures of the Caribbean",[2] the

---

[2] Guy TIROLIEN, BALLES D'OR (poem titled "Fruits dépareillés"), Présence Africaine, 1961, p. 37. Free translation from French.

Fig. 33.2 Joel Nankin's painting titled "ÊTRE (TO BE)" (Photograph by: Bernard Boucard. All rights reserved)

deportations of "peoples from abysses that have surged forth",[3] and still enduring chains of domination. How can we exist (or prove one's existence) in the world as a colonized person, a world where one's history, which is also that of all of humanity is scorned, hidden, and rendered conspicuously absent? As an artist, my commitment lies in unveiling the masks that obscure our potential for survival, rekindling our connection with the future and breathing life into it. Through the process of scarifying the canvas with "a triple will is tearing me

---

[3] Aimé CÉSAIRE, FERREMENTS (poem titled "Hors des jours étrangers"), Éditions du Seuil, 1960, p. 81. Free translation from French.

Fig. 33.3 Joel Nankin's painting titled "Et Rouge était la Ville" (And Red was the City) (Photograph by: Bernard Boucard. All rights reserved)

apart",[4] I expose the raw essence of the canvas. The drips of the Water element wash away the indelible mark of History, creating the subtle vibrations essential to capture the tension of the subject...

I declare my verticality as a Man open to the World, "against the sordidness of History…".[5]

---

[4] Guy TIROLIEN, BALLES D'OR (poem titled "Fruits dépareillés"), Présence Africaine, 1961, p. 37. Free translation from French.

[5] Aimé CÉSAIRE, cited by Madeleine ROUSSEAU, in Présence Africaine n°4, p.593. "Painting, one of the few weapons we have left against the sordidness of history. Wilfredo LAM is here to attest to that. And such is one of the meanings of Wilfredo LAM's painting, richer than any other: it halts the conquistador's action; it signifies his failure in the bloody saga of bastardization with its insolent assertion that something is now happening in the Caribbean." Free translation from French.

Joël Nankin A painter, musician, and political activist, Joël Nankin has made his life a struggle for a Guadeloupean identity. Nankin was born in 1955 in Guadeloupe, an archipelago of small islands nestled between the Atlantic Ocean to the east and the Caribbean Sea to the west. He both resides and creates his art within his Atelier, a sanctuary located in the heart of Lasserre, Morne-à-l'Eau. A self-taught artist, Nankin embarked on his artistic journey in 1989, following a transformative chapter of his life that saw him spend 6 years imprisoned as a political activist, a member of the militant autonomous organization *"Alliance Révolutionnaire Caraibe (ARC) — Caribbean Revolutionary Alliance"* located in Guadeloupe in the 1980s. This period of incarceration served as a crucible for his creative spirit, igniting a profound connection with the world of art. His preferred medium of artistic expression is painting, a craft he has mastered over the years, distinguished by his use of acrylics, Indian ink, and spray paint among other techniques. Through his vibrant canvases, Nankin weaves stories that resonate within the soul and celebrate the rich tapestry of life in Guadeloupe. He has risen to become an iconic Guadeloupean figure and one of the cofounders of the *Mouvman Kiltirel Akiyo (Cultural Movement Akiyo)*, an organization that, from its inception, has positioned itself as a militant force for cultural resistance and renaissance in Guadeloupe, forever changing the discourse on heritage and identity. In 2019, Nankin presented five of his works at La Biennale di Venezia. Guadeloupe was represented for the first time in its history with its own pavilion at the Biennale as part of the *"Personal Structures, Identities"* exhibition at Palazzo Mora Venezia.

34

Planetary Perspectives: Making Sense of the Sustainability Transformation through Art

Samuel Huber

We know from our own experience that the climate crisis is more than a set of numbers. Nevertheless, today's sustainability discourse mainly revolves around data, temperatures, targets, taxes, compensation, and emission trading schemes. Successes are assessed in CO_2 equivalents, proven by recycling rates and the percentage of secondary materials used in a new luxury car.

In regard to the climate crisis, we are going all in on technology and the potential solutions we hope it produces. Spearheading these efforts are experts such as scientists, technologists, engineers, and mathematicians, also known as the STEM disciplines. These brilliant people share the mission to significantly change the grim trajectory we are headed toward, but what if the climate crisis cannot be solved by technology? At least not by technology alone?

The more time I spend working on the sustainability transformation, the more I realize how the way we deal with its challenges is dominated by the rational language of quantity that attempts to put the complexity of our ecosystems into measurable entities. The exact sciences have regularly succeeded in providing answers to problems we could not yet come to grips with. Thus, our tendency toward what we can measure is fully understandable and helps us to grasp the enormity of the problem, even though this could mean that we decide to boil down the complexity of the world's interconnected ecosystems into a single two-degree target.

S. Huber (✉)
Zurich University of the Arts (ZHdK), Zurich, Switzerland
e-mail: samuel@forplanetstrategylab.com

However, of all the complex problems we face today, the climate emergency is by far the most wicked. According to Rittel & Webber (1973), wicked problems are a special type of system problems that do not present themselves in a clearly formulated and defined form. Instead, they are characterized by a lack of information, an overwhelming diversity of involved stakeholders, and an entangled mess of dependencies that are hard to isolate and trace. As a result, there is not a clearly defined problem with one single solution; instead, there is an ongoing process of understanding. This dynamic makes it difficult to describe wicked problems in a stable quantitative way. Moreover, they need to be continuously defined as they unfold over time. The problem therefore becomes a process.

Fortunately, since the earliest days of humanity, a widespread practice has existed that is well-suited to engage with wicked problems. Art is an oftentimes overlooked but crucial piece of the puzzle in understanding how we can transform our societies, economies, and ecologies to achieve a regenerative symbiosis. However, art cannot unfold in the sterile environment of scientific labs, which produce much of today's knowledge. Instead, art and creative practices thrive when embedded in the social and ecological fabric of our planet. Their diversity of perspectives and resulting integrative capacity perfectly complement the specialized knowledge we have accumulated to such an extent that transdisciplinary collaboration has become a quest for translation. Nonetheless, it is precisely such radical collaboration that is needed if we want to tackle the wicked problems of the climate emergency successfully. My story thus tells how art and creative practice have helped me to see beyond my own discipline in order to engage in deep collaboration with a variety of stakeholders—humans and nonhumans alike.

My story starts in New York City, or more precisely, on the rooftop of Manhattan's Summons Court. Nestled between Leonard Street and Broadway, the courthouse building and its renaissance-revival façade were crowned with a clocktower enclosed by four large clock faces. Each morning, long lines would form outside the building with people waiting for their court hearings. Each morning, the lines served as a reminder of the inequalities that riddle America's legal system to this day. Moreover, each morning, I would pass the long line, hush into the elevator, take it all the way up to the 13th floor, and be immersed in art.

Back in 1973, the underused top floor of the increasingly dilapidated building was occupied by an artist collective to create a home for New York's thriving art scene. Even 40 years later, when I finally found my way there as an intern, the Clocktower Art Gallery stood strong. It took in various artists and local talents by offering artist residencies, only to send their voices and messages around the globe again with its in-house art radio station. The Clocktower Gallery, led by MoMA PS1 founder Alanna Heiss, was a local institution. It not only preserved the oral history of the area and its artists but also offered refuge and neighborly help during hard times, a service which I observed first hand when Hurricane Sandy struck the city and left lower Manhattan in the dark.

Having grown up next to a forest on the sides of a hill (which, outside of Switzerland, most people would probably refer to as a mountain), I was always drawn to places with a view. Whenever the weather would allow, I would make sure to have my lunch breaks on the gallery's rooftop, which was accessible through the narrow stairs of the Clocktower. Whereas the building had since been walled in by much larger structures, the emptiness of the roof and the surprising angles one could catch in between the skyscrapers still rendered it a breathtaking viewpoint.

It was during one of these lunch breaks when I suddenly noticed a man watering a number of tiny pots with even tinier seedlings. As I went over, I realized it was David Horvitz, a conceptual artist whose work spans across a variety of mediums or materialities and who had apparently dedicated his time to plants for now. He had just started his residency at the Clocktower Gallery, and he was tending to 55 honey-locust trees, which he had germinated and potted. However, he was not an ordinary gardener. He had collected the seeds in Zuccotti Park, a prime location where the Occupy Wall Street protests had taken place during the previous year. In 2011, hundreds of people who called themselves the 99% had raised their voices against the rising economic inequality and the defining role of large corporations in keeping this exploitative system going. The seeds came from the very trees that had witnessed the anger, fear, and hopelessness of the people who had camped there for weeks on end. After the hurricane, most seed pods had been blown to the ground, where David collected them. Now, he used the Clocktower Gallery as an incubator, and when the weather was nice, he would let the seedlings breathe the somewhat fresh New York air on the rooftop (Figs. 34.1 and 34.2).

It took me many more years, many more experiences, and many more struggles to understand what was really happening with the 55 tiny trees. After my time in the exciting New York art scene, I slowly transitioned to the design field. In contrast to art, design, and especially design thinking, are heavily intertwined with business practices and their overarching quest to create value. Having moved to the Berlin startup ecosystem, I built apps, researched user patterns, and assembled elements into powerful platforms, all with the ultimate goal of generating value for users. As most users are

Fig. 34.1 David Horvitz with the germinated and potted seedlings of honey-locust trees (Photograph by: Samuel Huber. All rights reserved)

Fig. 34.2 David Horvitz watering seedlings on the rooftop of the Clocktower Gallery in New York City (Photograph by: Samuel Huber. All rights reserved)

also customers, our work seamlessly translated into business value. This clarity was godsent, as the breathtaking speed of the digital transformation made everyone look for something to hold on to, a lighthouse, a simple answer. There was so much to do. We had found our goal by creating value for users and by making sure that we could measure it: Optimizing retention metrics, net promoter scores, and the time spent on achieving a single task. It was almost like an obsession.

Only a drastic change of pace, which came about at the start of my Ph.D. studies, enabled me to see more clearly again. Moving on from endless to-do lists to suddenly being confronted with empty pages and open questions made me again realize how blind I had been. Whereas my struggle to optimize value for humans was an honorable undertaking, I had missed out on the fact that we humans do not exist within a vacuum. Instead, we are tightly embedded in an ecosystem. The heuristic that defined my early career was flawed. I had always been aware of stakeholders, but to me, these were equal to the powerful human actors who ran the show at the leading companies I was collaborating with. My studies made me see that there are many more stakeholders to consider: direct and indirect ones, powerful and marginalized ones, and human and nonhuman ones. My past practice had taken all of them for granted. If they had ever surfaced in my work, then it was simply by chance and probably not to their advantage. I realized I needed to take them more seriously and to deliberately make them appear in my practice, even if it meant that everything would become much more complex.

The 55 honey-locust trees at the Clocktower Gallery had been taken seriously even before they were born. David Horvitz saw them and their "parents," as he would call them, as silent participants in the 2011 protests whose message lived on within them. He would find people willing to exchange breaths with the trees. Their CO_2 for the plant's oxygen appeared to be such a simple transaction when I observed it for the first time, but now I see the beauty of it. Participants would just sit there in silence, together with the young tree, slowly blowing air in its direction. It was a rare moment of care and the realization that they were indeed one. The tiny trees and the humans, remembering together what had happened in the park during the Occupy Movement, the shared struggles and hopes.(Fig. 34.3)

Toward the end of his residency, David was looking for 55 people to each carry one tree and stop by Zuccotti Park to meet the parents one more time before the trees would finally find new homes in the gardens of museums, libraries, and educational institutions. There, they would continue growing as silent reminders of what could have been a tipping point. Recently, David Horvitz told me that one tree at Bard College was almost five meters

Fig. 34.3 Direct call from David Horvitz to exchange breaths with trees (Photograph by: Samuel Huber. All rights reserved)

(approximately 16 feet) high when he last visited it. I realized later that throughout the whole process, the trees were being treated as actors and as stakeholders in the proceedings of the city. They were part of the city. They had agency.

Today, I am convinced that it is precisely this very perspective that will have a wide-ranging influence on how we engage with the sustainability transformation. We need a planetary perspective that encompasses both human and nonhuman actors and that shows how they relate to our planet's ecological and societal systems. While quantitative practices excel at understanding the defined and static elements of such networks, they fall short when dealing with the dynamic and emergent qualities of the relationships involved. A planetary perspective goes beyond the quantitative descriptions of individual elements and emphasizes the intricate relationships that encompass them. Relationships that transcend human actors and intertwine them with their nonhuman counterparts. It is a language and a sensation that we, humans, cannot easily understand and that we first need to make sense of, not as individuals, but as a collective whole.

In the late 1960s, Canadian communication theorist and educator Marshall McLuhan (1968-1970) wrote to the readers of his newsletter that he thought of art as a special type of DEW line, a Distant Early Warning system that could reliably tell the existing culture what is beginning to happen to it. Greatly influenced by a world caught in the relentless grip of the Cold War, for it to now requires further explanation to resonate in the present day. The term DEW describes a chain of radar stations in the Arctic regions of Canada, and further down the coast, which had been set up to detect incoming Soviet bombers as early as possible. In this sense, art plays a crucial part in our collective quest to truly understand what is happening at the forefront of technology, society, and the planet. To benefit from this perspective, we must incorporate creative practices such as design and especially the arts in their many forms into how we deal with the sustainability transformation, the defining challenge of our time.

In my practice today, I come across an increasing number of organizations that no longer need to be convinced of the importance of sustainable business practices. As a result, an increasing number of businesses are deciding to include sustainability in their strategic goals. However, while applauded by their employees and investors for committing to making positive changes, they find themselves caught in the middle, unsure of how to proceed from that point. After all, the sustainability transformation is not accomplished by simply measuring carbon emissions, exchanging all virgin materials for recyclables or by setting up a service business model. Instead, it involves an honest reflection of the organization's value creation, how it is intertwined with its environment, and what kind of desirable future studies it is set to achieve. All these questions are not solely characterized by a technological dimension but also complemented with a meaning-driven dimension whose nuances are best understood through art and creative practice.

I was surprised to discover that many of the technological solutions needed for a regenerative future are at hand. Of course, most of them can and must still be improved. There are also futuristic technologies such as chemical recycling, which would allow us to break everything down into molecules once again. Nevertheless, these developments are often misused by those who wish to detract attention from the actions that need to be taken now. Subsequently, it is not primarily a question of creating fancy new technologies but how they can be put to good use within a team, an organization, and, most importantly, within an ecosystem, regardless of whether it is human-made or nature-made. Moreover, the climate emergency goes beyond the boundaries of single organizations and thus relies on transdisciplinary engagement. We do not need to create new things or new ideas; we need to understand how to integrate the existing elements across existing boundaries in meaningful ways. How can we collectively make sense of what we have at our disposal?

When operating in transdisciplinary engagements, there is no default language or single fact to guide organizations in making sense of their role in the sustainability transformation. To find clarity, they must connect with their potential futures. To cite McLuhan (1994, p. 108) again, "Our mechanical technologies for extending and separating the functions of our physical beings have brought us near to a state of disintegration by putting us out of touch with ourselves." Art, especially abstract art, can bring us in touch with ourselves and our ecosystem again. The tiny trees at the Clocktower Gallery established a common space that put protesters, policymakers, and successful businesspeople together as they were breathing, reflecting, and resonating with each other. All of them were New Yorkers. All of them, including the trees, were part of that very ecosystem that makes the city.

Art produces a skill set that is focused less on deep specialization but instead thrives more on the ambiguity of diverse perspectives and the necessary integrational capabilities that such a way of working entails. As we resonate in unison with our fellow human and nonhuman stakeholders, we can make sense of what was once out of reach, when our discourse was limited to facts and figures.

This story shall thus serve as a plea that art and creative practice should be valued alongside the existing STEM disciplines of science, technology, engineering, and mathematics. A NASA paper by Guy A. Boy (2013) justifiably argued that we need to move from STEM to STEAM by adding the arts to our way of thinking. This move, however, will not only make our approach toward the sustainability transformation more human but it will also provide leverage when considering the nonhuman perspectives that art can introduce to our ways of thinking and sensemaking. By doing so, we can gain the ability to adopt more balanced planetary perspectives, ones that make us view opportunities that go beyond human cognition.

There is no foolproof way of integrating art into your sustainability transformation. However, there are various ways to adopt planetary perspectives through leveraging the arts and creative practice:

- Be aware of what is there—Which actors are already on your radar? Which actors, human and nonhuman, have not yet been part of your practice? You will be surprised how many stakeholders are affected by the value creation of your organization. It is in your responsibility to enable them to exercise their agency.

- Make sense before you decide—We are putting too much emphasis on decisions. When uncertainty is high, we need to first make sense. This does not take place at the individual level; it is a collective achievement that can be facilitated by art and creative practice. Both allow us to be concrete and abstract at the same time; they can create the needed ambiguity for working with wicked problems.
- Tune your attention to the relations and not the boundaries—Sustainability is an intricate interplay inside a system and among systems. Do not focus on the boxes, but on the arrows that relate these systems with each other. This involves developing alternative ways to explore and describe relationships.
- Integrate existing value—The main reason why we keep creating new things is our difficulty to engage with what already exists and to apply this across disciplines. Art can help us to translate between various practices and boundaries, enabling us to integrate knowledge, practices, and actors in new and sustainable ways.

After all, there is no fixed recipe. Art's role in the sustainability transformation lies in its capacity to enable perspectives that go beyond human cognition. It can be extremely precise and dangerously vague at the same time. When dealing with wicked problems, however, this ambiguity is sometimes needed the most. In the end, art is also about having the courage needed to engage actively with things we don't quite understand. These include observations that only make sense much later in the future, just like in my case, when it took me almost a decade to understand the significance of the 55 honeylocust trees I had seen on the rooftop in New York City.

References

Boy, G. A. (2013). From STEM to STEAM: Toward a human-centred education, creativity & learning thinking. In *Proceedings of the 31st European conference on cognitive ergonomics* (pp. 1–7). https://doi.org/10.1145/2501907.2501934

McLuhan, M. (1968-1970). *Marshall McLuhan DEW-LINE newsletter*. Eugene M. "Tony" Schwartz.

McLuhan, M. (1994). *Understanding media: The extensions of man* (1st MIT Press ed.). MIT Press.

Rittel, H. W. J., & Webber, M. M. (1973). Dilemmas in a general theory of planning. *Policy Sciences, 4*(2), 155.

Samuel Huber is on a mission to introduce planetary perspectives to organizations and enable them to move toward regenerative value generation. He is one of the founders of the *For Planet Strategy Lab* that runs risky projects and daring experiments through a number of engagements. In addition, he is a research fellow at the Zurich University of the Arts (ZHdK), where he contributes his experience and his network from having worked in the startup ecosystems of Berlin, Tokyo, and Zurich. He was also a founding member of UBS Y, the future think tank of the world's largest wealth manager, worked long nights for ARTonAIR, a New York art gallery, and focused on development economics with Biovision. He was awarded the Dr. Peter Werhahn Prize for his Ph.D. dissertation, which focused on the topic of "Strategizing as Prototyping" from the University of St. Gallen's RISE Management Innovation Lab. Previously, his studies in sociology, economy, management, and design led him to the Universities of Zurich, St. Gallen, and all the way to Stanford and Keio in Tokyo. Website: www.samuelhuber.ch; www.forplanetstrategylab.com, E-mail: samuel@forplanetstrategylab.com, LinkedIn: https://www.linkedin.com/in/samuelphuber/

35

Chernobyl: The Path to Healing Human and Ecological Scars

Laurent Michelot

On Saturday, April 26, 1986, the explosion of Reactor Number 4 of the Chernobyl Nuclear Power Plant (ChNPP) changed the northern Ukraine landscape for centuries to come. A series of errors made during a routine test and the faulty design of Soviet RBMK reactors[1] led to an explosion followed by a fire, releasing large amounts of radiation, thereby contaminating the soil, water, and atmosphere with radioactive material equivalent to 20 times that of the atomic bombings of Hiroshima and Nagasaki. Radioactive salts of iodine, strontium, and cesium were projected into the atmosphere, leading to the contamination of 150,000 square kilometers in Belarus, Russia, and Ukraine, with clouds carrying radioactive isotopes[2] across Europe and

---

[1] RBMK is a Russian acronym (*reaktor bolshoy moshchnosty kanalny*) for high-power channel reactor. The Soviet-designed RBMK is designed as a water-cooled reactor with individual fuel channels using graphite as its moderator. (…). The combination of graphite moderator and water coolant is found in no other power reactors in the world. As the Chernobyl accident showed, several of the RBMK's design characteristics—in particular, the control rod design and a positive void coefficient—were unsafe. After the Chernobyl accident, a number of significant design changes were made to address these problems. (Sources: Muellner (2019); World Nuclear Association: retrieved from https://www.world-nuclear.org/information-library/nuclear-fuel-cycle/nuclear-power-reactors/appendices/rbmk-reactors.aspx; Retrieved 27 November 2020).

[2] Radioactive isotopes are widely used as tracers or labels for substances separated by thin-layer chromatography (TLC) for following the causes of chemical and biochemical reactions, determining the distribution of substances in a reaction mixture, elucidating metabolic pathways of drugs, pesticides, pollutants, and natural substances in human, animal, and plant tissues, and assessing the purity of isotopes. Source: Encyclopedia of Physical Science and Technology (Third Edition), 2003.

L. Michelot (✉)
Brussels, Belgium

reaching locations as remote as 500 kilometers from ground zero. Thirty kilometers of barbed wire fencing were quickly erected, creating the "Exclusion Zone" around the damaged power plant; 350,000 people were eventually evacuated.

Located in the heart of the Exclusion Zone, a few kilometers from the power plant, the ghost town of Pripyat serves as a reminder of the dramas that unfolded there and a testimony for future generations. Pripyat was founded in 1970 and was the ninth "Atomgrad"[3] (nuclear city) of the Soviet Union. It was a model city built to accommodate highly skilled Chernobyl power plant workers and their families. Its population rose steadily for over a decade, reaching 49,360 inhabitants (including approximately 17,000 children) at the time of the accident in 1986.

A jewel of Soviet urban planning, Pripyat was a theater of architectural experimentation. The city was pleasant to live in, with life revolving around its central square. In its shops, the inhabitants found everything they could have dreamed of, in contrast to many cities in the USSR at that time. Most of the inhabitants were young, and the numerous schools and kindergartens welcomed thousands of children, who made up roughly one-fifth of the total population. Pripyat also had a vast array of recreational facilities, the Palace of Culture, a cinema, several swimming pools, and a medical complex fitted with modern, state-of-the-art equipment.

On April 27, 1986, the day following the accident, all of Pripyat's inhabitants were hastily evacuated, never to return. As they entered the buses, they were instructed to bring only the bare minimum and told they would be returning in just a few days. No one expected a disaster of that magnitude. Despite efforts to decontaminate Pripyat by washing the buildings and eliminating the radionuclide, the residents' return was deemed impossible, and the city was condemned. It will forever remain a ghost town. Three hundred fifty thousand people from Pripyat and hundreds from surrounding villages had to abruptly leave their homes behind to relocate elsewhere in the Soviet Union (Fig. 35.1).

Over the decades, Pripyat has become an ecosystem of its own—a mix of concrete and vegetation, slowly blending together. It enables one to witness a large-scale experiment revealing how long a city can remain standing after human presence has abruptly departed. How long does it take before everything collapses and turns into dust? Pripyat serves as an ode to ecology atop

---

[3] An Atomgrad or Atomograd (Russian for "atom city") is a small industrial city (from 30,000 to 80,000 inhabitants) designed to serve the needs of large commercial nuclear power plants. Source: https://www.herder-institut.de/en/research-projects/individual-projects/atomgrad-kerntechnische-moderne-im-oestlichen-europa-1966-2017.html.

35 Chernobyl: The Path to Healing Human and Ecological Scars

Fig. 35.1 View from the central square of the ghost town of Pripyat, taken from the top floor of the Polissya hotel. From this elevated point of view, the silence and abandon of the place are striking. Below, there are rows and rows of empty buildings, and the empty square that brimmed with life three decades ago is now deserted and covered with trees. (Photograph by Laurent Michelot. All rights reserved)

the rubble of an industry that had once been the pride of a nation but no longer exists. Worldwide, Pripyat has become the symbol of human failure to tame the atom. Wandering inside this cold, silent city, you face history. It is like stepping inside a time capsule as you immerse yourself in Pripyat, a once prosperous Soviet city, now frozen in time, whose slogans and propaganda from a distant past emerge, covered by layers of dust. Despite the contamination of the zone and the dangers linked to crumbling structures, the Ukrainian government is now considering rehabilitating a section of the city and registering it with UNESCO to have it protected.

The Pompeii of modern times, slowly reclaimed by vegetation, Pripyat became a tourist hotspot in the 2010s. Before the war, tourism was reshaping the city. The annual number of visitors, pre-COVID-19, was approximately 100,000. Dark tourism, Urbex,[4] and the quest for fame and visibility on social media have turned a wasteland into a place to be seen. Pripyat's iconic landmarks, such as its Ferris wheel, amusement park, and swimming pool, are now recognized worldwide. In the end, Pripyat, a place reminiscent of another world and time, must serve as a reminder that it is our duty to ensure that another disaster of such enormous proportion can never happen again. It is still unknown how tourism will develop again once the war is over, as the zone is now littered with mines and other explosive devices that make visiting impossible for decades to come.

There is a before and an after Chernobyl: the scale of the disaster and its consequences, be it human or environmental, left a scar on the earth's surface, a trauma on a European scale, and eventually helped raise awareness about the destructive potential of the atom (Figs. 35.2 and 35.3).

The health-related consequences are still a subject of debate, as contradictory reports struggle to establish the exact number of people whose health was impacted by the accident. The official toll cites only 31 deaths as an immediate result of the explosion and the fire. However, according to a 2005 United Nations report, a projected number of 4000 people might eventually die due to radiation exposure, although this number has been disputed. Another 5000 may suffer from long-term health issues and disabilities, mostly among the 600,000 liquidators involved in cleaning the zone after the accident. Several reports show a rise in thyroid cancers and leukemia, mostly in Ukraine and Belarus, directly linked to the Chernobyl disaster. At least 1800 cases of thyroid cancer have been documented among children aged 14 and under when the accident occurred. According to several scientific studies, the thyroid gland is sensitive to radioactive iodine exposure, particularly in young children. The scale of the consequences may be even wider: the Kiev National Research Center for Radiation Medicine estimates that around five million citizens of the former USSR, including three million in Ukraine, suffer from health issues resulting from Chernobyl. In Western Europe, abnormal tissue

---

[4] Urbex stands for "urban exploration" and is commonly abbreviated as UE. "UE revolves around locating, documenting, and physically exploring (temporarily) abandoned and derelict (urban) spaces. (…). The UE imagery includes both spectacular high-contrast rooftop photos of cities by night and photos of derelict factories with assembly lines standing still, shutdown hospitals and schools with broken windows and cracks on the walls, or abandoned houses and mansions, where time seems to have stopped decades ago" (Klausen, 2017, p. 372). Source: Klausen, M. (2017). The Urban Exploration Imaginary: Mediatization, Commodification, and Affect. Space and Culture, 20(4), 372–384. https://doi.org/10.1177/1206331217720076.

Fig. 35.2 A school of the village of Mashevo, near the Belarus border. (Photograph by Laurent Michelot. All rights reserved)

growth rates, including cancers, have been higher in the areas that did not escape contamination.

Thirty-eight years after the disaster, ecological challenges remain. Dismantling of the ChNPP's sarcophagus or shelter structure covering the remains of the doomed reactor, storage of spent nuclear fuel, and polluted ground and radiation hotspots still endanger human life in the area. In 1986 at the time of the accident, the ChNPP's sarcophagus was hastily placed over Reactor Number 4. Made of 400,000 cubic meters of concrete and 7300 tons of metal, it had an estimated 30-year lifespan. At the beginning of the twenty-first century, the sarcophagus started showing worrisome signs of structural damage, and it was leaking severely. In 2016, a new sarcophagus called the New Safe Confinement or New Shelter was designed. Completed in 2019, this megaproject resulted in a massive arch-shaped structure measuring 108 meters tall and 162 meters wide. It is expected to last 100 years and allow the dismantling of the original shelter over several decades and the removal of the

Fig. 35.3 Discarded gas masks litter the ground of a school in Pripyat. Such masks were stored in schools and other public places in the event of an NBC conflict, in the midst of the cold war. Despite the dramatic aspect of the picture, no masks were used when the population was evacuated the day after the disaster, as they would have been irrelevant. (Photograph by Laurent Michelot. All rights reserved)

contaminated remains of the reactor vessel, including the debris and rubble under it. The ongoing war makes the task even harder, as the power plant is now under military control, with limited access to experts and workers.

Another ecological challenge is the storage of spent fuel assemblies coming from the other reactors. After the accident at Reactor Number 4, the three other one-site reactors continued working for years. The last working one, Reactor Number 3, was deactivated in 2000, exactly 14 years after the accident took place. In 2020, the authorities moved the first 21,000 spent-fuel assemblies from Chernobyl Reactors 1, 2, and 3 to the world's largest dry spent-fuel storage facility. The European Bank for Reconstruction and Development (EBRD) funded this project and announced it should have a minimum lifespan of 100 years.

Strontium-90 and Caesium-137, two major radioactive isotopes, are still present in the area, making the vicinity around the power plant unfit for human life. Thorough cleaning of the zone has proved impossible. Some areas such as the Red Forest were so heavily polluted with radioactive contamination that the trees died from radiation. These trees were buried in trenches and then covered with a thick carpet of sand, and finally, new pine trees were planted. Eventually, the forest grew back. However, more than 90% of the Red Forest's radioactivity is still concentrated in the soil, and massive fires such as those that took place in 2015 and 2020 could still potentially release radioactive material into the atmosphere (Fig. 35.4).

Devoid of inhabitants, the forsaken zone eventually became a haven for wildlife. Following the disaster, some plant and animal mutations, such as physical deformities, have been identified. Studies on the topic are still contentious, and the long-term consequences of the animals' exposure to radiation are currently unknown. Despite the presence of radioactivity, many species, such as wild horses, boars, beavers, moose, wolves, and even bears, are now returning to the area due to the absence of human activity and predators. Scientists and biologists in Ukraine and Belarus have been intensively studying The Exclusion Zone and the "Natural Radiological Reserve" that have naturally evolved. The absence of human settlements and lack of ecotourism enable wildlife to thrive undisturbed. On the Belarus side, the Polesie State Radioecological Reserve (PSRER) is home to many rare and endangered species, 70 of which are listed in the International Red Book (International

Fig. 35.4 View over the roofs of Pripyat, and, in the distance, the confinement arch covering the doomed reactor number 4 of the Chernobyl power plant. (Photograph by Laurent Michelot. All rights reserved)

Union for Conservation of Nature Red List of Threatened Species).[5] In Ukraine, a law passed in 2016 regulates the status of the Chernobyl Exclusion Zone, and a decree was signed to establish the 226,964.7 hectare reserve. This zone's objective is to preserve the Polissia region's most typical natural complexes in their natural states, stabilize the hydrological regime, rehabilitate areas contaminated with radionuclides, and facilitate the organization and execution of international scientific research.[6] The dangerous, contaminated environment, coupled with entry restrictions, protects flora and fauna from human-made damage. Due to its history, this zone is one of a kind and considered Europe's largest experiment in rewilding. In terms of area, it represents the third-largest nature reserve in mainland Europe.

I believe that in the end, the PSRER is the only positive legacy of the human-made disaster of 1986. By ensuring that this area remains out of reach of humans' destructive behavior, animals—including endangered species—have been given a chance to return, claim their territory, and live peacefully.

While horses, bears, and birds have found a peaceful haven for themselves, we humans are still living under the shadow cast by Chernobyl and under its consequences. Sadly, we are passing on that tainted legacy to the generations to come.

---

[5] Source: Deryabina, T.G., Kuchmel, S.V., Nagorskaya, L.L., Hinton, T.G., Beasley, J.C., Lerebours, A. and Smith, J.T. (2015). Long-term census data reveal abundant wildlife populations at Chernobyl. Current Biology Magazine, 25 (19) (2015), pp. R824-R826, https://doi.org/10.1016/j.cub.2015.08.017

[6] Source: Novikau, A. (2015). The evolution of the environmental movement in Belarus: from Chernobyl to global climate change. Environmental Sociology, (1), pp. 92–101, https://doi.org/10.1080/23251042.2014.1002187

35 Chernobyl: The Path to Healing Human and Ecological Scars

Laurent Michelot born in 1973 in Nancy, France, Laurent Michelot made his career in the advertising world as an art director. He now works in Brussels for one of the European institutions. With his camera, he has been covering the territory surrounding the Chernobyl Nuclear Power Plant since 2014, giving a glimpse, through his stunning images, of the wasteland now called the Chernobyl Exclusion Zone. Thirty-eight years after the 1986 disaster, his photographs show what remains of the city of Pripyat, where 50,000 people used to live before they had to be evacuated in just one day, leaving all their belongings behind. www.laurentmichelot.com, insta: instagram.com/pripyat_photos

36

The Colour Fools: Communicating Sustainability Through Music

Igor Shishlov

This chapter tells a story of The Colour Fools, an international music band that started in Barcelona just before the Covid pandemic. Through this project I wanted to combine my passions for sustainability and music while trying to find a new voice to tell the stories that reflect on our relations with each other, nature and the universe. The story highlight the power of collaboration, patience, and the arts in fostering a deeper connection to sustainability issues, despite the challenges posed by the consumerist society and the digital age's distractions.

With this in mind, it is crucial to find new ways of communicating sustainability and telling inspiring stories that can help people reflect on their lifestyles, their relationship with nature and each other, and hopefully inspire them to live more conscious lives. Moreover, telling impactful stories can help mobilize collective action in people by empowering them and making them feel part of a larger movement. Music, for example, has always been a powerful communication tool. Over the years, it has played an important role in various social movements, from civil rights to pacifism. Rock music in

---

I. Shishlov (✉)
Perspectives Climate Group, Freiburg im Breisgau, Germany

The Colour Fools, Barcelona, Spain

HEC, Paris, France
e-mail: shishlov@perspectives.cc

particular has a long history of exposing social injustice, promoting solidarity and inspiring the development of new collective identities.

Having worked on climate change issues for more than a decade, I have always been puzzled by the lack of engagement with this pressing societal challenge by most musicians. Having such a powerful communication tool and not using it to create space for reflection on climate change and broader sustainability topics seemed to me like a missed opportunity. This is one of the reasons why I wanted to combine my passions for music and sustainability, a dream that came true when I moved from Paris to Barcelona and started my own band, The Colour Fools (www.thecolourfools.com).

The story of The Colour Fools began in the year -1 BC (before Covid) when I met Pablo, an Argentinian designer, globetrotter, and experienced bass player who had also just landed in Barcelona. We had both "been to many places and walked many roads," collecting a baggage of "colourfool" experiences along the way. We started talking about the "ultimate questions of life, the universe and everything" and found a lot in common. When Pablo started talking about the dangers of our consumerist society and how everyone is running after "carrots" in their various manifestations, I knew that we would make a great team together, as by then I had already written a song precisely about that (watch the music video of "Rabbit, Run" here: www.youtube.com/@thecolourfools).

> *"Rabbit, Run"*
> Welcome to the race – run, rabbit, run
> Don't lose your pace – run, rabbit, run
> So many lips to kiss – run, rabbit, run
> And carrots not to miss – run, rabbit, run
> Rabbits like the speed when they feel adrenaline
> Rabbits like to breed, they got animal instincts
> And even when they sleep rabbits are aroused
> Daydreaming of the sweet carrots that they found
> Run run run, if you wanna win
> Run run run, in your spinning wheel
> Run run run, time is running out
> Run run run, till you're in the ground
> Tell me how it feels when you run, rabbit, run
> Do you think it's real when you run, rabbit, run?
> Go try and buy some time and run, rabbit, run
> Your lies are so benign – run, rabbit, run

Run run run, if you wanna win
Run run run, in your spinning wheel
Run run run, time is running out
Run run run, till you're in the ground
Rabbit, have you paid your dues?
The carrots are waiting for you.
You gotta run, rabbit
Run run run, if you wanna win
Run run run, in your spinning wheel
Run run run, time is running out
Run run run, till you shoot that gun
Run, rabbit, run
You gotta run till you're in the ground
Run, robot, run
You gotta run till you shoot that gun, run

Our discussions led us to the conclusion that the only way to save humanity from the looming decadence was to form a new music band that would raise people's consciousness and spread love and peace across time and space. Realizing that this fairly realistic goal might require a larger team, we started looking for like-minded musicians. The search for a drummer was long and thorny, as even the most skilled drummers in Barcelona could not feel the groove of our ideas, until we met Nicholas, a young Italian drummer who had just moved to Barcelona from Liverpool. From the very first rehearsal together, he understood and bought into our ideas and immediately became an integral part of The Colour Fools. The three of us started rehearsing and writing new "colourfool" stories, but even though it started to remotely sound like something people usually call "music," we all felt that something was missing, a secret sauce that would pull it all together. The universe seemed to agree and sent us Alexandra Wagner, a Polish virtuoso pianist, who completed the first lineup of The Colour Fools.

The band had not even had a chance to play its first concert when the Covid pandemic hit the world in early 2020. We decided to keep our spirits up and used the lockdown time to write new songs, using an online platform (www.soundtrap.com) that enables each musician to add and edit their parts, allowing for smooth remote collaboration. Reflecting on our Internet addiction that became particularly avid during the lockdown, we wrote a song about "scrolling" the never-ending social media feed (listen here: http://spotify.thecolourfools.com).

"*Scroll and Roll*"
>   Waking up in the morning
>   Checking on your endless feed
>   Information overloading
>   You gotta keep up with the speed
>   Writing a profound passage
>   Hundred forty characters
>   Interrupted by a message
>   It's a breaking news alert
>   Scroll and roll, this is all you need
>   Scroll and roll, this is how you feed
>   Scroll, scroll, scroll, scroll and roll
>   The screen is your big brother, it's here to satisfy
>   And feed with juicy colours, your salivating eyes
>   They gave you so much freedom to choose your time to waste
>   Until you find out your life is just a copy-paste
>   Your thumbs are moving faster
>   Your eyes are growing big
>   Kaleidoscope of lust and
>   The time grave that you dig
>   Scroll and roll, this is all you need
>   Scroll and roll, this is how you feed
>   Scroll, scroll, scroll, scroll and roll

With 12 songs in total, we recorded our first album in my coworking space in Barcelona (www.comusicwork.com) and started playing small concerts as soon as the Covid restrictions were lifted. By that time, we were joined by a new keyboard player Eddie from Sardinia (later succeeded by Matias from Chile), a Catalan singer Isa, an Argentinian saxophone player Adriano and a Spanish trumpet player Narciso, thus continuing our tradition of mixing people from different cultures and combining different music styles. As a cosmopolitan city with a large international audience interested in various social and environmental issues, Barcelona seemed the perfect place to tell our stories. Through our music project we met some inspiring people, made new friends, and received a lot of support and encouragement from our peers. After one of our concerts, I was approached by a young man who told me about Climate Sessions (http://www.linktr.ee/climatesessions), an amazing initiative by young environmental activists in Barcelona that creates space for artistic work related to the climate emergency. They invited us to perform at one of the Climate Sessions, and we decided to write a special song about climate change for the occasion called "Polar Bears."

"*Polar Bears*"
>Polar bears eat fish and chips
>Polar bears like to surf
>Polar bears move their hips
>When they dance all night long
>Polar bears drink whiskey straight
>Polar bears play black jack
>Polar bears flirt and mate
>But they never turn back
>Bears are on fire
>It's a slippery slope
>Bears are on fire
>They just want to be home
>Killing the bears, dividing their skin
>That's alright you can offset your sin
>Your indulgence - Article 6
>Polar bears will call dibs
>Bears are on fire
>It's a slippery slope
>Bears are on fire
>They just want to be home

We may not be able to save the world from climate change with a song, but I do believe that it is important to talk about sustainability not only through science and media but also through the arts. Science is crucial to our understanding of the world and to devising solutions to societal challenges, but people also need an emotional connection to these causes and inspiration to act, something that music and other forms of art can provide. On a more personal level, for me music is a great way to reflect on life and our relationship with each other and the universe. In our fast-moving consumer society, full of psychological manipulation and artificially imposed desires, the arts provide a refuge and a sane space to gain new perspectives on the world and help to face the absurdities of our existence.

My experience with The Colour Fools has taught me several life lessons. The first one is the importance of joining forces with like-minded people. Without my bandmates, who have also become my close friends, I would never be able to launch such a project. As in any ambitious endeavor, there may be moments of doubt and it is the energy and support of the team that can help overcome these difficulties and not give up. I have also learnt that good things take time. Our Western society is geared toward instant gratification and quick fixes to the problems, but in many cases, it takes a lot of patience and perseverance to achieve something worthwhile. Finally, I have learnt to accept my own limitations and to stop looking at other people's talents and successes with envy. Having met some amazing musicians on this journey, I have gained a good deal of humility and learned that music—and life for that matter—is not a sport and not a competition. Art is not about being the best, it is about finding and revealing your own voice and telling your own story. I hope that the story of The Colour Fools will inspire others to also look for and reveal their voice, tell their unique story, and make their own contribution to a better future through the arts.

Igor Shishlov is the Head of Climate Finance at Perspectives Climate Group, a climate policy consultancy and research firm. He has more than a decade of research, advisory and leadership experience in climate policy and climate finance. Since 2016, Igor has also been teaching Climate Change Economics at HEC Paris, where he is currently the Executive Director of the Climate and Business Certificate program. He holds a PhD in Environmental Economics and an MSc in Sustainable Development. In addition to his work on climate policy, Igor is a singer and guitarist in The Colour Fools, an international music band that he founded in Barcelona together with Pablo Garcia and Nicholas Sardo in 2019.

37

An Ecological Path: From Science to Music and Painting

Emilia Jücker

This story traces a life full of discoveries and experiences revolving around ecology.

The Philosophical Side of Ecology

Originally considered only a branch of biology, ecology is now a science in its own right. The subject has evolved dramatically. Ecology as a science is approaching such a level that it now not only dramatically exceeds the understanding of almost all other natural sciences and perhaps even social sciences but also represents a new degree of their synthesis. In this way, as a result of its own development, it comes closest to philosophy. It is my opinion that the key questions facing modern ecology are best approached through this lens.

There are certainly differences in ecologists' understanding and approach to their subject. However, we can say that the concept that unites all the dominant points of view is the concept of an ecosystem. But what is an ecosystem?

Eugene P. Odum in Fundamentals of Ecology writes: "The development of an ecosystem (…) can be defined by (…) three parameters: (1) an orderly, predictable process of community development (…) with changes over time in species structure and processes occurring in the community; (2) (the development) occurs as a result of changes in the physical environment caused by

---

E. Jücker (✉)
Hamburg, Germany

the community, i.e., the succession is controlled by the community, although the physical environment...sets the limits to which the development may reach; (3) the culmination of development is a stabilized ecosystem in which there is maximum biomass...and maximum symbiotic links between organisms."

Now, replace the word "community" with "society"!

The term "global ecosystem" refers to the relationship and mutual dependence of society and nature. The development of the global ecosystem is, like any ecosystem, an objective, internally regulated process, whose ultimately stabilized state can be predicted. This development is carried out mainly by society, although its parameters are dependent on the environment, i.e., nature.

The culmination of the global ecosystem is a stable state in which the connection between society and nature has become so inseparable and organic, and their dependence is so strong that any further change will be destructive.

Classical trends in the analysis of ecosystems, however, do not provide a sufficiently clear answer as to what should be the further fate of ecosystems after they have reached their climax state, their stabilization. Is it possible for this state to be viewed as the beginning of something new? Or will the climax of the ecosystem be inevitably the beginning of the end? If humanity could master and regulate the growth of its needs, could a stable condition be maintained?

These questions require a philosophical approach to answer, because that is where we analyze the essence, the nature of humanity itself, not only as an independent unit but as a part of a global system.

Ecology and philosophy are probably facing the need for an alliance. Such an approach could have significant implications in both theoretical and practical terms, and we could find answers to our questions in some surprising new places.

My Grandfather: The Roots of My Love of Nature

Love of nature from which man is born...

My roots on my father's side are in Rabisha, a village in the northwestern part of Bulgaria. My father was born there, and his father, and his father as well. My father was the first to leave the village in 1935 and went to study and live in the city. I was born in Sofia, a city of over a million people, but my love of nature comes from Rabisha, the land of my forefathers.

Picturesque lush green fields, dense forests, tranquil meadows, fertile soil, imposing Balkan mountains, serene lakes, and rivers full of fish. Underneath the wide blue skies, there lies a tiny Balkan village nestled along the banks of the Danube. Here, hot summers and cold winters make for four distinct seasons of delicious homegrown foods.

My grandfather, Nedelko Ivanov Nedelkov (Неделко Иванов Неделков), born in Rabisha at the turn of the twentieth century, came from a prosperous, large family. He stood out as a gentle and affectionate person, refusing to align with his father's relentless pursuit of economic interests. He married for love—revolutionary at the time. He loved animals, too, and gave all the farm animals names—again, very unusual for the time! And he couldn't bear to slaughter them.

During my childhood vacations, I often visited my grandparents' village. My grandpa would play his duduk, a type of wooden flute, and tell me stories from the old days. He spoke of his love for my grandmother, whom he married when she was only 14, and with whom he had two sons. Only one survived, my father, who went on to become one of the founders of the environmental protection movement and a pioneer in ecological education in Eastern Europe.

My grandpa was as loving and delicate as nature itself. And it is from him that my deep appreciation and love for nature began took root.

My Father: From the Past, a Positive Message for Today

My father, Ivan Nedelkov Ivanov (Иван Неделков Иванов), was a pioneer in environmental protection in Eastern Europe. He was a chemist with a degree from Sofia University in Bulgaria. In 1970, he created the first programs in ecology for the high schools and technical colleges of Bulgaria, and he was the first in Eastern Europe to establish a certification system for environmental protection controls.

He introduced me to chemistry when I was a little girl, and he made it magical. I especially loved the colors and how substances came together. I used to smash the flowers in my mom's garden and paint everything, including myself, with green paint. This helped me to understand flowers and their colors; later, in my research, I would do experiments with flower extractions. But when I was young, my mother worried about me, especially when my highschool philosophy teachers came to our home for philosophy talks with me. My father was happy—he transferred his great love of learning and of plants, soil, and ecology to me. How important it is that parents are understanding and encouraging their children and that they trust them! (Fig. 37.1).

Fig. 37.1 Memories of my father, Ivan Nedelkov Ivanov

My father was always burning for knowledge, updating his information, developing his vision. He often changed jobs. At one point, he transferred from the Central National Laboratory to the Central National State Council of Waters in Sofia. He saw that the intense push for development was leading to uncontrolled pollution. This was unacceptable for my father as a chemist and as a budding ecologist. He helped to set up the first water-purification stations in Bulgaria before changing his job again to the Ministry of Education.

His strong opinions got him kicked out of the communist party, and thereafter he was restricted in his work. He was permitted no job that involved writing; I remember him selling tickets for a traveling circus. Our family didn't always have enough to eat. My father was not sleeping nights, and my mother had serious health problems. However, our family stayed firm together, and our parents managed to give us a wonderful, sunny childhood.

After struggling for 15 years, things began to change in Bulgaria. We found educated, supportive people who helped my dad return to his work. He established the first organized control system for the protection of natural parks, the regulation of noise pollution, ecological requirements for city buildings, and more. He continued to work even after retirement and lived a life of love for people and nature into his 90s.

My final picture of my father is one of strength and persistence, his life one of love for nature, his evolution toward a modern and emotional style and his respect for young people and creativity, his practical and natural vision for the good of humanity and long-term progress. Thinking for the future—that is the positive message for today.

My Academic Research and Chernobyl

I graduated from the Chemical-Technological University in Sofia with an MS in chemical engineering in 1979. I had a good analytical mind, so after graduation, I was taken on as a research fellow at the same university for 5 years. I assisted on many projects that were interesting to me, but after a while it wasn't enough. I wanted to head up my own project, something I could dedicate myself to for a long time.

I applied to earn a PhD at the Academy of Sciences in its new Ecological Institute—a center for joint environmental projects between Bulgaria, UNESCO, and the UN. For the next 6 years, I conducted research at the institute and wrote my dissertation: "Ecological Conditions and Biogeochemistry of Manganese in the Eastern Part of the Sofia Basin," a qualitative and quantitative analysis of the manganese cycle in the region. Manganese biogeochemistry is a function of ecological conditions, and my supervisor and I described its qualities and effects, particularly in relation to other chemical reactions in plants, for the years 1985–1989. The Chernobyl disaster occurred in 1986: this suddenly required our research to include additional data for the new ecological conditions. We conducted this extra work in secret, for fear of censorship.

I defended my doctoral research to a specially-assembled international commission to the Institute of Plant Physiology at the Bulgarian Academy of Sciences in Sofia. Ecology was a very new subject for the VAK (Higher Attestation Commission of State of Bulgaria, which oversaw higher academic degrees). The material was, in fact, so new that few researchers qualified to critique it at the institute; specialists had to be brought in from other research centers.

The defense was held in a large hall, with 21 professors selected for the secret vote. About 700 people came to hear it; even the corridor was full, and the door was propped open so that they could listen in. Manganese was known to be important because of the metallurgical component in the air pollution, and Chernobyl's effects were of concern to everyone.

There were a lot of questions. In addition to the commission's inquiries, I fielded over 400 questions from the public, many of which were particularly challenging. It became evident that manganese pollution indeed poses a significant risk to human health. Finally, after 3 h of addressing these questions, the session was halted so that the voting process could begin. I received 20 votes out of 21 in my favor. However, it is the face of the ordinary people in the audience, some of whom had traveled long distances to be there that I will always remember—people deeply concerned yet feeling powerless.

Following my doctoral defense, I continued to publish and expand my research horizons. I ventured to the Netherlands where I specialized further, completed five post-doctoral positions, and spent time in the United States working at the Climate Stress Laboratory within the US Department of Agriculture Beltsville Agricultural Research Center (USDA BARC) in the Washington area. My academic journey eventually brought me to Germany, where I concluded my research in genetics and medicine.

Alongside my scientific endeavors, I have translated some of my ecological work into art. As an artist, I also explore the realms of social ecology and philosophy. Yet, amid all these experiences, I will never forget the individuals present at my PhD defense. They serve as the true source of inspiration and motivation in research. This, indeed, is the purpose of research and science—to improve people's lives. Much like the harmonious order of nature, everything should harmonize in balance to create a functional ecosystem.

Painting: My New Passion

I have painted with pleasure all my life. High-speed painting has always given me energy and a way to connect with people. Currently, living in a different country, speaking different languages, painting and design is my shortcut to communication. Drawing and painting are part of my everyday life—inside the studio, while traveling, partaking in club activities, meeting with friends, experimenting in the laboratory or field as part of my profession. This has always been my way to screen, analyze, and synthesize my environment in visual form. My project of the last 3 years has been "Painting to Music," about which I would like to tell you a story.

At the end of one very heavy year, I went to a classical concert. It was a late evening directly after work, and the concert was in a big cathedral in central Hamburg. We sat down late because there were so many people and such small doors. The philharmonic orchestra played a long oratorio, which was practically unbearable: no intermission, no air in the cathedral, very loud and very brightly lit...how can I escape, I thought, when I had been formally invited to this concert? And I "escaped" by drawing all over the written program.

The next day, I was observing my "tracing long street of music" drawings from the concert. It formed a figure. So, I got the idea to analyze what the composer had "formed" with his music. It was the beginning of my new project: painting to music.

I began to listen through my body, following classical music with hand tracings. As with all my projects before, I painted by hand at high speed. With this new project, I was also moving my hand—so what was new? New was: I was drawing not with my own speed or rhythm, not from my thoughts, but with the music and its form—its form, not mine. Never mind that the paintings came from me.

I would analyze my drawn lines later to figure out what was there. The figures and combinations formed interesting shapes, perhaps like something from the composer's imagination: the works of Chopin very often recalled women's heads, flowers, imaginary figures corresponding to the rhythm...

Fig. 37.2 shows my first live painting of clasical music during the concert given by famous Hamburg pianist Marina Savova (Brahms waltz, op.39, 120 × 100 cm, acrylic, oil, mixed media).

Fig. 37.2 Emilia Jücker visualizing Brahms Waltz, opus 39—A synesthetic expression; Photograph by Emilia Jücker: All rights reserved

One last question: could an elementary analysis of our environment performed with sensitivity have any relationship to painting? If this could be made more understandable to people (like painting with music was for me), would they love nature more? Painting may have an ecological aspect: it is something from our environment that has a certain biological effect on us, as an artist's paintings may have an effect on an observer.

Emilia Jücker has a Ph.D. in biology with a specialization in ecology and conducted research on the biogeochemistry of manganese after the Chernobyl disaster. She later worked in applied ecology and genetic engineering at institutions such as the University of Delft and the United States Department of Agriculture. Returning to academia in Germany, Emilia taught chemistry and biology at several prestigious institutions. Today, Emilia combines her lifelong passion for painting with environmental themes using biological and geological materials. She is investigating the neurobiological mechanisms of social bonding, exploring the relationship between music and color, and experiencing the effects of music on the brain, possibly influenced by synesthesia, a rare neurological condition. Emilia has performed in numerous exhibition-concerts with concert pianist Marina Savova in Hamburg. In various occasions, she has also painted in public at the Hamburg State Opera as well as at the Elbphilharmonie during live concerts and performances.

38

Art of Change 21: Uniting Art and Ecology for a More Sustainable Future!

Alice Audouin

How long has a connection between art and the environment existed? When considering this, it is essential to differentiate "environment" and "nature" as the former includes the notion of protecting nature, a concept that emerged in the nineteenth century. In my opinion, this enduring relationship truly became a prominent part of the history of art in the early 2000s. During that period, contemporary art, with its contextual and conceptual dimensions, was increasingly influenced by the pressing concerns of global warming, which had become particularly alarming and subject of intense media attention.

At first, this unprecedented and irreversible movement involved only a handful of avant-garde artists. Overtime, it expanded to encompass various forms of environmental consciousness, including topics such as biodiversity, pandemics, and, more importantly, the Anthropocene Epoch, characterized by significant environmental consequences resulting from human activity.

In 2004, when I organized the first symposium in France dedicated to this subject at UNESCO Headquarters, titled "L'artiste comme partie prenante" ("The artist as stakeholder"), I reached out to contemporary artists who were addressing the issues of global warming and sustainable development. This pioneering initiative allowed me to identify around 100 artists at the time. Fast forward 20 years, and environmental issues have assumed a central role in contemporary art. A dynamic movement now involves young artists, numerous thematic exhibitions, and biennials focused on environmental

---

A. Audouin (✉)
Art of Change 21, Paris, France

issues. Moreover, there is a notable drive within the sector to reduce its own "carbon footprint." My database has expanded significantly, now comprising almost 3000 artists whose work engages with this theme.

How can we most accurately describe this movement? Is it best described as ecological art, environmental art, or anthropocenic art? None of these terms appears entirely fitting. Perhaps this is because the phenomenon implies a long-term perspective and exerts an impact on the very conditions of life on Earth, extending well beyond the notions of ecology and the environment.

The first generation of artists, emerging in the midst of the Anthropocene Epoch and the ongoing ecological crisis, is deeply committed to these pressing issues. They have, as Albert Camus put it, "embarked in the galley of the times." For this new generation of artists, confronting the ecological crisis has become a major contemporary issue. They do not consider ecology as merely inspirational subject matter but rather as a crucial, fundamental, aspect of their very relation with the world.

The artists are changing humanity's role in the world in a number of ways: through acts of cocreation with the living world, an anthropological approach to renewable energies, works that influence the struggle for climate justice, long-term objectives, the promotion of postcarbon communities, the quest for improving health and memory, a representation of the living world, that transcends the traditional "phylogenetic tree," and the use of novel organic materials. Their work represents humanity's interconnectedness with other species and suppressing human arrogance as they pursue greater conviviality and equity.

What Is the Path to a Solution, and What Are the Major Steps?

For this new generation of "eco-artists," the environment is not simply a theme they address in their work, but the definition of their relationship with the world. They are reinventing a sense of community and collective values. From ecofeminism and postanthropocentrism to interspecies relations, they are playing their role as members of the avant-garde to the full, optimistically paving the way for a future where cooperation will triumph over competition.

Above and beyond the environmental issues they tackle, these artists bring a new energy and suggest different, more convivial ways of thinking and being that are light years from the clichés of punitive environmental policies. They resynchronize our relationship with time by linking human and geological time, rethink our habitat by considering mankind as one species among many, combat patriarchal and extractive strategies by seeking to replace them with a more ethical, holistic, and shared approach to the world, teach us how to take collective action, create and safeguard resilient places, foil political and economic policies that pay scant attention to their consequences, and give us back control in a globalized world by making us stakeholders in charge of the common good.

A number of artists are also concerned about the environmental impact of their art. They have realized that the materials (concrete, glass, acrylic paint, etc.) and equipment they use (kilns, software, etc.), as well as how they transport artworks count more as causes of the environmental crisis than solutions. In 2009, Long Horizons: An Exploration of Art + Climate Change, a pioneering series of essays on the subject, was published by Julie's Bicycle. Among other content, Anthony Gormley shared with readers his confidences and commitments: "I am responsible for managing my own impact, including the carbon footprint of the studio and all its activities." Gormley had already calculated his carbon footprint, reduced his use of air freight and insulated his studio, where he was getting ready to install solar panels. Since then, examples of good practice among artists, motivated in particular by the COP21 in Paris, have been multiplying. Examples include artworks being transported from Germany to Japan without using planes, artists calculating the carbon footprint of installations (Olafur Eliasson) and exhibitions powered by solar power (Julian Charrière).

It is not just the artists; the art sector is also changing as industry professionals become more aware of the globalized nature of their activity and its reliance on air transport. In addition, certain key locations (in coastal or vulnerable areas such as New York or Hong Kong) are threatened by rising sea levels and extreme weather. There is a groundswell of support with initiatives by galleries (Gallery Climate, Coalition, Galleries Commit, etc.) and art curation focusing on the environment both at biennials (Taipei, Helsinki, Korat, Kochi, etc.) and museums (Garage, ARoS, Barbican, Gropius Bau, Palais de Tokyo, lille3000, etc.). Art Paris art fair is a pioneer in that it is the first fair to carry out a life cycle analysis and implement measures to reduce its environmental impact, a dynamic to which I am proud to have contributed.

I have always been convinced that the worlds of creativity, social entrepreneurship, and activism are, in fact, united. They are certainly united in the common will to drive societal change, making it possible to bring about the world of tomorrow and allowing the emergence of promising and innovative ideas. However, what path should be taken to raise awareness, to create citizen mobilization around climate issues? How can we best express the desire for a more ecologically healthy future?

My Positive Takeaways

During my career, I experienced many ways to tackle climate change issues, through collaborative actions, prizes, talks, collective workshops, and exhibitions.

As the founder and chair of *Art of Change 21*, I truly believe in the power of art and cooperative thinking.

Created in 2014, ahead of COP21, the not-for-profit organization *Art of Change 21* connects contemporary art with major environmental issues, highlighting and supporting the important role of art to raise awareness and provide our society with new alternatives and solutions.

Patroned by renowned artist Olafur Eliasson, its modes of action include: exhibitions, debates, prizes, workshops, artist-led campaigns, and events during COP, in collaboration with major environmentally-focused artists including Tomás Saraceno, Mark Dion, Julian Charrière, Minerva Cuevas, Romuald Hazoumé, Janet Laurence…

Art of Change 21 also publishes Impact Art News, a bimonthly online publication in English & French dedicated to news regarding art and environment.

"Le Conclave": Implementing Cocreating Processes

"Le Conclave" of *Art of Change 21* was an unprecedented event that brought together artists, social entrepreneurs, and youth involved in the ecological transition and sustainable development. The goal of the Conclave is to relate art and sustainability and to generate new kinds of solutions, with one leading conviction: drivers of change are part of the solution to the environmental crisis, but without the participation of artists, it will be difficult to make the ecological transition. Artists' imaginations and creativity, their ability to innovate and accelerate change, make them major players in this great transformation toward the "postcarbon" world that we are trying to create for cities, businesses, consumers, and more.

The two conclaves organized by *Art of Change 21* in 2014 and 2017 mixed committed artists (Laurent Tixador, Minerva Cuevas, Opavivara Coletivo, Ibrahim Mahama, Wen Fang, Romulad Hazoumé, et al.), social entrepreneurs (David Kobia of Ushahidi, founder of GoZero Waste in China Elsa Tang, the ethical fashion designer Tiffan Pattinson from Hong Kong, et al.), and young leaders or activists involved in environmental movements such as Afroz Shah from India. From Brazil to China, throughout the United States, New Zealand, and Kenya, I invited these actors to play the game—not to compete but to highlight their common projects and their initiatives in order to exchange and imagine together ideas for innovation and social and environmental transformation.

How does a conclave work? Let's take the first session, Le Conclave 2014. It included 21 participants, including seven artists, seven independent innovators (social and solidarity entrepreneurs, eco-innovators, actors for the sharing and collaborative economy, "open source" energy participants, do-it-yourselfers, upcyclingers, etc.) and seven young leaders for mobilization against global warming from 12 countries.

These actors, all committed to sustainable development, were accompanied by a cocreation coach, Stéphane Riot, by an evaluation committee made up of experts and by me; these experts evaluated in real time not only the ideas for action on the ecological, financial, and logistical levels but also from the ideas' power to mobilize and influence. By the end of 2 days, the first session had given birth to our flagship project, Maskbook.

Maskbook

Art of Change 21's flagship project, Maskbook, was born precisely from this cross-fertilization of ideas. It was during a discussion at Le Conclave 2014 with the Chinese artist Wen Fang about the censorship of the social network Facebook and air pollution in China that the idea of the name was born: "In China we don't have Facebook," he said, "but since we all wear anti-pollution masks, it should be called Maskbook!"

Maskbook is the first participatory international movement with the health-pollution climate-pandemic link that uses the mask as a symbol. Its objective: to raise public awareness of the major issues linking health and the environment by utilizing the creative talent hidden in each of us. In 5 years, Maskbook has gathered more than 7000 portraits from citizens of more than 40 countries, the best of which are available at the online gallery maskbook.org.

Maskbook also has more than 200 mask-creation workshops, over 15 international exhibitions, and more than 60 international masked personalities! Maskbook was chosen to launch World Environment Day in 2019 by the United Nations Environment Program (UNEP), propelling *Art of Change 21* onto the large screens of the world's largest cities, and in 2020 by the French government to celebrate 5 years of the Paris Agreement and the COP21. What a great honor for our organization that was actually born for the COP21! The short films that we produce, which are very visual and highly adapted to social media, and our ability to reach a young target audience play a major role in the Maskbook system. Our ability to mobilize citizens digitally has also enabled us to continue to act during the pandemic; we only had to press a button to switch from offline to online.

This is the full force of the tremendous power of artistic creation, because who is better than artists in turning the potentially anxiety-provoking image of a mask into a symbol of the fight against climate change and an expression of optimism and commitment?

My goal has always been not only to work with artists but also to awaken the artist within each of us. As the German artist Joseph Beuys said so well, "Every Man is an artist," and that everyone has within himself "a power to shape that he must know and develop," to make his life a work of art in perpetual re-creation and to be an actor for the change that is taking place, and today, the needed transition requires change to take place, and therefore creativity!

Integrating artists into the heart of the process was pioneering. Today, I see a multitude of exhibitions, debates, conferences, multidisciplinary projects with scientists and researchers, and the creation of networks and collectives, all united around a common idea that has carried me for 20 years now: to rethink the role of art and artists as drivers of alternative and more sustainable, more supportive, and fairer futures.

Art Prizes to Support Eco-Artists and Sustainable Practices

The "Planète Art Solidaire" prize was created from the conviction that environmentally-engaged artists have the power to reveal a new generation of artists and spotlight artists who speak more than ever of their time, which is what *Art of Change 21* tried to do by rewarding the efforts of 21 young environmentally-minded artists impacted by the health crisis, selected by a prestigious jury. A total fund of 42,000 euros was awarded to the artists, amounting to 2000 euros each. This prize was supported by Maison Ruinart.

After the success of the Planète Art Solidaire, *Art of Change 21* continued its commitment to French artists through the Eco-design Art Prize (Prix Art Eco-Conception). It aims to promote the culture and practice of eco-design in artistic creation and brings together for the first-time artists and experts in this field, focusing on processes and bringing eco-design initiatives at the forefront of change.

The 12 winners of the Eco-design Art Prize were revealed on 10 January 2023 at the Palais de Tokyo. They were chosen by a prestigious Jury from 36 finalists previously chosen by a selection committee from 278 candidates.

The eco-design method goes further than just calculating the carbon footprint by including other environmental issues, such as biodiversity, water, climate, or scarcity of resources. It intervenes at the beginning of the creation process, at the time of the design and production of the work, all the way until the eventual "end" of the work, i.e., the full life cycle. While the acceptance and diffusion of more ecological practices is spreading rapidly in the art world, the aim here is to provide genuine scientific and technical expertise.

The award consisted of a coaching in eco-design at the Palais de Tokyo by professionals and experts recognized and invested in the art sector over a period of 3 days and in groups. In addition, two of the twelve artists among them will also benefit from a Life Cycle Analysis (LCA). Calculated by eco-design engineers, the LCA provides a complete scientific evaluation of the impact of a creation on the main environmental issues. The reward (the coaching and the two LCAs) is worth €40,000 in total. In addition, at the end of their support, the artists will be able to request a bonus of €1000 for their time commitment.

Within the framework of this accompaniment, materials, production techniques, transport, display systems, and conservation were all explored to identify innovative and less impactful alternatives. The main results of this process will be made public.

Art Exhibition to Link Science and Art

Exhibition "Biocenosis21," IUCN World Congress, Marseilles, 2021

Biocenosis (a scientific term inaugurated by the German biologist Möbius in 1877), or community, corresponds to all living beings (animals, plants, fungi, bacteria, etc.) established in the living space and linked by reciprocal dependence. At a time when biodiversity is collapsing in the face of the destruction of natural spaces and global warming, *Art of Change 21* activated an artistic biocenosis at the heart of the IUCN World Congress. Biocenosis21 brought together 14 French and international artists who are the most inspired and committed to biodiversity within (Marie-Sarah Adenis, Art Orienté Objet, Thijs Biersteker, Julian Charrière, Marcus Coates, Abdessamad El Montassir, John Gerrard, Jérémy Gobé, Caroline Halley des Fontaines, Camille Henrot, Janet Laurence, Lin May Saeed, Tomás Saraceno, Michael Wang) and gave carte blanche to Photoclimat.

Sensitivity, together with the process of cocreation and a multidisciplinary approach, are principles shared by the projects that I have been leading for nearly 7 years now with *Art of Change 21*. These principles are ingredients that I believe are essential for reaching and mobilizing young people and others on major environmental issues. This is a new way to communicate about topics that are still very often misunderstood and are, for some, anxiety provoking.

As Art Curator: The Power of Hope

Driven by the conviction that exhibitions are essential to the development of a new imaginary, I curated a number of exhibitions based on environmental themes: "Novacène" (Gare Saint Sauveur, Lille, 2022), "Art and the environment" (Art Paris, Paris, 2022), "Vita Extremis" (Patinoire Royale Valérie Bach, Brussels, 2022), "Biocenosis21" (IUCN World Congress, Marseilles, 2021), "Warmingland" (Paris City Hall, 2018), and "Post-Carbon" (Groupe La Poste headquarters, Paris, 2015).

My last major exhibition, Novacene, welcomed 90,000 visitors in Lille, Gare Saint Sauveur (May–October 2022).

Jean-Max Colard and I formed the curatorial duo commissioned by lille3000 to imagine a major exhibition on the theme of nature and the environment. We have accordingly chosen some principles: to choose both emerging and established artists who are among the most advanced in the "paradigm shift," to steer clear of the "good feelings" of ecology and to challenge the subject by thinking about ecology "beyond nature," as the philosopher Timothy Morton. Our starting point was "Novacene," James Lovelock's last book—which is both visionary and terrifying but also looks forward to a post-Anthropocene world with a certain technophile optimism. We decided to adopt its forward-looking approach and, to some extent, its technical perspective. We both knew that projecting ourselves into the post-Anthropocene was neither new nor original because civilizations and empires rise and fall, as Jared Diamond and before him Paul Valéry underlined in La Crise de l'Esprit (The Crisis of the Mind). Instead, it gave us an opportunity to look objectively at our contemporary "thermo-industrial" world, to stimulate imaginations, and, most importantly, to bring together this powerful generation of artists to highlight their movement's reach and intensity. The "Novacene" exhibition focuses on a post-Anthropocene world, enabling us to detach ourselves from our contemporary world and see the beginnings of progressive change and explore the means by which this new paradigm can be attained. As the book is set in a utopian future, "Novacene" depicts—with some humor—our current world as a bygone era, disrupted by ecological disasters. The exhibition explores this future civilizational era through the eyes of committed and visionary contemporary artists. The drive to attain a low carbon-based future and foster more harmonious relations between humans and "other-than-humans" depends on fundamental changes within our societies, our perception of the world, and our relations with the living world and raises new ethical dilemmas that will need to be addressed. Enriched by the most current reflection on the environment, including its social and anthropological aspects, the "Novacene" exhibition highlights the ways in which artists can propose alternative models and lifestyles and shed light on an emerging shift. Those artists were Allora & Calzadilla, Art Orienté Objet, Guillaume Aubry, Bigert & Bergström, Bianca Bondi, Julian Charrière, Omar Victor Diop John Gerrard, Anna Komarova, Taisia Korotkova, Fabien Léaustic, Jeeyoung Lee, JP Mika, Haroon Mirza, Marie-Luce Nadal, Otobong Nkanga, Lucy + Jorge Orta, Damon Sfetsios, Maarten Vanden Eynde, and Zheng Bo.

I will end by insisting again on the fact that artistic creation and imagination are formidable assets in the fight against the environmental crisis. Acting together is crucial. Mixing talent is essential, as is finding creative solutions together. Combining social and environmental issues and integrating multiple stakeholders is what any committed artist already does naturally. They hold the key to tomorrow's world.

Alice Audouin, a pioneer in sustainable development initiatives since 2001, has been actively engaged in exploring the intersection of Art and the Environment since 2004. She founded *Alice Audouin Consulting* in 2016, specializing in sustainability, art-sustainability connections, and responsible communication. With a diverse client base from luxury and cultural sectors, Alice brings a wealth of experience, previously serving as sustainable development director of Havas Media (2005–2013) and Marketing and Communication director of Novethic (2000–2005), a CSR and sustainable finance research center she helped create under the auspices of Caisse des Dépôts Group. Alice is also the founder and chair of the not-for-profit organization *Art of Change 21*, endorsed by

Olafur Eliasson in 2014. Under her leadership, international projects like Maskbook have trived. A trailblazer in France, she organized the first international symposium on the theme "The Artist as stakeholder" at UNESCO in 2004 and recently presented a climate-oriented exhibition (Julian Charrière) and discussions at COP28 under the banner *ART AT COP 28*. As a curator, she orchestrated three impactful shows in 2022: "Novacène" that welcomed 90,000 visitors (Gare Saint Sauveur, lille3000, Lille, France), the guest curator for the Art Paris 2022 fair on "Art and the Environment," and the curator of "Vita Extremis," the retrospective of the duo Lucy + Jorge Orta (Patinoire Royale Valérie Bach, Brussels, Belgium). Alice, a published author with four books, including a novel, is the chief editor of *Impact Art News*, a newsletter on art and sustainability published by *Art of Change 21*.

In recognition of her contributions, Alice received the medals of "Chevalière de l'Ordre du Mérite" in 2016 and "Chevalière de l'Ordre des Arts et des Lettres" in 2023. Website: https://artofchange21.com/, Facebook: Art of change 21, Twitter: @artofchange21, Youtube: Art of Change 21, Instagram: @artofchange21

39

Who Am I? A Plural Identity, Hybrid, Ambiguous, Interconnected

Brigitte Bernard-Rau

– Krik?[1]

---

[1] In the French Caribbean, storytelling plays an important role. An oral tradition, this form of expression is used to share funny stories and annecdotes about everyday life. Between tales, songs, and riddles, the storyteller engages the audience with a "Krik", "Yékrik", and "Mistikrik" to make sure everyone is listening. The audience responds with a "Krak," "Yékrak," and "Mistikrak." To maintain attention, the storyteller then interrupts the performance with resonant calls: "Yékrik" or, later in the story, "Yé Mistikrik." The listeners would respond in unison: "Yékrak," or "Yé Mistikrak." Occasionally, the storyteller would ask, "Is the court asleep?" and the collective answer would be, "No, the court is not asleep." If the court

---

The population of the French West Indies or French Caribbean (Antilles Françaises) forms a rich tapestry of diverse origins. Historically, the Arawak and Caribbean Indians inhabited the islands of the archipelago first, then the white settlers (« blan frans », in French creole) from mainland France and other European colonial powers occupied them. They brought in Africans (« nègs » and « négresses ») through the transatlantic slave trade, between the sixteenth and nineteenth centuries. The white descendants of the first settlers, known as « blan péyi » or « béké », continued to live on the islands together with the descendants of the African slaves who, in the meantime, became free men and women in the middle of the nineteenth century. A small group of white people living in remote areas, often less affluent, and colloquially known as « blan-matignon » were also part of the mix. Further contributing to this intricate mosaic are the « coolie-malaba » or « zindien », representing the Asian population, mainly of Indian origin, brought in when slavery was abolished, as well as communities of refugees from Syria and Lebanon (« siriyin »). This diverse mix has given rise to a hybrid population, a « melting pot » or a « fusion ». From these diverse backgrounds, the French Caribbean has inherited various terms, some flattering, others derogatory and offensive, to categorize, in the creole language, individuals according to their mixed ethnic ancestry: « nèg rouge, chabin (male), chabine (female), chabin doré, chabine dorée, creole, milat (male), milatresse (female), câpre (male), câpresse (female), bata zindien ».

B. Bernard-Rau (✉)
University of Hamburg, Hamburg, Germany
e-mail: info@thesustainabilitystories.com

- Krak!
- Yékrik?
- Yékrak!
- Mistikrik?
- Mistikrak!
- Is the Court asleep?
- No, the Court is not asleep!
- So, ladies and gentlemen, if the Court is not asleep, let your soul be instructed by a story!

ଌ ଌ ଌ ଌ ଌ

ଌ ଌ

>   I stay Here
>   I go to Paris
>   I travel around the World
>   I am … "Tout-Monde"[2]
>   Fly butterfly, fly
>   Fly Creole child, fly
>   For the finest, down in the locker lies.
>   I am … "Tout-Monde"
>   Yesterday, Tim-Tim Bwa Sek, Teddy and Burnet,
>   Camino de Santiago, Bridget the Fidget
>   Then Martine à la neige, redet über Goethe
>   Stand up, little ones, let's do the waggle dance
>   I am … "Tout-Monde"
>   Mixed continents, Mixed bloods,
>   Mixed countries, Mixed joys
>   Mixed head,
>   Papillon volé
>   Sé volé i ka volé
>   I am … "Tout-Monde"

---

was awake, the storyteller would declare, "Let it listen once more to what I am about to tell," and the storyteller would continue.

[2] "Tout-Monde" is derived from the works of French writer, poet, philosopher, and literary critic Edouard Glissant, born in Martinique. Glissant introduces this new concept in the novel "Tout-monde" (Gallimard, 1993) and the essay "Traité du Tout-monde" (Poétique IV) (Paris: Gallimard, 1997), which has been translated into English by Celia Britton in 2020 under the title "Treatise on the Whole-World" (Liverpool University Press, 2020).

Jump from rock to rock
From Schloß to cathedral
In the center reunite
But mainly at the periphery
Transcend my boarders
I am … "Tout-Monde"
Slide Creole child, slide
Leave this unique and poor you,
Relate, Curse, Kiss the Other
And go on "Tout-Monde" to discover
That
You are … "Tout-Monde"
Thus, sweep your landscape
Teach your seas a thing or two
Savour your bittersweet Cythera apple,
Your sea grapes too
Shout in border-languages
That
We are … "Tout-Monde"!

– Kric?
– Krac!
– Yékric?
– Yékrac!
– Mistikrik?
– Mistikrak!

I Have a Dream

I have a dream
    Deeply rooted in my relation to the world
    A plural world
    Where the Self is bound to the Other
    Not to become the One
    But the All

I have a dream
    Full of new engagements, new shared realities
    And imagined futures
    I have a dream
    For All
    I have a dream

—Brigitte Bernard-Rau

GPSR Compliance
The European Union's (EU) General Product Safety Regulation (GPSR) is a set of rules that requires consumer products to be safe and our obligations to ensure this.

If you have any concerns about our products, you can contact us on

ProductSafety@springernature.com

In case Publisher is established outside the EU, the EU authorized representative is:

Springer Nature Customer Service Center GmbH
Europaplatz 3
69115 Heidelberg, Germany